English Local History

An Introduction

English Local History

An Introduction

K A T E   T I L L E R

ALAN SUTTON

First published in the United Kingdom in 1992 by
Alan Sutton Publishing Ltd
Phoenix Mill · Far Thrupp · Stroud · Gloucestershire

First published in the United States of America in 1992 by
Alan Sutton Publishing Inc · Wolfeboro Falls · NH 03896–0848

British Library Cataloguing in Publication Data

Tiller, Kate
  English local history.
  I. Title
  942

  ISBN 0 86299 958 8

Library of Congress Cataloging in Publication Data applied for

Typesetting and origination by
Alan Sutton Publishing Limited.
Printed in Great Britain by
The Bath Press Ltd., Avon.

Contents

Preface

This is a book about local history which ranges broadly in terms of place, people and time. By its nature local history generates information and ideas which are printed, recorded or recalled in publications and individual memories widely scattered throughout the country. My task in seeking to bring some of these diverse historical experiences together would have been impossible without the interest and help of many colleagues, friends and students.

John Blair, James Bond, Ralph Evans, Rex Leaver, Dennis Mills, Mary Prior and Sandra Roe have all read chapters and provided valuable comments. Joan Dils and Mary Hodges have nobly read more than one chapter and provided a wonderful combination of good advice and kind encouragement. Guidance on matters medieval from Christopher Dyer and Jennifer Thorp was also much appreciated. Very special thanks are due to James Bond for producing many of the maps, plans and diagrams specially drawn for the book, as well as numerous photographs. Any errors remaining, despite their help, are my own.

Linda Rowley typed successive drafts of the main text and I am grateful to her, and to Rachel Saunders and Rosemary Cottis for their help and skills. Grace Briggs checked proofs with humour and precision. Peter Greenland processed many photographs.

This book would not have become a reality without two other ingredients. Firstly thanks are due to Alan Sutton for taking the book on so promptly and encouragingly, and to Roger Thorp and Clare Bishop, editors at Alan Sutton Publishing, for their efficient and friendly work. Secondly my husband Liam has, over a period of some three years and amidst the often hectic pressures of our respective professions and of a growing interest in golf, never ceased to support me. For his practical help, from photography to indexing, and his affectionate tolerance of incursions made by 'the book' into our home I am deeply grateful.

Illustrations play a major part in this book and I am happy to acknowledge permission to use pictures as follows (figure numbers are given):

Aerofilms 28, 50, 126; Archives Division, Birmingham Library Services 59; Mick Aston 106; Berkshire Record Office 92, 108; Bodleian Library, Oxford 23 (R.Pal. 5.4b (O.S.), Item XXIII);

James Bond 8, 9, 14, 15, 16, 17, 19, 20, 22, 25, 27, 29, 31, 32, 34, 35, 40, 42, 43, 45, 49, 51, 54, 60, 62, 63, 68, 72, 73, 81, 88, 93, 101, 114; Geoffrey Bryant 64; John Chandler 77; Brian Davey 141; Doncaster Library and Information Service 2, 3, 76; Essex Record Office and Sir John Ruggles-Brise 111; Helena Hamerow 11; Hampshire Record Office 65; Hitchin Museum and Art Gallery 100; Trevor Hussey 27; the Vicar of Kidmore 117; Lancaster City Museums 130; Lincolnshire County Council, Recreational Services, Usher Gallery, Lincoln 13; Longman Group UK 18; the Warden and Fellows of Merton College, Oxford 57; Stuart Miller 66; the Open University 74; Oxford University Press (reproduced by permission from P.D.A Harvey, *A Medieval Oxfordshire Village*) 3; Oxfordshire County Council 36; Oxfordshire Photographic Archive, Oxfordshire County Council 86, 102; Mark Priddey 99; Public Record Office (Crown copyright, reproduced by permission CP 25/98/55/1167 and E210/162, 163) 46, 48; Anthony Quiney 94, 95, 127, 128; Elizabeth Roberts, Centre for North-West Regional Studies, Lancaster University 129; Somerset County Council 33; Margaret Spufford 84; the Vicar of St Mary's, Taunton 75; M. Steiner 44; T.R. Theakston Ltd 26; Liam Tiller 24, 41, 67, 70, 96, 109, 112, 113, 116, 131–3, 135; Michael Turner 107; Geoffrey Tyack 97, 125; Stanley West 12; The Wharram Research Project 61; Angus Winchester 58. Photographs 10, 21, 37, 38, 39, 52, 53, 55, 69, 71, 79, 83, 115, 118, 136, 138, 139 were taken by the author.

Introduction

Local history has two essential ingredients – people and place. Together they have interacted to produce changing, but particular, historical experiences in the many differing areas of England. The result is a rich, but possibly confusing, diversity. The material and documentary evidence of local lives in the past stretches from the archaeological and landscape clues of prehistory and the earliest written records of the Saxon period to the present day. English local historians need to be able to pick their way through this outstandingly rich body of material. This they can do through the shared agenda of questions that has developed in English local history, questions which are relevant whatever place is being studied. This book aims to provide a guide which illustrates the diversity of the available evidence but which also points to pathways through a potentially distracting jungle of information.

An obvious starting point is curiosity about a particular place. The 'local' in local history is readily defined by geographical area, by a spatial demarcation line. Yet this is only part of any definition of 'local'. Without the people physical place is a passive ingredient, devoid of historical significance. Local history also has to be about the shared concerns and interests, whether in consensus or conflict, of the people living within an area. In other words local history is primarily about the origin and growth of community, about how, why and when local communities changed, and perhaps have now disappeared.

The common agenda for local history arises from this concern with people, place and community. It includes such basic and shared questions as who lived here? How many of them? How, when and why were settlements made? Did they grow, decline or shift? How has human agency moulded the landscape? Did the physical setting, in turn, affect people's lives? What work did men, women and children do? How were they governed and educated? Did they take part in religious worship? What were their social relationships and attitudes?

Here is a starting point for reconstructing the history, both public and private, of a place, of seeing how and why people acted as they did in the overlapping spheres of their lives, which may range from those of the individual, family or household to links with county, regional and national influences. In pursuing all of this a continuing grasp on the essential questions of local history will help to keep the emerging picture in focus and to identify manageable topics to tackle as a next step along the way.

How should you start to build up that picture? Doing local history is like tackling a very large jigsaw puzzle, where all the pieces are not kept in the same box and some may ultimately turn out to be missing. The first chapter of this book suggests how you can start to work out the approximate size and shape of the picture and some of its main features by critical use of the substantial amounts of local history already in print. Then, having seen the gaps and biases in the work of others, having defined and refined the questions you want to answer, and having gained a preview of some of the available sources, you will be ready to plunge into the original evidence both documentary and material. Subsequent chapters are designed to help you to do this by distilling the patterns of experience for local communities in successive periods of English local history. Major themes and causes of variation are discussed to illustrate how specific local circumstances and wider factors have worked together to produce particular local experiences. No community functioned as a sealed unit. Its members will also frequently be members of other groupings – of kin, or trade or religion, for example – that go beyond the geographical bounds of immediate locality. The local historian needs to maintain this wider awareness alongside a tenacious grasp on his or her own place. Each chapter will balance the survey and overview sections with case studies of actual communities and a discussion of sources.

Local history research need not, and should not, be a solitary pursuit. In becoming a local historian you are joining many thousands of other enthusiasts who share your curiosity, and who frequently have useful knowledge, expertise and ideas. In most areas there are networks linking the great variety of people active in local history. Links with these networks will come through local studies libraries, record offices, museums, university extramural and WEA classes, and local or county local history, archaeological or family history societies. From these contacts will come information, the chance to acquire useful skills (from reading early handwriting, to surveying buildings, to using micro-computers), and to compare methods and results. Quite apart from such practical advantages most local historians will enjoy the sense of shared recovery of a common past.

Finally never under-estimate your possible contribution to new knowledge and understanding in local history. It is now a subject open to a wide range of interests and skills, which, with the sort of guidance on approaches, sources and methods which this book aims to provide, can find ample expression. Local knowledge is vital. Expertise in botany, architecture, statistics, photography, computing and many other fields may all be turned to great use.

Many places have never had a local history written; the others need gaps filled and revisions made in what has already been done. In an age of narrow specialisms, the subject comprehends rather than excludes, always provided you are willing to think out the questions, to track down evidence, to collect and analyse it carefully and systematically, and to formulate some basic answers to what will be a growing number of questions. In this way you can hope to reconstruct the lives of people and places, avoiding both fusty, antiquarian compilations of unconnected facts, and abstract, jargon-laden models of those lives. I hope this book will help you to do this.

THE ANTIQUITIES OF WARWICKSHIRE

ILLUSTRATED;

From Records, Leiger-Books, Manu-scripts, Charters, Evidences, Tombes, and Armes:

BEAUTIFIED

With Maps, Prospects, and Portraictures.

By Sir *WILLIAM DUGDALE.*

MANTUAN,

Cuncta aperit secreta dies, ex tempore verum Nascitur, & veniens ætas abscondita pandit.

The SECOND EDITION, in TWO VOLUMES,

Printed from a Copy corrected by the AUTHOR himself, and with the Original Copper Plates.

The whole revised, augmented, and continued down to this present Time;

By *WILLIAM THOMAS*, D. D.

Sometime Rector of *Exhall*, in the same County.

With the Addition of several Prospects of Gentlemens SEATS, CHURCHES, TOMBS, and new and correct MAPS of the COUNTY, and of the several HUNDREDS, from an Actual Survey made by HENRY BEIGHTON, F. R. S.

ALSO

Compleat LISTS of the Members of Parliament and Sheriffs taken from the Original RECORDS;

AND AN

ALPHABETICAL INDEX and BLAZONRY of the ARMS upon the several PLATES.

LONDON:

Printed for JOHN OSBORN and THOMAS LONGMAN, at the *Ship* in *Pater-noster-Row:* And are Sold also by ROBERT GOSLING, at the *Crown* and *Mitre* in *Fleet-street;* and WILLIAM RATTEN, Bookseller in *Coventry.* MDCCXXX.

CHAPTER ONE

Beginning Local History

Where to begin

The best place to start is the printed information already available
for your chosen place of study.

This may save you considerable effort; it will establish what
information is known, what sources have so far been recorded, and
how they have been interpreted. Duplication can be avoided and
gaps in knowledge ripe for investigation or, alternatively, hotbeds
of local historical controversy, pin-pointed. Thus the printed
history is at once a quarry and a jumping-off point for further
research. However, do not take all you read as gospel, or be afraid
of sometimes challenging what you find in print. One of the
bugbears of local history has been the unquestioning repetition of
'facts' with little clear foundation, just because they have once been
published. If you know that the soils in a particular part of your
parish are unsuitable for wheat growing, despite what a local
booklet on earlier agriculture suggests, or if you are suspicious of
the triumphantly Anglican tone of a nineteenth-century history of
your town when it comes to assessing the strengths of nonconformity, by all means investigate further. You will find that printed
local history falls into a number of phases of development, each
with its own form and emphases. A guide to these is given below;
the types will soon become familiar and this awareness will help
you to read critically what you find.

Another major reason for starting with printed materials is their
relative accessibility. Unlike original documents, they do not need
to be transcribed from sometimes difficult original handwriting, or
translated from Latin or other languages. Printed histories are kept
in repositories usually nearer to the average searcher's home and
open for longer hours, including Saturdays, than is the case with
other sources. You will find that three basic distinctions are made
in the location of local history sources – between printed materials,
original documents, and field evidence and artefacts. Each of these
is commonly found in a different place – respectively the local
studies library, the record office, and 'the field' and/or museums.

1. (OPPOSITE) The title-page of
the second edition of Sir
William Dugdale, *Antiquities of
Warwickshire* (1730), illustrating
the interests and concerns of
a leading early antiquarian.
Despite their limitations such
works remain a useful quarry
for modern local historians.

Local studies libraries, or local studies sections within public libraries, look after printed materials. Here you will find probably the largest concentration of histories of your study area. This will not just be in the obvious history of 'your' place, but also in volumes covering larger areas of which it was part, usually a hundred, county or a region or in the observations of travellers, like Daniel Defoe in the early eighteenth century. Equally it may be the subject of more recent articles or pamphlets. Guide books and trails are common. A local studies library is the easiest place in which to build up a bibliography of what is available using a printed list of items, or working through the library catalogue. Always ask if there is anything particularly recent or useful on your topic. Local studies librarians are knowledgeable and in-touch. They are also very busy and local history is a boom area for publishing, so they may know of something not yet catalogued, or on exactly your theme in a neighbouring town or village. Useful information and ideas gleaned from similar studies of other places may help your work considerably; comparing and assessing the typicality of local experiences is an essential part of local history. This concentration of material will be found in the central library of your city, town or county. Although many branch libraries have useful, if modest, on-the-spot local collections these usually offer only part of the picture.

You will also discover in main local studies libraries other major pieces of your jigsaw in the form of original printed sources, usually eighteenth-century and later; these include news-papers, directories, maps, photographs, posters and pamphlets. These, like manuscript documents, count as 'primary' sources and we shall return to them in discussing research on the eighteenth and nineteenth centuries. The initial emphasis is on using the library's secondary sources to establish you safely on the local history road, having first built up a good, clear map of where you are going.

It is impossible to generalize about how much printed history may be found. Even the 'standards' like the Victoria County History (VCH) do not cover every parish or county as yet, and where they do the nature of the coverage varies greatly according to the date of publication. The rule must be to make the most of what you have got. Establish a method of collecting materials from the start. For example, a cumulative slip index of references will yield increasing returns and avoid future frustration when, as is inevitable, you need to refer back to earlier readings. In some localities there may be an embarrassing amount of material, in which case you should note references and sources used but give priority to the most relevant items, starting with a VCH volume if available, then other recent books, pamphlets and articles. Work out from these, cross-checking between accounts.

Collect references on a standard sized slip (paper will do), and with standard layout showing always author, title, date and place of publication, journal title and volume if relevant, and page numbers if only certain sections apply. If you regularly use the same library their classification mark noted here can save you time. Similar information should appear on your more detailed notes. This method ensures that you, and anyone else, can always get back to the original source of information or opinion, when wanting to follow a point further. It also avoids those vaguely attributed or wholly unsupported statements that will irritate you in others and which get local history a bad name.

Once in amongst the stock of your local history library, you will often form strong impressions of the characters and preoccupations of your predecessors as local historians. Their work will likely have generally recognizable features, depending on when it was produced, by what kind of person it was written, for what reason, and using what sources. These distinguishing characteristics should enable you to identify the different species of local historians.

The earliest local history accounts

The earliest written 'history' in which you are likely to find specific mention of a particular place will probably not be a volume devoted to that town or parish or village. In the case of *The Anglo-Saxon Chronicle* or later medieval chronicles mention is usually confined to some major military or political event with which a place was connected, and conveys little about the place itself. Only in the fifteenth and sixteenth centuries do written accounts reflecting a concern with the intrinsic interest of individual places begin to emerge. These take the form of itineraries dealing primarily with the physical description or topography of places visited by the authors; they say little of the people, past or present. However, the paucity of early material means local historians must wring the maximum possible use out of such coverage. The earliest available itinerary is William of Worcester's, compiled from notes of his journeys in 1477–80 and references from monastic and private libraries. William had interesting characteristics in common with many present-day local historians: he absorbed himself in the subject after retirement (from the service of Sir John Fastolf in Norfolk) and he returned to familiar territory, his birthplace, Bristol. His itinerary includes a street-by-street description of that city, distances between towns, and detailed descriptions and measurements of buildings, especially large churches and monasteries. There is an emphasis on the West Country and Wales, southern England and East Anglia.

Wider ranging, and a constant source of reference, are the

itineraries of John Leland (1506–52) in or about the years 1535–43. In 1533 Leland had received the King's commission to search the libraries of monasteries and colleges for the work of old writers. He was determined to record and preserve as much as he could of the evidence and learning, books and documents to be found in the monastic and church institutions then being dismantled. As he toured England and Wales he made notes, later written up into descriptions of town and countryside, interspersed with historical information. He wrote about castles, markets, towns, cities, churches and other principal buildings, the houses of great men, street plans, building materials, bridges, rivers and watercourses, and the use of land – for common field arable, enclosed arable, meadow, waste, wood, forest or parks. Leland's ambitions for a comprehensive description of the English realm to lay before his royal patron never came to fruition, and not all places are recorded in equal detail. Nevertheless much can be gleaned from the editions of Leland's itinerary produced by eighteenth- and twentieth-century editors.

The tradition of observant and literate travellers was a tenacious one. The best-known and most accessible of Leland's successors include Celia Fiennes (1662–1741) and Daniel Defoe (?1660–1731). Although contemporaries their views of England at the turn of the seventeenth and eighteenth centuries vary. Celia Fiennes, an un-married gentlewoman, travelled the length and breadth of England, mostly on horseback, between 1685 and 1703. She kept a first-hand account of what she saw for herself, not for a patron and not for publication. Her writing is often breathless and certainly unpolished, and she records a somewhat random series of observations on the contemporary scene, with little of the antiquarian's preoccupation with earlier inhabitants or archaeological and archi-tectural remains. The landscape, the farming, the food, the state of the roads, the quality of accommodation at the local inn, the manufacturers, the decay or decline of the local economy, the churches but also the dissenting meeting-houses (Celia came of good parliamentarian stock), the houses of merchants, gentry and aristocracy, and the state of country house architecture and gardens may all be gleaned from *The Journeys of Celia Fiennes*.

Daniel Defoe's *Tour through the Whole Island of Great Britain*, published between 1724 and 1726, is very different from Celia Fiennes's private reactions. It is a work firmly intended for publication, and written by a businessman, journalist and employee of politicians to reflect in particular contemporary commerce, trade and employments. Like Celia Fiennes, antiquities are not his chief concern:

> . . . my business is not the situation or mere geographical
> description of [a place]; I have nothing to do with the longitude
> of places, the antiquities of towns, corporations, buildings,

charters, etc. but to give you a view of the whole in its present
state, as also of the commerce, curiosities and customs . . .

In practice Defoe did not always resist the temptation to include
antiquarian information. Unlike Celia Fiennes his observations
were not gleaned first hand on actual journeys, but consist of
recollected information and ideas arranged in the form of thirteen
letters (including Wales and Scotland) each describing a notional
itinerary. For some places, most likely towns, it is possible to bring
together such observations for periods when little other 'local
history' is available.

Such a place is Doncaster in the West Riding of Yorkshire, a
town outwardly dominated by late eighteenth- and nineteenth-
century developments to its churches, its public buildings and the
Great Northern Railway. Only surviving street names reflect the
earlier, medieval town centre.

It is here that the early travellers come into their own. In his
Itinerary[1] John Leland recorded in detail the churches, castle site,
college of priests, friary, bridges, bridge chapel, gates, local soils
and building materials of Doncaster at the end of the Middle Ages.

I notid these things especially yn the towne of Dancaster. The
faire and large paroch chirche of S.George, standing in the very
area, where ons the castelle of the toune stoode, long sins clene
decayid. The dikes partely yet be seene and foundation of parte
of the waulles. There is a likelihod that when this chirch was
erectid much of the ruines of the castelle was taken for the
fundation and the filling of the waullis of it.

There standith an old stone house at the est ende of the chirch
of S.George now usid for the town house: the which, as sum
suppose, was a pece of the building of the old castelle or made of
the ruines of it.

There is in the declining *in area castelli* a prati litle house buildid
of tymbre as a college for the prestes of the toun.

There was another paroche chirch yn the towne yet standing,
but now it servith but for a chapelle of ease.

There was a right goodly house of White Freres in the mydle
of the towne now defaced: wher lay buried in a goodly tumbe of
white marble a Countes of Westmerland, whos name, as one told
me, was Margarete Cobham. The image of the tumbe is
translatid ynto S.George Chirch, and by it as the crounet is made
she shold be a duches.

There was a house of Grey Freres at the north ende of the bridg,
communely caullid the Freres Bridge, conteyning a 3. arches of
stone. Here I markid that the north parte of Dancaster toune, yn
the which is but litle and that mene building, standith as an isle: for
Dun ryver at the west side of the towne castith oute an arme, and
sone after at the este side of the town cummith into the principal

streame of Dun again. There is also a great bridge of 5. arches of stone at the north ende of this isle: at the south ende of the which bridg is a great tournid gate of stone, at the west side wherof is a fair chapelle of our Lady, and therof it is caullid S. Mary Gate. At the est ende of this bridge be 2. or 3. great milles as at the water.

There appere no tokens, as far as I could lerne or se, that ever Dancaster was a waullid toun; yet there be 3. or 4. gates in it: whereof that in the west side is a praty tower of stone, but S. Marie Gate is the fairest.

The hole toune of Dancaster is buildid of wodde, and the houses be slatid: yet is there great plenty of stone there about.

The soile about Dancaster hath very good medow, corne, and sum wood.

Later visitors included Celia Fiennes in 1697,[2] who wrote:

Doncaster is a pretty large town of Stone Buildings, the streetes are good; there is a handsome Market Cross advanc'd on 20 steps at least, the Church is neate and pretty large, several little Monuments; this town stands on the River Don which gives name to the town, here is also a good large Meeteing place; we were here the Lord's day and well entertained at the Angel.

Unlike Leland she describes the Market Cross. Since his time it seems more building in stone had taken place and a dissenting place of worship been established.

Daniel Defoe[3] noticed other things:

Doncaster is a noble, large spacious town, exceeding populous and a great manufacturing town, principally for knitting; also as it stands upon the great northern post-road, it is very full of great inns; and here we found our landlord at the post-house was mayor of the town as well as post-master, that he kept a pack of hounds, was company for the best gentlemen in the town or in the neighbourhood, and lived as great as any gentleman ordinarily did. Here we saw the first remains or ruins of the great Roman highway, which, though we could not perceive it before, was eminent and remarkable here, just at the entrance into the town; and soon after appeared again in many places.

This town, Mr Cambden says, was burnt entirely to the ground, anno 759, and is hardly recovered yet; but I must say, it is so well recovered, that I see no ruins appear, and indeed, being almost a thousand years ago, I know not how there should; and besides, the town seems as if it wanted another conflagration, for it looks old again, and many of the houses ready to fall.

Despite his concern with contemporary commercial developments Defoe records his debt to the work of the first generation of antiquarian historians. He has read the *Britannia* (1586) of William

2. (OPPOSITE, ABOVE) 'The faire and large paroch chirche of S. George', Doncaster described by John Leland in the 1530s, but destroyed by fire in 1853.

3. (OPPOSITE, BELOW) Baxter Gate entrance to Doncaster Market Place, c. 1800.

Camden, a leader of that group, who wrote of the two streams of the river Dan, the various forms of the town's name, of the ancient tower near St George's Church, and of the great fire of 759. Local historians have often repeated such episodes from their predecessors, but what was the original source?

Defoe clearly thought that Doncaster in the 1720s was ripe for new building and development. Pevsner's description, in that invaluable, late twentieth-century gazetteer *The Buildings of England* suggests that this in fact happened in the late eighteenth and earlier nineteenth centuries, but he found the town centre in the 1960s had 'a general atmosphere of slumminess and neglect which fails to create a picturesque effect'.[4] Successive phases of decay and development, revealed in printed sources, start local historians on the task of uncovering the cause and effect of earlier periods of change and continuity. Like Defoe they will need to turn to the antiquarians.

The county historians

In the 1570s English counties, and the places within them, began to be described in maps and in words. Between 1574 and 1579 Christopher Saxton engraved the series of county maps of England and Wales which became the first national atlas. In 1576 William Lambarde published the first county history or survey, *The Perambulation of Kent*. By the time Sir William Dugdale, widely thought to be the most outstanding of all county historians, brought out his *Antiquities of Warwickshire Illustrated* in 1656 he could cite as his predecessors not only Lambarde, but Carew on Cornwall, Burton on Leicestershire, Somner on Canterbury, and a forthcoming volume by Erdswicke on Staffordshire. Thus Dugdale was emulating, and excelling amongst, a school of antiquarians who had for the first time established the detailed and specific study of particular places and families, and had laid down an approach to local history which was influential into the early twentieth century.

This antiquarian history was local history for the county gentry, often written by county gentry. These were frequently 'new' men who had taken advantage of plentiful opportunities to acquire landed wealth and status, particularly in the second half of the sixteenth century. Such men were hungry for information about their patch, its antiquity and importance, and by extension their own place and importance. Dugdale, while himself a newcomer – 'for my father was the first', a Lancashire man from Clitheroe, marrying into Warwickshire – was keenly aware of the function of the new local history. He dedicates his history to

'My Honoured Friends The Gentry of Warwickshire . . . Wherein you will see very much of your Worthy Ancestors, to whose memory I have erected it, as a Monumental Pillar . . . My principal ayme having been, by setting before you the noble and eminent actions of your worthy ancestors, to incite the present and future ages to a virtuous imitation of them.'

These antiquarians wrote in the idiom of a post-Renaissance classical education. Dugdale likened his labours to those of Tacitus and Thucydides. He emphasized monuments and tombs by analogy with the Roman reverence for dead ancestors. William Camden (1551–1623), a founder of this school, set out in *Britannia* to reconstruct the geography of the Roman province. This work, organized in county chapters, was first published in Latin in 1586 (first English edition 1610), and was prone to classical analogy, as for example 'that Geffrey Chaucer our English Homer'.

The contents of this type of county history reflect the outlook of their writers, and their sponsors. For Dugdale the important ingredients were the descent of the manor, pedigrees of the lord's family, tombstones, monuments and heraldry, the church and its fabric, a list of incumbents, religious houses, hospitals, chantries and churches. Entries were arranged by the ancient administrative sub-units of the county, the hundreds, and within them by parish. Where there was more than one settlement in a parish the place with the church was treated first and then the hamlets, 'whether depopulated or otherwise . . . setting forth a succession of their ancient possessors by which the rise, continuance and decay of many families, with their most venerable actions, are manifested'. The parochial entries were preceded by a general introduction to the county and its history. The emphasis was also on careful use of original documents. Despite the disruptions of the Civil War Dugdale's twenty years of research uncovered a great deal of material and his careful marginal notes of sources set an example of attribution to later generations.

It was not unusual for antiquarians to amass extensive collections of notes, manuscripts and drawings but never to publish them as planned. Many such collections are now in libraries and record offices and include otherwise unknown material, including records of lost documents, archaeological finds, or buildings, stained glass, monuments etc. Local historians from the sixteenth to the early twentieth centuries have left such deposits but these are rarely listed and indexed and require detailed work in order to use them effectively. Often previous researchers have used these antiquarian archives and so material is in print, although not in works by the original collector. Look out for this in later histories of the area studied and in the volumes of the county or other local historical, archaeological and record societies. For example, Roger Dodsworth (1585–1654), a famous early antiquary, planned a history of his home county of Yorkshire, an English baronage, and the *Monasticon Anglicanum* (records of dissolved monastic houses). He published nothing in his lifetime but Dugdale used his notes, and subsequently published the *Monasticon*. Dodsworth's papers were deposited in the Bodleian Library, Oxford as early as 1673 and were later used for publications on the history of Agbrigg Wapentake by the Yorkshire Archaeological Society (1884), of medieval Lancashire *Inquisitions post mortem* by the Chetham Society (1875–6), and by Thoroton for his *History of Nottinghamshire* (1677).

County histories in the antiquarian mould continued to be published into the nineteenth century, and in some respects are continued by the Victoria County Histories. Some, like Dugdale, were revised and reprinted in later editions. By 1800 only seven counties were without such histories. At the beginning of the nineteenth century the Lysons brothers planned a series of standard county histories, each with the familiar general and parochial history sections. However, their *Magna Britannia* reached only six volumes (1806–22), covering counties alphabetically up to Devon.

The quality of county histories varies considerably in terms of sources covered and the effectiveness with which they are used. Coverage may seem narrow to modern local historians, and interpretations coloured by the class and priorities of the writers. Much material, including extensive extracts from original documents, may be reproduced with little explanation or interpretation. These are faults of the antiquarians but their labours still provide a primary reference point.

4. Romanesque carving on the Norman font at Avington recorded in Daniel and Samuel Lysons, *Magna Britannia. Berkshire* (1813).

Parish and town histories

There can be little real doubt that a Parochial History of England would be a very valuable work, by bringing to light, and preserving much information which, from its local and particular character, is not to be found in any history of a more general nature.

Hon. and Revd Henry Alfred Napier, *Historical notices of the parishes of Swyncombe and Ewelme* (1858)

The first parish history was published in 1695. That and the town history became the commonest form of local history writing in the prolific days of the Victorian and Edwardian periods, and examples of the genre continue to appear today despite the emergence of 'modern' local history.

The parish was seen as the natural smallest unit of study, as it had been within the increasingly large and expensive multi-volume county histories. It embraced a settlement or settlements and their associated farming land in a unit likely to go back at least to the twelfth century; besides this continuity it was the parish which was the principal unit of record keeping, both civil and ecclesiastical, from at least the sixteenth century. The fact that a large number of parish historians were clergymen undoubtedly reinforced this parochial perspective. It was such men, rather than the gentry and lawyers who figured largely in earlier antiquarian writing, who appear frequently as parish historians in the eighteenth and nineteenth centuries.

The character of most parish histories was apparent from the very first of the kind. In 1695 White Kennett published his *Parochial Antiquities attempted in the History of Ambrosden, Burchester and other adjacent parts in the Counties of Oxford and Buckinghamshire*. Kennett was the Vicar of Ambrosden in Oxfordshire, the first in a long line of Anglican parsons who devoted their extensive leisure and often considerable learning to uncovering the history of their own parishes. They were well placed for the task. Large amounts of evidence were readily to hand, in parish, manorial, and estate records held locally. To this they applied a scholarly background. Some, like Kennett, had contact with leading antiquarians of the day, energetically pursued national and monastic records, and built up libraries of county histories and the increasing number of published texts of documents, like Dugdale's *Monasticon Anglicanum*, which printed charters granting property to monasteries. Archaeological finds were brought to them. Some conducted their own excavations. These clerical antiquaries were collectors, often jackdaw-like accumulators of both gems of information and unconsidered trifles. Some failed to render this amassed

5. The Revd H.J. Gepp, one of many clerical local historians, outside his vicarage at Adderbury, Oxfordshire. His history of Adderbury was published in 1924.

material into written history, others did so, sometimes without distinguishing the gems from the trifles.

Parish historians cast their net widely. Most felt a need to delve into earliest origins despite uncertain evidence. Kennett touches on 'the primitive Britains' before proceeding, with increasing confidence, to the Romans, Saxons and Normans. Like others of his kind he does not confine himself to local events, or even events of local significance. Whenever a famous individual or family, or a body such as a monastic house is connected with the story it is likely that a potted history will appear. This very much affected the length and balance of 'parish' histories. For example Henry Napier's history of Ewelme and Swyncombe is largely the history of the Chaucer and de la Pole families and their chequered role in fourteenth- and fifteenth-century English history. As a result we learn little of the population at large, the houses and landscape of the villages, or the fields and farming. Little is said of the period post *c.* 1500. All too often in parish histories national history elbows local history aside rather than illuminating it.

It is not surprising that antiquarian local histories are history from the top down. As with the county histories this reflects by and for whom they were written. Clerical authors frequently took a partisan view. Kennett began his researches in order to defend disputed rights over local church charity lands. His task broadened but his perspective remained that of maintaining 'veneration to the Church of England'. He wrote of his parochial antiquities with a sense of preserving for posterity the knowledge of a past unappreciated in a philistine present, when

> idle witty People . . . think all History to be scraps and all Antiquity to be Rust and Rubbish . . . I then appeal to Posterity; for I believe the times will come when Persons of better inclination will arise, who will be glad to find any Collection of this nature, and will be ready to supply the Defects, and carry on the continuation of it.

Kennett's parish history was not immediately followed by a flood of others. It is in the nineteenth century that we find large numbers of individual parish histories coming from the presses. The outburst of local historical and archaeological activity which this betokened in turn reflected wider changes. Intellectual interest in the origin and development of institutions, from field systems to borough corporations, was high. At a time of change and reform, enthusiasm for systematic and thorough investigation of the past and its possible relationship to the present was marked. Railway and building developments brought new archaeological discoveries. A new and wider range of educated middle-class readers and participants in local history emerged. Local history was part of local identity and was sought after. The need to record and restore buildings was recognized. Mechanized and relatively cheap printing provided a means of disseminating discoveries, and disseminated they were.

'The dead hand of the seventeenth-century squire still guided, until recently, the hand of the living antiquary.' So W.G. Hoskins, doyen of modern English local history, has written. [5] The printed output of the nineteenth and much of the present century often shows this in a lack of clear narrative and an absence of questions posed or answered about the place and its people. Events take place, people and institutions come and go, seemingly for no apparent reason. There remains the tendency to undiscriminating collection of raw ingredients, never brought together or prepared to form a finished dish within a balanced menu. Frequently the choice of ingredients is familiar. The place-name and its etymology (linked insecurely to the date of origin of the settlement), selected gobbets of sources like Domesday Book and churchwardens' accounts, the church building, famous sons; sometimes the ingredients are not fresh – the descent of the manor drawn from an earlier county history. What may be new will be more recent history, often given in some detail, for example railway building, new schools, municipal reform or population growth. Here an element of interpretation may appear, portraying the nineteenth century as the acme of progress, the culmination of a remorseless march of civilization. Such triumphalist tones should trigger caution in the modern reader, but at least here is a line of argument that helps later local historians to frame questions about the development of their town or village. Did it experience smooth linear progress to Victorian prosperity and stability or did dislocation or decline intervene at any stage? How much of a peak of fortunes was, for example, 1850?

Towns as well as rural parishes attracted this type of history, again emphasizing matters manorial and the records of parishes within their bounds. For chartered and incorporated boroughs the institutional aspects of town government loomed large. Again the nineteenth and early twentieth centuries were peak times for the production of printed volumes and articles or pamphlets. Some towns did have histories published earlier than any parish volumes. Stow's famous *Survey of London* (1598) was followed by works on Great Yarmouth (1599), Canterbury (1640), Stamford (1646), Newcastle (1649) and Scarborough (1660). However, most towns had to wait at least until the eighteenth century for a history, and more until the nineteenth.

The antiquarian enthusiasm of the Victorians also expressed itself in the organization of societies and clubs. Many of the county historical, archaeological and architectural societies are products of this era, and survive today in varying degrees of vigour. For the local historian in search of source materials their journals may be of considerable use. The societies made forays around their counties, looking at churches and major antiquities. Descriptions, sometimes accompanied by plans and documentary excerpts, were then published, along with the texts of papers delivered during the winter on a catholic range of topics, often including natural history. These volumes, and those of the county record societies, which specialize in publishing the texts of major documents, continue to be great use.

The VCH

Victorian self-confidence, in terms of local history, culminated in the founding in 1899 of the 'Victoria History of the Counties of England', otherwise known as the VCH (Victoria County History). The aim was, and is, to write an outline local history of the whole of England, county by county, and place by place. By 1989 two hundred volumes had been completed. These represent completed coverage of eleven of the thirty-nine ancient English counties plus one riding of Yorkshire. A further twelve counties are currently in progress, while the remaining counties have no coverage (Northumberland and Westmorland) or only general volumes without place-by-place histories.

The VCH is recognized for its consistent methods and high scholarly standards. Where its volumes exist they will be a first reference for local historians. There are two types of volume, first the general, containing essays on major themes in the county's history, for example, religious history, agriculture, industries, population (with summary tables of decennial census totals 1801–1901), and Domesday Book (with a reliable English translation of this much-used source); and secondly the topographical containing parish histories, arranged by hundred or wapentake.[6] This structure is not the only way in which VCH followed the earlier tradition of county histories. This was particularly apparent in its first phase of activity, 1899–1914, when VCH was very much a gentleman's history, manifesting the familiar concerns with manorial history, advowson,[7] parish churches, charities, Roman and earlier remains. This remained the case through the inter-war period which, for the VCH as for English local history as a whole, was relatively quiescent. Since 1947 the pace has changed with two or three VCH volumes published each year, largely written by full-time professional staff. The format of the parish histories has been modernized by expansion to include economic and social history, the history of population, landscape and the physical growth of settlement, education, religious nonconformity, and local government. Entries have grown. Whereas 'early' counties were completed in up to four volumes, general and topographical,

6. The VCH. The Victoria History of the Counties of England takes its name from Queen Victoria, whose arms continue to adorn the title-pages of what has become the standard reference work for historians of particular localities.

VCH counties now take up at least twice as much space. The parochial unit has been retained but amendments have been made. Initially ancient ecclesiastical parishes were used even if this meant that, for example, the major industrial town of St Helens in Lancashire appeared only briefly and as a subsection of the township of Windle, itself a subsection of the ancient parish of Prescot. Since the mid-1950s the VCH parish is the civil parish, the modern successor of the ancient parishes or of townships within them. Large towns are dealt with as a whole, including, since the 1960s, built-up areas of adjoining, formerly rural parishes.

7. VCH coverage to the end of 1991.

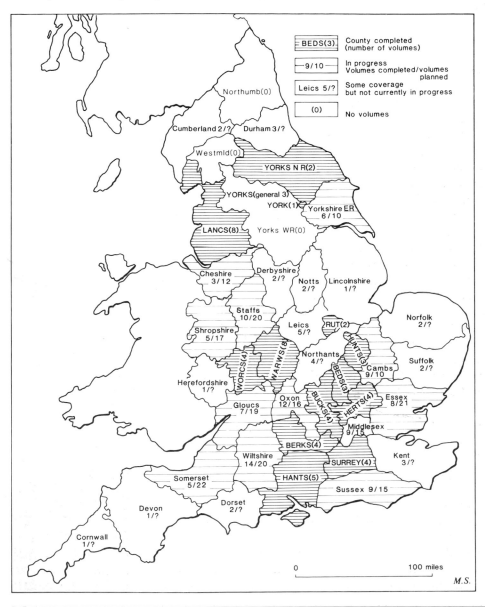

BEDS(3) — County completed (number of volumes)

9/10 — In progress Volumes completed/volumes planned

Leics 5/? — Some coverage but not currently in progress

(0) — No volumes

Northumb(0)

Cumberland 2/? Durham 3/?

Westmld(0)

YORKS N R(2)

YORKS(general 3)
YORK(1) Yorkshire ER 6/10

LANCS(8) Yorks WR(0)

Cheshire 3/12 Derbyshire 2/? Notts 2/? Lincolnshire 1/?

Staffs 10/20 Norfolk 2/?

Shropshire 5/17 Leics 5/? RUT(2)

Northants 4/? HUNTS(3) Suffolk 2/?

Herefordshire 1/? WORCS(4) WARWS(8) Cambs 9/10

BEDS(3)

Oxon 12/16 BUCKS(4) HERTS(4) Essex 8/21

Gloucs 7/19

Middlesex 9/15

BERKS(4) Kent 3/?

Wiltshire 14/20 SURREY(4)

Somerset 5/22 HANTS(5) Sussex 9/15

Devon 1/? Dorset 2/?

Cornwall 1/?

0   100 miles

M.S.

Local history today

Since the 1950s English local history has taken on a new face. When, on the publication of the VCH's two hundredth volume, Christopher Lewis summed up what a VCH parish or town history should aim to do,[8] he also summed up the 'new' agenda for all local historians:

> The account of any place must record systematically the main features of its history: the fluctuations in population, the succession of principal landowners, how the inhabitants have made a living and in doing so altered the environment around them, how they have worshipped and how their life as a community has endured over hundreds of years. It must draw attention to what is different and what is typical about that one place in relation to its neighbours, to wider regions, and to the county at large. It must be a store of references for the national historian who may be interested in the career of only one landowner or the growing of a single crop, but satisfying for the local historian who is a native or resident of the place. It must be accurate in every respect.

In throwing off the restrictions of approach and method inherited from earlier antiquarians local history has been opened up. It is now concerned with the community as a whole, and with all the people in it, not just the landed or the rich; with non-Anglicans as well as Anglicans; with women and children as well as men; with urban, suburban and rural places; and with all occupations and trades. Chronologically the recent past has become important ground for study, for example through recording recollections of the inter-war and Second World War periods. Local history is being studied by a much wider range of people drawing on a more varied range of materials; oral history is one, another is landscape history. Here, as in many other ways, the influence of W.G. Hoskins has been of utmost importance. Going beyond the old traditions of descriptive topography he urged us, notably in his *The Making of the English Landscape* (1955), to go out and get mud on our boots. The English landscape, in its fields, hedgerows, trackways, woodlands, moors and watercourses, and in its villages and towns and their street patterns, plot layouts, and buildings, vernacular as well as polite, was there to be read as a whole. This was a matter not just of isolated features, but of a palimpsest, a fabric on which successive generations had left the evidence of their lives and activity, and which could be interpreted by patient peeling back of those cumulative layers. This approach did not eschew documentary research; well-known sources could be looked at afresh, for example medieval manorial court rolls and custumals for evidence of farming practices, but this should be interpreted alongside direct investigation of soil conditions, surviving ridge and furrow earthworks, fieldnames, patterns of trackways on early maps, or dating of hedges from botanical evidence. Landscape history has provided some of the most striking examples of the integrated and holistic approach of modern local history. Many counties are now covered by separate volumes in a series, *The Making of the English Landscape*.

Impetus has been lent to local history by shared questions. Few local historians find in practice that they want, or are able, to produce a history of their place from earliest times to the present day at one fell swoop. Rather they need to start by identifying a theme of importance and interest to focus their efforts. One productive example has been population studies. The questions are basic. How big was this place? Did the size of its population fluctuate? If so when and why? From these first order questions stem more detailed lines of enquiry. Did the community experience sudden crises of mortality? If so were these due to epidemics or to dearth? How was disease transmitted? For example, did outbreaks follow trade routes, or come in through a local market or occur when Civil War troops came to the area? Were there longer term trends in death rates or birth rates? The main source of answers is likely to be parish registers, dating in the earliest cases from 1538. Research in this field over the past twenty years has shown just how valuable it is to bring together local and national perspectives. A major project was led by CAMPOP (The Cambridge Group for the Study of Population and Social Structure) with the aim of describing and interpreting English demographic change using parish registers and, from 1841 to 1871, national censuses. Almost all their parish register data were extracted (from 404 registers) by amateur local researchers working on their 'own' registers. Specific comments were made on each register by the Cambridge team, a permanent record put on computer at CAMPOP, and a book, *The Population History of England 1541–1871*, which is a bench-mark against which to compare all subsequent local findings, produced from the total analysis. Distinct phases of demographic growth, stagnation and crisis emerged, and relationships were suggested between population levels and actual behaviour – when people got married, when they built new houses, when they migrated. The resulting methods, ideas and comparisons have helped many local historians to understand their particular place, and in doing so to add to the general picture. In this kind of local history the two-way links between local and wider studies have a natural momentum, far removed from the unconnected chunks of national events superimposed on local matter which characterized earlier histories.

This is reflected in much recent local history writing which focuses on an important theme as it applied in a particular place. Such studies appear in the growing number of local journals, in national journals like *The Local Historian* and *Local Population*

Studies, and in books and pamphlets. Your local studies library should lead you to these.

The 'new' local history attempts to rediscover the physical and mental landscape of local people in the past. Their horizons will vary with economic and social position, place and time. An individual's life and thinking may be encompassed by a single small town, a suburb, a village, or a larger parish area. In 'the classic slum' of early twentieth-century Salford a few adjoining streets marked the horizon. For others, as on the Norfolk coastal estates of Sir Nathaniel Bacon of Stiffkey in the late sixteenth century, a group of parishes covered by the Bacon estate defined a world of ownership, employment, housing and marketing. As patterns of migration in the seventeenth- and eighteenth-century countryside show, many people operated in a circuit of five to ten miles, encompassing their own and adjoining settlements and often the nearest market town. For labouring people this was the area in which they normally found marriage partners, work and housing. The world of the gentry was also that of the estate and parish, but beyond that they were part of a wider county network, with direct links to regional capitals, like Norwich, and to London. A figure like Nathaniel Bacon moved in several different spheres and could be the link transmitting influences from national to local level, and vice versa, for example, as part of the political patronage system. Perceptions of locality therefore varied, with status and also with sex (women were in many periods more mobile through marriage and employment in domestic service), with education, with occupation (a miller with his fixed capital was less mobile than a shoemaker), and with age (the young generally moved most). What is 'local' will not always prove to be circumscribed by an administrative area, like the parish, and links with a wider world will be frequent. County, regional and national experiences will affect life in the localities.

The rewards of the 'new' local history are great. However, the demands of not just collecting information but of turning it into local history can seem daunting. All historians feel this. Professor Ladurie has suggested that there are two kinds of historian, truffle hunters and parachutists.

> The truffle hunters are those supremely professional practitioners who are precise in their historical vision, addicted to their archives, and high-minded in their search for what they believe to be the truth. They usually know a great deal about very little, are meticulously accurate in their footnote references, and deliberately eschew broad generalizations or speculative hypotheses, on the grounds that they are inconsistent with the exacting requirements of real scholarship.
>
> The parachutists are, by definition, a very different breed. They range more audaciously across the centuries, and survey a

far broader panorama of the historical landscape. They are concerned with deep underlying causes rather than with super-ficial phenomena, they venture wide (and sometimes wild) generalizations, they move very rapidly from one topic to another, and their work relies more on secondary resources than on detailed research. [9]

Local history is prone to produce extreme examples of both kinds. There is the lofty but rather stressful position of the parachutists, which engenders sweeping and rapid generalizations. This ap-proach may come from those who see local history as national history writ small, bringing theories into which local evidence will be fitted, rather than testing ideas and models against that evidence. Then there is the nose-to-the-ground position of the truffle hunters, given to grasping an incomplete diet of tasty morsels, and never raising their heads sufficiently to see the shape of the surrounding woodland. The local historian needs to balance the best elements of both perspectives, collecting ideas and information and then finding a good stable viewpoint from which to form an overview of his or her patch.

Starting with the printed histories and sources is the best first step. From that basis we can now begin to tackle the questions and original evidence generated by successive phases of local experience, and relate them to the wider context provided by the work of others. The following chapters aim to illustrate ways of doing this, beginning with the earliest period of local historical record, the Saxon.

References

1   L. Toulmin Smith (ed.), *The Itinerary of John Leland in or about the years 1535–1543*, vol. 1 (1907), pp. 34–5.

2   C. Morris (ed.), *The Journeys of Celia Fiennes* (1947), p. 75.

3   P. Rogers (ed.), *Daniel Defoe, A Tour through the whole island of Great Britain* (1971 edn.), p. 481.

4   N. Pevsner, *The Buildings of England. Yorkshire, The West Riding* (1967 edn.), p. 185.

5   W.G. Hoskins, *Local history in England* (3rd edn., 1984), p. 30.

6   In the East Midlands and North the wapentake was the equivalent of the hundred in the South.

7   The advowson was the right to appoint clergy to a church. Local historians will encounter many specialist terms. An invaluable reference work is John Richardson, *The Local his-torian's encyclopaedia* (2nd edn., 1986).

8   C. Lewis, *Particular places. An Introduction to English local history and the Victoria County History* (British Library, 1989), p. 64.

9   Quoted by David Cannadine, *The Guardian*, 6 November 1987.

o – ingas

+ – ingaham

· – by

CHAPTER TWO

The Saxon Centuries: Prehistory into History

To understand local history often involves going back a long way. Much may be recovered, despite subsequent layers of change. The period of earliest local historical record, the Saxon, clearly shows this. The six centuries between the departure of the Romans and the Norman Conquest (*c.* 400–1066) have left extensive traces of lasting relevance. Among them are many present-day place-names, settlement patterns, field systems, manors, estate and territorial boundaries, increasingly large and unified kingdoms and ultimately a single English Kingdom, the familiar units of shires, hundreds, wapentakes and tithings, the coming of Christianity, the establishment of cathedrals, monastic and minster churches, the subsequent emergence of smaller, local churches, and – closely linked to Christianity – the growth of written records. All these developments were under way before 1066.

Six hundred years is a long time, as long as from the Black Death of 1348 to the present day. It would be foolish to picture the Saxon period as a single phase of experience. The fifth and sixth centuries were very different from the seventh and eighth, and again from the ninth and tenth.

Early Saxon England: settlements and place-names

Evidence is sparse and our understanding of this early Saxon period uncertain. Sources are confined to archaeology (particularly evidence from pagan burial sites), place-names, and a few, unreliable or retrospective accounts in texts and annals. Despite this many local historians will have a very definite picture in their minds, one which may well need radical revision in the light of recent research bringing together the findings of archaeology, history, geography and place-names. For example Christopher Taylor's commentary on W.G. Hoskins's interpretations of Saxon settlement in the 1988 edition of his classic account, *The Making of the English Landscape*,

8. (OPPOSITE) Place-names are major clues to the Saxon period but need careful interpretation of written references, archaeology and topography. On this basis the distribution of names in *–ingas* and *–ingaham* is no longer believed to map new settlements made by advancing Anglo-Saxons. Less problematical is the coincidence of names in *–by*, Norse for settlement, with areas of Scandinavian settlement.

first published in 1955, shows how our understanding can change.

The old picture of the Saxon period focused on the collapse of civilization as the Romans left Britain, and on the onslaught of Saxons, Angles and Jutes from north Germany and Denmark. Each of these groups was seen as having a distinct tribal and ethnic identity, reflected in the patterns of settlement and customs, such as inheritance, which they established in the different areas which they settled. The progress of their settlements, and the tribal nature of their societies, characterized by personal loyalty to a chief, was reflected in the names of the places which they established in their gradual colonization. Thus the suffixes –*ingas* and –*ingaham* added to a man's name, as in Reading and Wokingham in Berkshire, or Hastings and Gillingham in Kent, mean 'the followers of Read (or Haesta)', and 'the homesteads of the followers of Wocca (or Gylla)', and represent early stages of territorial assertion by the Anglo-Saxon incomers. Place-names were used as an indicator of where the immigrants, bringing with them field systems and village plans from their homelands, created a new landscape. These new places had to be reclaimed, firstly from a land of collapsed clusters of civilization – of ruined villas, towns and roads, and of shattered political and administrative structures – and secondly from a countryside still containing large amounts of uncleared ancient woodland. The Saxon settlement was thus seen as the beginning of English village communities (the early Saxons were not an urban people), in a setting of largely unimproved nature with some surviving vestiges of an imposed Roman occupation.

The evidence now available reveals a much earlier phase of human intervention, dating to the Neolithic period (5000–2500 BC), which had already transformed much of England from an untamed, post-glacial land covered in woods, to a landscape extensively cleared and settled for farming. Prehistoric and Roman England sustained a growing population in a much exploited countryside, with fields, farmsteads, estates, villages, towns and tracks. Some estimates put the population by the third century AD at four million, a level not subsequently attained until the thirteenth century.

Most local historians hear only at second hand of the evidence supporting this view. In order to find out what specific information exists for your locality use the resources of local sites and monuments records, usually organized on a county basis by museums or planning departments. These typically contain information about individual finds, excavated sites, earthworks and cropmarks, as well as (chiefly for later periods) standing buildings. Their records frequently show the value of fieldwork by local amateurs; for example, our knowledge of how intensively the Romano-British countryside was settled, with many scattered farmsteads, hamlets and associated fields, as well as villas and towns, owes much to

9. Fieldwalking: collecting pottery and other man-made fragments from the autumn or winter ploughsoil. The distribution of finds is recorded by dividing the field into a grid of squares marked by rods.

fieldwalking by local groups, looking for pottery and other objects in ploughsoil, and carefully recording their exact location and distribution. Many are the long winter's evenings spent by fieldwalking local historians, on the next stage of washing finds ready for identification.

Archaeological finds have been used in conjunction with other evidence, like place-names. For example, the marked lack of coincidence between early Saxon archaeological remains and places with *–ingas* and *–ingaham* names discredited the earlier idea that these places plot the location and date of early immigrant settlements. Indeed the notion that the emergence of a place-name, datable from its linguistic form, also indicates the beginnings of that place is now treated with extreme caution.

Place-names make a fascinating and complex study. They can reveal Latin, Celtic, Scandinavian or Saxon influence, they may incorporate personal names, indicate various land uses such as woodland, summer pasture, or dairying, mark crossing places, the presence of churches or fortifications, or the location of meeting places. The possibilities are vast. So are the pitfalls. How does the non-specialist know that Clavering in Essex is not, like Reading and Hastings, an *–ingas* name? The skills needed are those of the philologist, probing the earliest and purest linguistic form of a name. All local historians should find place-names interesting and relevant, but most will turn gratefully to the work of the English Place-names Society, and the books of scholars like Margaret Gelling, for interpretations.

10. Ingoldisthorpe, Norfolk. 'Thorp', as this place was recorded in Domesday Book of 1086, is probably a Danish name, an outlying hamlet or farm, to which a Scandinavian personal name was subsequently added as a first element.

The Saxon settlement is now seen as a process of adoption and adaptation to living in a country that had already been intensively occupied. It was not a matter of starting from scratch in an empty land. Nevertheless the early Saxon period was a time of far-reaching disruptions. Life was localized and violent, compared with what had gone before and what was to follow. There was a substantial fall in population, perhaps by a half or a third to two to three million. By the end of the sixth century the invaders were in permanent control of half of Britain, having moved west up the Thames Valley and from East Anglia, and northward from Wessex. Remaining British influence centred in Wales and the West Country.

Mid-Saxon England: kingdoms, central places and minsters

In the seventh century a pattern of kingdoms emerged. The most important were Kent, Sussex, Wessex, East Anglia, Essex, Mercia and Northumbria, the Heptarchy. Some smaller, local kingdoms still survived; their leaders had the status of sub-kings. The significance of these developments for the local historian is firstly that a greater degree of organization was emerging, with known if not always stable structures to which local experience may relate; and secondly that there is enough written evidence to construct some general narrative, and even, in the form of the early charters, to find individual documents referring to named people and places. Despite these developments much remains uncertain. Over-kingship was contested, control fluctuated, and power depended on military force and the continued command of personal loyalty from a military aristocracy. This loyalty was reinforced by gifts to those followers, a relationship demonstrated in the grants of lands and rights recorded in charters. The mid-Saxon period probably saw the beginnings of local structures of authority reflecting these realities of power.

These local areas took the form of recognized territories, centred on a royal manor house or *tun*, run by a royal official and visited from time to time by the king and his retinue. As John Blair writes, 'Each modern county contains several such sites, some given away by place-names such as Kingston, others less obvious. It was these "central places", not towns or even villages, which were the main local foci of early and mid-Saxon society. The scattered inhabitants of the district looked for law and government to the king's great hall with its surrounding buildings. Here too they paid their dues and other public burdens in accordance with a complex system of assessment.'[1] An organized relationship of protection and exaction was developing. For example, assessment was made by the hide, a measure notionally related to the area necessary to support a free

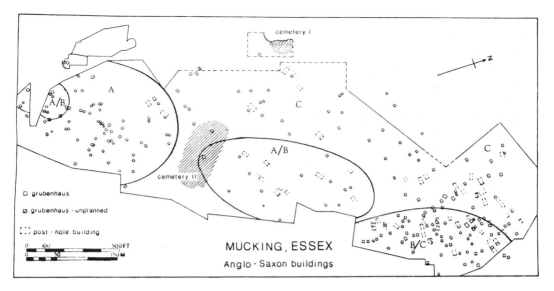

cemetery I

z

A

A/B

A/B

C

C

cemetery II

C

□ grubenhaus
⊠ grubenhaus - unplanned
⌐⌐ post - hole building

0   100   500FT
0   50   150M

B/C

MUCKING, ESSEX
Anglo - Saxon buildings

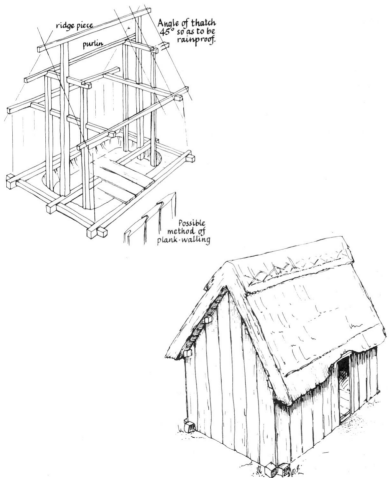

ridge piece   Angle of thatch
                     45° so as to be
    purlin   rainproof.

Possible
method of
plank-walling

11. The shifting nature of Anglo-Saxon settlement is shown by the internal evidence of the excavated site, at Mucking, Essex. Grubenhauser are the sunken-floored, timber huts characteristic of the periods represented at Mucking, i.e. A fifth century, A/B fifth/sixth, B/C sixth/seventh, and D seventh.

12. West Stow, Suffolk is another early and mid-Saxon settlement. Here excavation was followed by reconstruction of what was a small village of three to four families, settled by 450 and abandoned by 750. With no permanent internal property boundaries house-sites shifted. Homes were arranged in groups, each of a hall and five to six small out-houses, single rooms with underfloor spaces, possibly for storage or ventilation. A few had hearths, and one a clay-built oven. These houses were used for sleeping, storage, and for weaving and potting.

peasant and his household for a year. However it was not yet akin to the feudal lordship, peasant labour services and complex agricultural organization familiar in medieval manors. The areas involved were generally much larger and are called 'multiple estates' by historians. They took in numbers of settlements or scattered farmsteads, and frequently exploited the complementary farming specialisms of different parts of the estate. Their populations were relatively dispersed, and settlement was isolated or randomly grouped in unplanned and small clusters.

Many Saxon 'central places' also contained a Christian minster church. By *c.* 660 only the Isle of Wight and Sussex were unconverted to Christianity. This profound change was the outcome of a two-pronged process of conversion, from Rome and from the Celtic church in Ireland. Augustine's mission from Rome to King Aethelbert of Kent had begun in 597, and was followed by the dispatch of other missionaries. It was very much a conversion from the top down and it is difficult to know how quickly changed beliefs penetrated to all the people. Pagan and Christian elements continued to co-exist. The other source of conversion was the Celtic missions, coming from Ireland to Scotland and then Northumbria, beginning in the 560s. The missionaries established monasteries, and churches in royal vills, and became influential outside Northumbria, as for example when Cynegils, King of the West Saxons became a Christian on the marriage, in 635, of his daughter to King Oswald of Northumbria. In 664 at the Synod of Whitby King Oswy of Northumbria decided to accept the authority of the Roman rather than the Celtic church. This was the beginning of Christian England, although the country remained politically disunited.

A gradual stabilization of the organization of the English church began. A diocesan structure was established. A network of local minsters grew up, and by 750 hundreds existed. However, just as the secular central places and estates also emerging at this time were not like medieval manors, so minsters and their parishes were unlike later parish churches. Instead of local churches in local villages, each with its own priest, each minster church was manned by a group of priests who went out to serve the people of an extensive surrounding area, which might coincide with a large multiple estate. It was within this structure that local churches, and eventually local parishes, subsequently evolved. So how does the local historian identify the minster churches and parishes of her or his area?

Minister churches administered the basic rites of baptism and burial, and took the dues like mortuaries associated with them. They also collected the tithe, a levy of one-tenth of all produce. Even when more local chapels, often to become parish churches, began to appear the original minster or mother churches continued

13. Stow, Lincs. The church of St Mary, painted by Frederick MacKenzie (1787–1854). This picture provides valuable evidence of how the building looked before restoration by J.L. Pearson in 1851, when the roof pitches were raised and an external stair turret 're-built' in the angle between transept and nave.

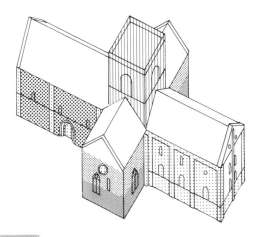

Anglo-Saxon: Bishop Aelfnoth (c.975)

Bishop Eadnoth II (1034-1050)

Early Norman: Bishop Remigius, c.1070

Late Norman: Bishop Alexander, c.1150

Perpendicular, c.1400

Victorian, John Loughborough Pearson, 1848-1865

14. For much of its history St Mary's has been the parish church of a relatively small community yet the building remains a fine example of a large, cruciform Saxon church of minster status, created to serve a large area. Its early importance is reflected in the four main building phases, all pre-1200.

to claim these functions. Vestiges of this may appear in records as late as the nineteenth century and provide clues to the identity of Saxon minster churches, for example where rights of burial were claimed, or practised, by a church other than the immediately local one. In some areas dependent churches had no burial ground and corpses were transported long distances to the former minster. Easter processions by parishioners from neighbouring churches are another clue, as are references to the 'mother church'. A church surrounded by others that are first recorded as chapels is also a likely candidate, as are those with a large number of priests. Tithe payments from former daughter churches may have been exacted. The fabric of the church may give indications. An early font, carefully preserved, can be a symbol of baptismal rights, jealously guarded. A cruciform church plan with central tower may indicate early status, while the high level of a churchyard can show that it was filled with more than just the local dead.

15. A Norman font preserved in a church of probable minster status at Hook Norton, Oxfordshire. Biblical and pagan figures (signs of the Zodiac) are both portrayed.

In 731 Bede completed his *Ecclesiastical history of the English people*. This work, by a monk in the Northumbrian monastery of Jarrow, is an unprecedented source for later historians. It was also a measure of Anglo-Saxon learning, which came to be internationally recognized at this time. Bede's *History* is a record of the Christianization of England, which also shows how the concept of an English nation or people had come to be recognized. However, a single English kingdom was still to come.

Late Saxon England: unity, instability and emerging local institutions

From the mid-eighth century to the mid-tenth the political story is that of the emergence of a single English kingdom, rooted in the dominance of the royal house of one of the existing kingdoms, and of the far-reaching effects of successive Viking incursions.

These events had very direct impacts on many local areas, and contributed to longer-term patterns – of strong governmental institutions, and of differences between English and Viking areas of the country. The period also saw rising population levels, the growth of nucleated rural settlement and related field systems, an increase in towns and trade, and a reformation in monastic and local church life. This can be traced from an increasing range of documentary sources – chronicles, histories and saints' lives, charters, writs, wills and law codes, and from the continuing archaeological record, particularly pottery and coins, but also metalware, weapons, jewellery, bones, textiles, and the sites of houses and churches.

During the eighth century the main political theme is the

attempted political overlordship of Mercia, and the dominance of King Offa of Mercia (757–96). Offa called himself King of the English. By 786 he achieved control of all the kingdoms south of the Humber. Offa's concept of over-kingship was reflected in many ways. He developed the royal council or Witan, he established a capital at Tamworth, and saw the nearby cathedral of Lichfield elevated to an archbishopric. He produced a systematic and widely-used coinage. Mercia had international political and trading contacts with Scandinavia and the Carolingian Empire. Power relationships within England are recorded in the Mercian charters of this period, which granted land to churches and aristocrats. The idea of 'bookland', land for which a written charter gave legal title, became established. After 749 reciprocal duties of the landowners to build bridges and fortifications appear. The sheer extent of the fortifications built by Mercia in defence of its territory is perhaps the most striking proof of all of the extent and effectiveness of its kingly control, and the ordered power which under-pinned it. Offa's Dyke stretches from the Severn Estuary to the Irish Sea coast of North Wales. This massive construction runs over terrain up to 1,400 feet above sea level. Excavation has shown how it was topped by a stone wall in parts, while areas were burnt and cleared for its building – an organized effort of truly impressive proportions.

16. Offa's Dyke.

17. Offa's Dyke at Llanfair Waterdine, Shropshire.

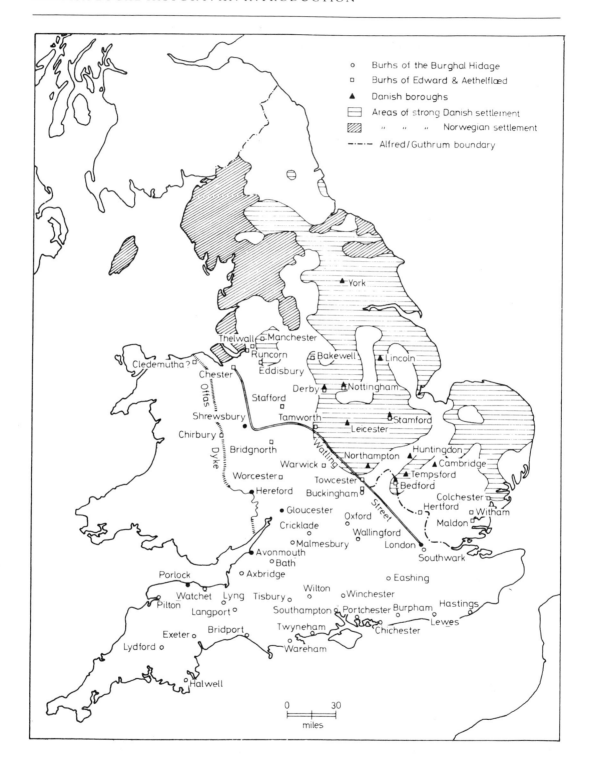

Burhs of the Burghal Hidage
Burhs of Edward & Aethelflæd
Danish boroughs
Areas of strong Danish settlement
" " " Norwegian settlement
Alfred/Guthrum boundary

York

Thelwall Manchester
Runcorn Bakewell Lincoln
Cledemutha? Eddisbury
Chester Derby Nottingham
Offas Stafford
Shrewsbury Tamworth Stamford
Chirbury Leicester
Dyke Bridgnorth Huntingdon
Warwick Northampton Cambridge
Worcester Towcester Tempsford
Hereford Buckingham Bedford
Watling Colchester
Gloucester Hertford Witham
Cricklade Oxford Maldon
Malmesbury Wallingford Street
Avonmouth London
Bath Southwark
Porlock Axbridge Eashing
Watchet Lyng Tisbury Wilton Winchester
Pilton Southampton Portchester Burpham Hastings
Langport Chichester Lewes
Exeter Bridport Twyneham
Lydford Wareham
Halwell

0   30
miles

Mercian dominance, for all its seeming substance, did not outlast Offa. In its place came Wessex, to whose King, Egbert, Mercia itself fell in 829. Even Northumbria acknowledged his lordship. However, English rivalries were overtaken by the threat of Viking raids. These began in 789 and culminated, in 865, in full-scale invasion and settlement.

There were two main routes of incursion, and two main types of resulting settlement: the Norwegians came round the north of Scotland to the Western Isles, Ireland, Scotland, north-west England, Wales and Cornwall; the Danes came principally to the east and south coasts of England and to Gaul. In the 860s, after subduing Northumbria and East Anglia, the Danes turned to Wessex. Their initial military success drove Alfred, King of Wessex from 871 to 899, back to Athelney, in the Somerset marshlands. Alfred's counter-attacking victory at Edington, Wiltshire in 878 did not get rid of the Danes, but it stopped their expansion. The Danish leader, Guthrum, accepted Christian baptism and withdrew to East Anglia in 880. A subsequent treaty between Alfred and Guthrum resulted in the division of the country between the Scandinavian settlers and the English. The dividing line ran from the Thames estuary north and west to Chester, following Watling Street for much of the way. Alfred ruled Wessex, including London, and part of the former Mercia, but the kingdoms of Mercia, East Anglia and Northumbria disappeared. In this area, known later as the Dane-law, Viking settlement was widespread. Bishoprics and monas-teries were disrupted. In the longer term the Vikings left a lasting legal and linguistic mark, seen in place-names (particularly those with the elements –*thorp* and –*by*), manorial organizations, land measurement, law, and social differentiation.

Alfred's surviving English kingdom has attracted greater atten-tion, not least because we know most about it. In the relative peace of the final years of his reign Alfred's court became the centre of a revival of literacy and learning. It was probably there that the main contemporary source for the period, *The Anglo-Saxon Chronicle*, was compiled, *c.* 892. This year-by-year account of important events begins, in understandably rather sketchy style, in 60 BC and continues, incorporating entries by post-Alfredian chroniclers, until 1042. An example from the text appears in the Monks Risborough case study below. Although the Chronicle deals with events throughout the country it gives prominence to the West Saxon kingdom and its dynasty. This has contributed to the heroic, proto-nationalistic view of Alfred's Wessex conveyed by many later historians, local and otherwise.

Even given the bias in the sources the achievements of Alfred remain impressive. His military successes were consolidated by his organization of military and naval forces. His marshalling of resources is clear from the network of *burhs* or fortified towns,

18. (OPPOSITE) Late Saxon England (from H.R. Loyn, *Anglo-Saxon England and the Norman Conquest*, by permission of Longman Group U.K.).

established to defend Wessex by the 880s and recorded in the Burghal Hidage, a document of the early tenth century. There are thirty-three known *burhs*, the present-day street plans of which frequently show the careful planning of the ninth century in their regular, gridded layouts, based on a 66-foot measure. These defensive centres were manned by a force conscripted from a designated surrounding area. Sixteen men could defend twenty-two yards of wall. Each hide, a unit familiar from the mid-Saxon period, was required to supply one man. From the number of hides of the supplying area it is therefore possible to calculate the length of the fortifications of a *burh*. In towns where surviving ramparts enable this calculation to be checked, for example at Cricklade, Southampton and Porchester, it has proved to be accurate. Landholders providing men to the defences could use the fortified area, and often built 'town' houses there to store marketable produce from their land. *Burhs* became centres for trade and marketing as well as defence. They were part of a growing economy, which accompanied the other developments in military, political and educational life in Alfred's Wessex.

Alfred's inheritors drew on this strong Wessex to reconquer the Danelaw. Aethelflaed, sister of Edward the Elder (889–924), built a series of Mercian *burhs* as the bounds of Wessex were extended and consolidated. By 920 the English frontier was at the Humber. Northumbria had been subject to attacks by Norwegians from Ireland, who established themselves in York from 918 to 954. When Eadred of Wessex invaded Northumbria in 954 and ejected the Norwegians a single kingdom of England was finally achieved, and the royal house of Wessex became the royal house of England.

These political developments were endorsed by a more national, unifying style of kingship in which law-making, providing justice, keeping peace and encouraging trade were important. The status of the king was reinforced by religion, expressed in a well-organized church hierarchy. Through the Witan, or royal council, nobles and bishops were involved in the king's government. At a more local level the system of shires was crystallized during the reign of Edgar (959–75), sometimes drawing on existing units such as the area of hides linked to a *burh*. The shires were entrusted to a group of leading magnates, the ealdormen. Shires were broken down into hundreds or (in the Danelaw) wapentakes for legal and administrative purposes. Shire and hundred courts were held. Law enforcement depended at the most local level on the tithing, a group of ten, mutually-responsible households. Also under Edgar the coinage was reformed, consolidating a nationally-accepted currency. The study of coins suggests a shift in numbers minted from the south to the north, with large numbers struck at mints like York, Lincoln, Derby, Leicester, Nottingham, Tamworth, Stafford, Shrewsbury and Chester. This is taken to indicate a general increase in the

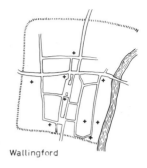

Wallingford

Cricklade

Oxford

Rectilinear Saxon burhs

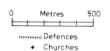

0 Metres 500

.... Defences
+ Churches

19. Saxon *burhs*: planned layouts of the ninth century reflected in the street plans of Wallingford, Cricklade and Oxford.

wealth of northern regions, and an expansion in overseas trade from York, Lincoln and Chester. A measure of the way in which coins passed from hand to hand is the fact that of the stray losses found today as many as two-thirds are not from local mints.

A final important feature of Edgar's reign was the monastic reform movement. This was part of a European phenomenon, but also reflected the imperfections of existing English monastic houses. The reform was supported and funded by the king and his nobles. It began with three new foundations, under the Benedictine rule, at Glastonbury and Abingdon in the 940s, and then at Westbury on Trym. Some fifty houses were to be founded or refounded under the influence of these three, and played an important role in many localities, not least through their extensive land holdings. Despite renewed proof of the insecurity of the English dynasty, and the persistent threat from Scandinavia (producing Danish kings of England from 1016 to 1042), the local historian reflecting on the late Saxon period will find much of lasting relevance. It was a period when growing political unity and economic revival were accompanied by population increase. In the most populous areas nucleated villages developed from earlier scattered settlements, 'often as a result of conscious planning, perhaps accompanied by a total reorganization of agriculture and the growth of the fully developed open or common field system'.[2] As well as villages and field systems there were more manors and manorial lords. The old multiple estates were being broken down into smaller units as lesser thegns received grants of land. Relationships within such manors, villages and field systems became more regulated and stratified; lords made more demands on their tenants and exploitation of available land by an increased population became more intensive within the technology available. This pattern was most marked in Midland and Southern Central England, the heartland of open field farming, which has been distinguishable from woodland and pastoral areas of England ever since. We shall return to this distinction in later periods.

Towns also grew, in population and functions, with markets, tradesmen, specialist craftsmen, gilds, churches and suburban areas.

In these towns and villages private local churches were established, especially after c. 1025. These were often expressions of seigneurial status by manorial lords; some also reflected the decline of the old centralized minster system, or a desire by increasingly coherent village and town communities to have direct access to the rites of the Church. Whatever the particular local circumstances it is from the period 1050 to 1150 that a significant building, or perhaps rebuilding, of local churches in stone occurred. This phenomenon straddles the Conquest and much building at local level continues local, pre-Romanesque architectural traditions. Recent studies of

20. A silver penny of the reign of Edgar reading EADGAR REX ANGLO(rum) and, on the reverse, bearing the name of the moneyer, Aethelsige and the mint, Shrewsbury (abbreviated to SCRO).

church fabric have suggested that some buildings previously assumed to be 'Norman' may in fact belong to this earlier tradition. This burgeoning network of local churches grew within the interstices of the declining minster *parochiae* and before the development of local parish units. That story belongs, as we shall see, to the eleventh and twelfth centuries.

The other great legacy of Saxon to Norman England lies in the field of governmental institutions. The Normans comprehensively displaced the English aristocracy – only two Englishmen were top landowners in 1086, only one a bishop and two abbots of major abbeys by the following year, but they did adopt from the Saxons 'integrated systems in which the distribution, assessment and measurement of land, the gradations of society, and the institutions of government were elaborately related together'.[3] Amongst these systems was the *fyrd*, a militia which, by the end of the tenth century, meant every five hides had to equip and provide a man for military service. They also included the shire, the sheriff (shire-reeve, representing the king in the county), the shire and hundred courts, the geld or taxation system, and the royal writ, an authoritative expression, authenticated by a seal, of the king's will, usually to the local sheriff or bishop. The Normans also took over and adapted the coinage.

Some nineteenth-century constitutional historians and early local historians have interpreted certain Saxon institutions as lineal ancestors of modern and democratic institutions. The shire court is seen as pre-figuring the medieval House of Commons, which thus has its roots in early Germanic institutions, free of the subsequent Norman yoke. You may encounter vestiges of these enthusiastically perceived continuities in some local histories, but there is little evidence to suggest participating local community structures. The sources say little of the lesser landholders and cultivators of Saxon society, whom some historians have seen as participants in these courts and gatherings. What we do know, from national and local documents, and from art and archaeology, is an increasingly organized hierarchical society, in which military power still dominated. That power, and the personal allegiances it commanded at successive levels, was being translated into permanent institutions, ecclesiastical and secular, and into landholding patterns. Saxon society was an unequal one, in which differences of social stratification became more distinct. Far from being the Dark Ages, a stark and uncivilized prelude to a new and different medieval world, the Saxon centuries in England left a clear and emphatic imprint on the later history of our local communities.

21. St Martin's, Wareham, Dorset has many features characteristic of non-minster, stone-built, Saxon churches: small nave and chancel, steep roofs, high walls, long-and-short work at the corners, and a few, small windows.

Using Saxon sources: landscape and documents

The importance in local history both of using printed information, and of integrating evidence from landscape as well as documents, has already been stressed. How to put this into practice is shown in this case-study of a parish whose written history, like many, begins in Saxon times.

The first specific, written reference to Risborough (now Monks Risborough) in Buckinghamshire, comes in an Anglo-Saxon charter dated AD 903. This is one of around 1,600 charters which conveyed land or rights either from kings to senior churchmen, lay aristocrats or religious houses, or – at the next stage down – from an ecclesiastic or noble to his followers. The earliest charters date from the 660s, but the majority of those surviving, often in later medieval copies, came from the ninth, tenth and eleventh centuries. Those most prized by local historians include detailed boundary perambulations, some 840 in all. These describe the exact extent of the property granted, using recognized features in the local land-scape. Not all counties are equally well endowed with charter boundaries; Buckinghamshire has six, of which Monks Ris-borough is one.

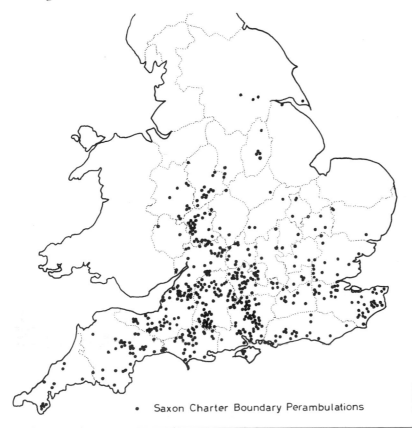

• Saxon Charter Boundary Perambulations

22. Places described in Anglo-Saxon charters with boundary clauses.

From this charter[4] we can locate Risborough in the fluctuating political hierarchies of the early tenth century as part of the former Mercia, now under ever-stronger Wessex overlordship. The charter grant is by Alfred's successor, Edward the Elder, with his sister Aethelflaed, Lady of the Mercians, and her husband Aethelred to ealdorman Aethelfrith. The estate, of thirty hides, is confirmed to Aethelfrith, all of whose charters of inheritance had been destroyed by fire. The established importance of the written record, and of 'bookland' is clear in Aethelfrith's determination to obtain substitute charters validated at the very highest level. His new charter also spells out the exact bounds of his thirty hides. This estate boundary can be traced on the ground, and later became that of the ecclesiastical parish of Monks Risborough, a unit that survived in this form until 1934. The resulting area was a typical scarp-edge parish or estate. It ran from upland chalk hills in the south-east down a steep escarpment, at the foot of which, on lower greensand and a spring line, lay the principal settlement, with to the north-west an area of rich but wet and low-lying pasture land. There can be no substitute for going and looking on the ground, in order to gain a real understanding of how the unit of land described in such a document may have worked as a place to live, to win a livelihood, and yield what was required of it by the king and by Aethelfrith. Charter boundaries provide the local historian with the earliest opportunity for that matching of archival and field experience which can be one of the most rewarding of all local history ventures, as W.G. Hoskins vividly conveys:

> . . . there is at least one feature in the countryside which is of Saxon origin and often remains more or less intact. I refer to the boundary banks of large Anglo-Saxon estates, which one learns to recognize by laboriously tracing the points named in the surviving charters. This exercise gives one a truer and more detailed knowledge of the English countryside than any other pursuit, not excluding fox-hunting. By the time one has scrambled over hedges, leapt across boggy streams in deep woods, traversed narrow green lanes all but blocked with brambles and the luxuriant vegetation of wet summers, not to mention walked along high airy ridges on a day of tumultuous blue-and-white skies with magnificent views of deep country all round – by the time one has done this, armed with a copy of a Saxon charter and the $2\frac{1}{2}$-inch maps, the topography of some few miles of the English landscape is indelibly printed on the mind and heart. And at the same time, one has the constant intellectual exercise of fitting the frequently obscure landmarks of the charter to the ground one is traversing, and the mental excitement of making some unmistakable identification and of revealing to oneself the age of some ordinary feature of the scene – a ditch, a hedge, a piece of marsh, a pond, or what you will.[5]

23. (OPPOSITE) The Risborough charter of 903. Most of the text – invoking the Supreme Father, recalling the loss of earlier charters, confirming and witnessing ealdorman Aethelfrith's claim to the thirty-hide estate – is in Latin. The key boundary clause (top of lower page) is in the Old English vernacular.

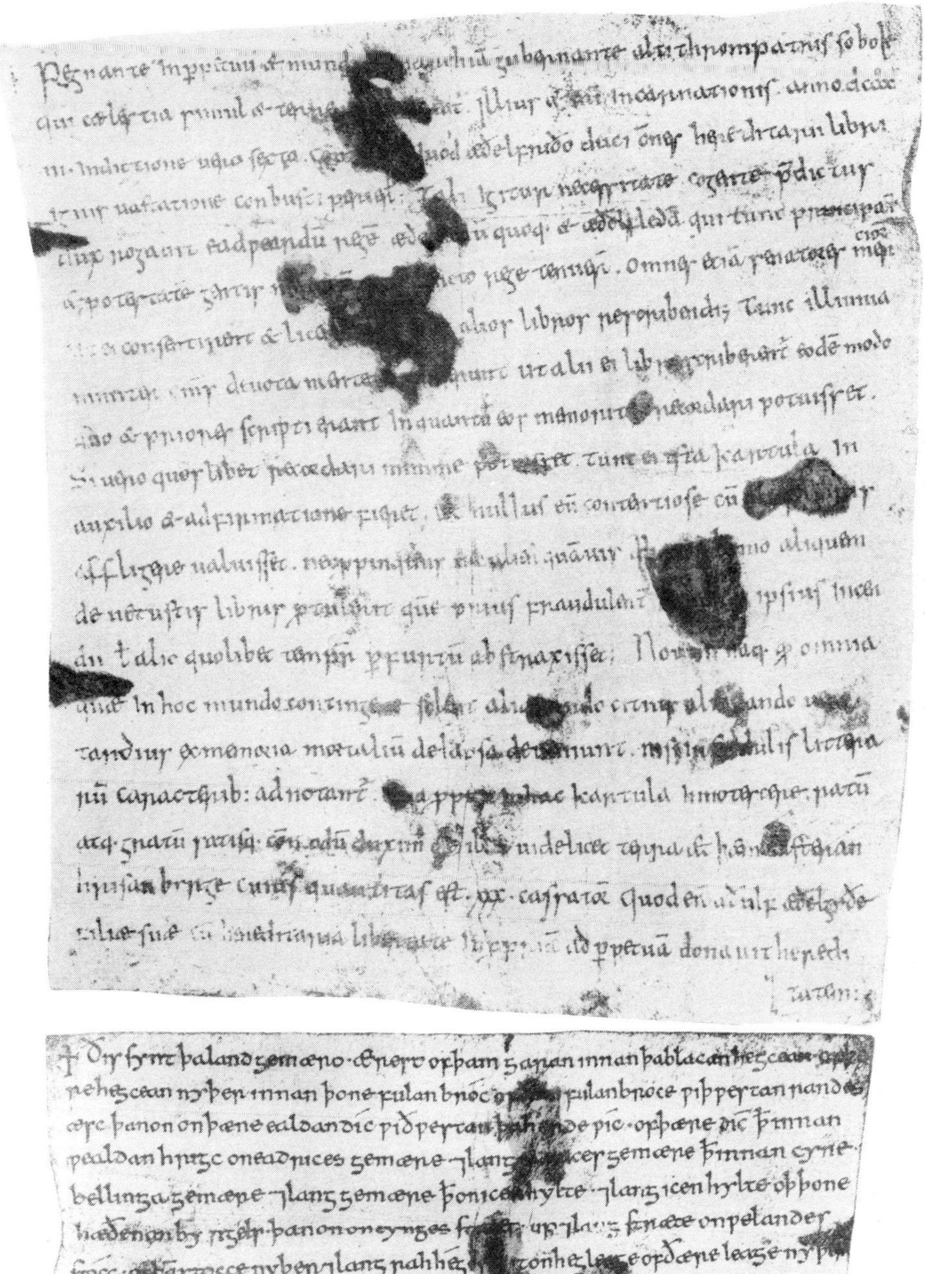

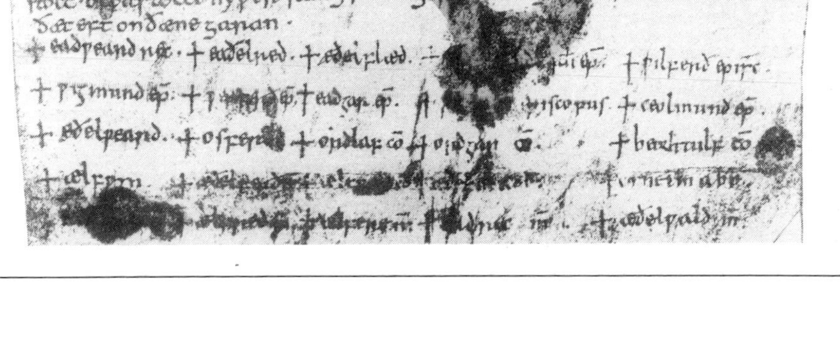

24. (ABOVE) The line of the Black Hedge continues to mark the charter boundary of 903 and the later parish of Monks Risborough in the present-day Buckinghamshire landscape.

Dinton
Waldridge Manor

Eadric's boundary ridge

N

Kimble

Owlswick

Old ditch

Foul Brook

The Ash Tree

Icknield Way

Heathen Burials

The King's Street

Monks Risborough

Lower Cadsden

Weland's Stump

Roe deer hedge

Green Hailey

Hay clearing

The Black Hedge

0   Km   3

The gore

25. Risborough bounds from the charter perambulation (after M. Reed).

The points chosen to mark a perambulation tell us much more than the mere shape of the holding. Those for Risborough are shown below in italics and on the map opposite.[6]

1.   *First from the gore.* It is likely that here the gore is the pointed angle of the boundary itself.

2.   *Into the Black Hedge.* The Black Hedge has been surveyed and dated (see below). It is so thick that for long stretches it has a footpath running through the middle.

3.   *From the hedge down into the foul brook.* The hedge can still be followed down to the Icknield Way. From this point it has disappeared under residential development but its course can still be traced along property boundaries as far as the brook.

4.   *From the foul brook to the west of the ash tree on the river bank.* Beyond the foul brook the stepped pattern of the boundary seems to indicate that it was going between existing furlongs of arable land.

5.   *From there to the old ditch west of the herdsman's building.* It is possible that the herdsman's building, or *wic*, is now called Owlswick (Ulfr's *wic*), from the Scandinavian into whose possession it fell at some later date.

6.   *From the ditch into wold ridge.* The boundary then makes a right-angle turn to climb the ridge. Any woods there have long disappeared. Only the name of Waldridge Manor still preserves their memory.

7.   *To Eadric's boundary.* Two estates at Waldridge are recorded in Domesday Book, one of half a hide and the other of two hides and one virgate. It is possible that Eadric held one or other of them late in the ninth or early in the tenth century.

8.   *Along Eadric's boundary into the boundary of the people of Kimble.* The point where the parishes of Dinton, Great Kimble and Monks Risborough meet.

9.   *Along the boundary to Icknield.* The boundary then turns south-east and, still marked by a series of hedgerows, it makes its way over the A4010 road to the Upper Icknield Way.

10.   *Along Icknield to the heathen burials.* The boundary follows the Icknield Way for only a very short distance. There is now no visible trace of the heathen burials.

11.   *From there to King's Street.* The King's Street is the narrow road that rises through a steep-sided valley to Lower Cadsden, after which it becomes a footpath.

12.   *Up along the street to Weland's stump.* Is this a reference to the mythical smith Wayland? If so, iron working in the Chilterns is less improbable (see Roman iron bloomery site at Great Missenden, less than three miles away).

13.   *From the stump down along the roe deer hedge to hay clearing.* The boundaries here are still marked by hedgerows and Green Hailey preserves the name of the hay clearing.

14. *From the hay clearing down back to the gore*. Much of the rest of the boundary is now marked by minor roads.

Some features we cannot hope to find, for example the ash tree, yet the fact that a single tree of a recognized species should have been so distinctive a landmark suggests a cleared landscape. In other areas there are indications of woodland, now lost (6), or implied, as in parts of the upland where there was a clearing (13 and 14). The existence of a field-layout of parallel furlongs is suggested by the boundary shapes in the middle of the estate (4), while in the lower part of the estate the terrain, matched with name evidence at Owlswick, suggests land use for pasture. Road patterns are indicated by references to the Icknield Way and 'King's Street'. Continuing awareness of previous pagan inhabitants is shown by the use of the heathen burials as a marker and the name Weland's stump. Just as continuities from previous periods to the tenth century emerge, so too the evidence of later sources helps in interpretation, for example the later place-names of Owlswick and Green Hailey, and landholding information in Domesday Book (7). Finally there is the remarkable present-day survival of a seemingly impermanent kind of boundary mark, the Black Hedge, to which we shall return.

The story of Risborough as deduced from Anglo-Saxon charters is not finished in 903. By 994 the estate, together with its charter, was in the hands of Sigeric, Archbishop of Canterbury. Grants to churchmen were frequent, but it is also possible that a disproportionate number of records of such holdings were made and have survived because of the extensive record-making and careful record-keeping practised by ecclesiastical bodies. Certainty of the corporate inheritance of their records also made for greater archival immortality, a fact reflected in the large part played in historical research by the records of monasteries, archbishops and bishops and, later, colleges rather than individual lay families. However, Archbishop Sigeric was not immune to attack from the pagan Danish armies, who in 994 threatened to burn Christ Church, Canterbury unless he bought them off. He sent urgently for help to Bishop Aescwig of Dorchester, who responded with ninety pounds of silver and two hundred mancuses of gold. In return the Archbishop gave the Bishop the estate of Risborough, a transaction which was recorded in a new charter, granted by King Aethelred. This subjected the estate only to the three dues common in later charters, the *fyrd* (military service) and the maintenance of bridges and fortifications. In understanding transactions such as this do not forget the value of more general sources, particularly *The Anglo-Saxon Chronicle*. Its entry for 994 makes very clear the terrifying circumstances of that time.[7]

In this year Olaf and Swein came to London on the Nativity of St Mary with 94 ships, and they proceeded to attack the city stoutly and wished also to set it on fire; but there they suffered more harm and injury than they ever thought any citizens would do to them. But the holy Mother of God showed her mercy to the citizens on that day and saved them from their enemies. And these went away from there, and did the greatest damage that ever any army could do, by burning, ravaging and slaying, both along the coast, and in Essex, Kent, Sussex and Hampshire; and finally they seized horses and rode as widely as they wished, and continued to do indescribabie damage. Then the king and his councillors determined to send to them and promised them tribute and provisions, on condition that they should cease that harrying. And they then accepted that, and the whole army came then to Southampton and took winter quarters there; and they were provisioned throughout all the West Saxon kingdom, and they were paid 16,000 pounds in money.

Then the king sent Bishop Ælfheah and Ealdorman Æthelweard for King Olaf, and hostages were given to the ships meanwhile. And they then brought Olaf to the king at Andover with much ceremony, and King Ethelred stood sponsor to him at confirmation, and bestowed gifts on him royally. And then Olaf promised – as also he performed – that he would never come back to England in hostility.

Bishop Aescwig, who had helped to save Christ Church in 994, on his death in 1002 willed Risborough back to Christ Church and the Archbishop. What exactly happened has been somewhat clouded by the existence of two more seeming charters, dated 995 and 1006, purportedly granting Risborough to Canterbury. These are amongst those texts established as spurious by the experts, who carefully test the fabric, language and wording of charters to establish cases of fraud. Forgery, particularly by monastic houses seeking to establish their claim to land, is not uncommon. In the case of Risborough it seems there were over-zealous attempts to invest proof of a true title to the estate with the added weight of a full charter. So the thirty hides at Risborough became *Monks* Risborough. Its archepiscopal lordship gave it a special status into the Middle Ages, and until the nineteenth century. Monks Risborough became a 'peculiar', a separate jurisdiction not owing suit to the secular shire court, and with its own ecclesiastical jurisdiction, for example in matters of probate. Many such exceptions to the general pattern, which may seem confusing or inconvenient to the local historian – detached parts of counties are another – stem from similar early patterns of ownership.

How do you discover whether there is a similar charter or charters for a place you are studying? P.H. Sawyer's *Anglo-Saxon charters: an annotated list and bibliography*[8] lists all known charters, as well as writs, wills and associated documents. It gives the date,

26. Theakston Peculiar ale owes its name to the ecclesiastical jurisdiction of the Peculiar of Masham, Yorkshire, whose seal was adopted by the local brewery. For local historians peculiars, and other unusual jurisdictions, may affect the location of sources such as wills and court records.

grantor, grantee(s) and grant, explains what manuscript and printed versions are available, and comments on the vexed question of authenticity. The two most comprehensive collections of published texts of charters, by Birch and by Kemble,[9] date from the nineteenth century, although a modern edition is now slowly under way.[10] There is a reasonable chance that individual charters, or those from a particular county or area will have been published, in the regional series begun by Finberg,[11] or in county or occasionally more local journals. Using these published texts and comments it will usually be unnecessary, indeed inadvisable, to try and go back to original documents in Latin and Saxon vernacular. Having exploited your charter(s) to the full, linking them if possible to wills, writs and chronicle sources, and to the landscape, you should know more about the politics, personalities and lordship of your place, about early local place-names, and about landscape and land use.

Particular features may demand further work. At Risborough the Black Hedge claimed attention. This formidable boundary marker, thirty feet wide in places with a double hedge and central ditch still discernible in parts, marches emphatically between Monks and Princes Risborough parishes. Some 480 yards were surveyed in detail by the Natural History Section of the Bucks Archaeological Society.[12] The line of the surviving hedge was clearly that of the hedge mentioned in the charter of 903, but how old is what we now see? This was tested using the technique of dating popularly known as Hooper's Hedgerow Hypothesis (HHH). Dr Max Hooper first suggested in the 1960s[13] that the age of a hedge could be related to the number of woody species it contained. Numbers of hedges from Devon to Lincolnshire, whose ages were known from documents, were examined, and a relationship between their age and their botanical composition was found, based roughly on one species per hundred years of growth. Dr Hooper's method requires the counting of woody species from one side of the hedge in a number of sample lengths of thirty yards. To calculate from the resulting observations the degree of correlation between number of species and age Dr Hooper produced a regression equation:

$$\text{Age of hedge} = (110 \times \text{number of species}) + 30 \text{ years.}$$

HHH has since been the basis of much local history fieldwork and the source of great debate. Obviously there are local variables other than age and number of species that may affect a hedge, not least soil, altitude, natural colonization of other species, and management or lack of it. In order to improve accuracy several studies have formulated local regression equations, based on data from at least twelve dated hedges in the study area. On this basis, Dr Hooper himself found, for a small area on the Huntingdonshire–Northamptonshire border, that only 15 per cent of all variation in

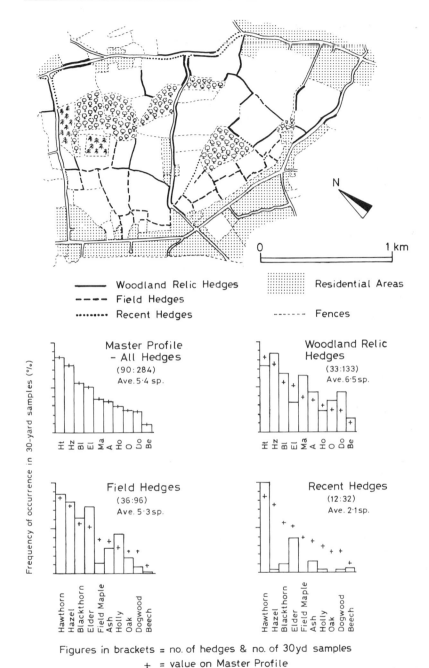

Frequency of occurrence in 30-yard samples (%)

**Master Profile
– All Hedges**
(90:284)
Ave. 5·4 sp.

Ht Hz Bl El Ma A Ho O Do Be

**Woodland Relic
Hedges**
(33:133)
Ave. 6·5 sp.

Ht Hz Bl El Ma A Ho O Do Be

Field Hedges
(36:96)
Ave. 5·3 sp.

Recent Hedges
(12:32)
Ave. 2·1 sp.

Hawthorn Hazel Blackthorn Elder Field Maple Ash Holly Oak Dogwood Beech

Hawthorn Hazel Blackthorn Elder Field Maple Ash Holly Oak Dogwood Beech

Figures in brackets = no. of hedges & no. of 30yd samples
+ = value on Master Profile

—— Woodland Relic Hedges
- - - Field Hedges
········ Recent Hedges

Residential Areas

- - - - Fences

N

0   1 km

27. (OPPOSITE) Analysing the
number and identity of plant
species in local hedges can
help to explain the history of
land-use and landscape, as
in the study of Naphill,
Buckinghamshire, described
here.

hedge composition was due to factors other than age; Trevor Hussey's study of Emmington in Oxfordshire leaves 20 per cent unaccounted for.[14]

Using Hooper's method at Risborough BAS found that the Black Hedge was indeed extremely old. It was not of uniform age, average numbers of species ranging from 11.13 to 8.25 in different sections. This puts the oldest parts as seventh- or eighth-century and already old when recorded in the charter.

Hedges of all ages can tell you much about your local history and are worthy of survey. Trevor Hussey has done this for Naphill, up on the Buckinghamshire Chilterns, near Risborough. This wooded, hilly countryside, with dispersed farms and small settlements, does not conform to the pattern of community evolution suggested by the open-field arable and nucleated villages of the nearby Midland plain. It has often been said that areas like the Chilterns developed by piecemeal assarting or clearance of small, separate fields immediately around settlements. The hedges at Naphill suggest rather that initial woodland clearance was on a larger scale to form big fields, and that those were sub-divided by later hedges into the small fields we now see. This picture is based not only on numbers of species, but also on the actual species in the hedgerows. The earlier hedges, around the big fields cleared from woodland, have the woodland herbs growing in and near them which are associated with 'woodland relic hedges'. Bluebell, primrose, wood anemone, wood spurge, yellow archangel, wood melick grass and dog's mercury are all considered 'indicator' species in this way. As for the hedges themselves, Hussey has constructed 'species profiles' from ninety Naphill hedges and has found not only more species in the older, woodland relic hedges, but different species. These are the shrubs unlikely to be colonizers, and thus indicative of older hedges – hazel, holly, spindle and field maple. This is true of Naphill and of studies in the West and East Midlands, yet hazel and field maple seem to colonize recent hedges more easily in Kent and East Sussex.[15] So the methods and the possible relationships are known but the opportunity and need for more local studies remains. Hedgerow studies are a prime example of how pieces of the local history jigsaw may fit together – from Saxon charter to present day hedgerow, from botanical identifications to statistical methods, from earliest records to recording, appreciating and perhaps helping to preserve surviving hedges.

References

1   John Blair, 'The Anglo-Saxon period', in K.O. Morgan (ed.), *The Oxford illustrated history of Britain* (1984), p. 65.

2   C. Taylor, in W.G. Hoskins, *The Making of the English landscape* (1988 edn.) pp. 40–2.

3   J. Campbell (ed.), *The Anglo-Saxons* (1982), p. 241.

4   A facsimile is printed in *Facsimiles of Anglo-Saxon manuscripts*, Part 3, XXIII (Ordnance Survey 1884). See also M. Gelling, *The Early charters of the Thames Valley* (1979), pp. 74 et seq.

5   W.G. Hoskins, *The Making of the English landscape* (1988 edn.), p. 61.

6   Comments based on M. Reed, 'Buckinghamshire Anglo-Saxon charter boundaries', in M. Gelling, op. cit., pp.180–1.

7   Quoted in D. Whitelock (ed.), *English historical documents*, vol. 1 (2nd edn., 1979), pp. 235–6.

8   P.H. Sawyer, *Anglo-Saxon charters: an annotated list and bibliography* (Royal Historical Society 1968); see also D. Whitelock (ed.), op. cit., pp. 369–82; and K. Bailey, 'Anglo-Saxon charters and the local historian', in *The Local Historian*, 17 (May 1986), pp. 71–7.

9   W. de G. Birch, *Cartularium Saxonicum* (1885–99); J.M. Kemble, *Codex diplomaticus* (1839–48).

10 *Corpus of Anglo-Saxon charters*: A. Campbell (ed.), vol. I Charters of Rochester, (1977); P.H. Sawyer (ed.), vol. II Charters of Burton Abbey, (1979); other volumes in preparation.

11 H.P.R. Finberg, *The Early charters of Devon and Cornwall* (1953).
    ——, *The Early charters of Wessex* (1964).
    C.R. Hart, *The Early charters of Eastern England* (1969).
    ——, *The Early charters of Essex* (2nd edn., 1971).
    H.P.R. Finberg, *The Early charters of the West Midlands* (2nd edn., 1972).
    C.R. Hart, *The Early charters of Northern England and the North Midlands* (1975).
    M. Gelling, *The Early charters of the Thames Valley* (1979).

12 See A.H.T. Baines, 'The Boundaries of Monks Risborough', in *Records of Bucks*, XXIII (1981), pp. 76–101.

13 See M.D. Hooper, *Hedges and local history* (Standing Conference for Local History, 1972); E. Pollard, M.D. Hooper and N.W. Moore, *Hedges* (1974).

14 T. Hussey, 'Hedgerow history', in *The Local Historian*, 17 (May 1987), pp. 327–42.

15 ——, loc. cit., pp. 333–4.

28. The pattern of medieval open-field farming revealed by surviving ridge and furrow earthworks at Byfield Hill, Northamptonshire. Created by the plough turning the furrow inwards from the border with the next man's strip, ridge and furrow is best preserved in fields later put down to grass. The hedges of later enclosures are superimposed on the strips and furlongs.

29. Peasant lives have been increasingly reconstructed through local studies. This occupation for the month of February is based on a late thirteenth-century English calendar.

CHAPTER THREE

Medieval Local Communities

The year 1066 is probably the best known date in English history. It has often been understood as the beginning of the Middle Ages, but just how important a watershed was the Norman Conquest in the lives of local communities? The invasion of 1066 undoubtedly wrought major dynastic and political changes, yet it took time for invasion to become conquest. The Domesday survey, that remarkably comprehensive stocktaking of Norman England so much referred to by local historians, was made in 1086, twenty years on from William's victory at Hastings. Only then was his authority sufficiently secure to embark on this judgemental recording. Even so Lancashire was not separately listed, while Durham, Northumberland, Cumberland and Westmorland escaped scrutiny. The transition of these years has been summed up[1] as one from conquistadors to landlords. At the top of society changes are certainly apparent with almost total replacement of those in leading positions of lay and ecclesiastical authority by Normans. These new figures, as Domesday Book records, were firmly located in direct line of dependence on the king, from whom they held their land, in return for allegiance and obligations. Feudalism, in its classic sense of owing military service, was established. Written records of those obligations were increasingly made in Latin rather than Old English. Yet there was no cultural crusade to expunge English ways. Rather the Normans adopted whatever means enabled them most effectively to exercise control and exact maximum returns. For example, compiling the exhaustive detail in Domesday Book would have been impossible without the use of existing mechanisms like the shire and hundred courts. In this way a national survey, of which no other regime in Europe would have been capable at this time, was completed in under a year. Behind the dramatic façade of conquest the local historian will find significant continuities from Saxon England.

Each local settlement in medieval England existed within a framework of parallel patterns of power and jurisdiction. There was the basic unit of feudal lordship, the manor; the ecclesiastical hierarchy of parish or chapelry, rural deanery, archdeaconry and diocese linked ultimately to the authority of Rome; and the chain of civil power through vill or tithing, hundred or wapentake, and shire or county to the crown. In some towns there was also borough jurisdiction. Manor, church and crown all affected local experience. As institutions they generated the bulk of source material available for medieval local studies. Their records, taken together with the evidence of landscape and buildings, reflect events, and changes in the economic reality and social relations of local life. Local historians will therefore find reconstructing past patterns of ownership and power, jurisdiction and authority, essential to finding evidence and to understanding the medieval picture. This chapter begins with an outline of the main features and trends to look for locally, taking the perspectives of manor, church, crown, the landscape, and town and commercial life. This will be followed by local case studies, and by a brief survey of available sources.

Manors, lords and tenants

The Domesday Book entries for each county are organized not by place but under the names of the king's tenants-in-chief and principal tenants, the key relationship in the new regime. Under the names of these individuals come entries for manors, the units through which they in turn exercised lordship, assuming the power to grant land and rights to peasant tenants and exacting in return goods and services in kind, cash and labour. Like military service, manors were not new in post–1066 England, but existing institutions which were encompassed in a tighter net of stated obligations. New faces appeared in the upper reaches of the hierarchy but lower down the social scale there was no wholesale change of personnel. The feudal network did not produce a single type of local lord. Of landholdings in 1086 (based on the percentage of annual revenue recorded in the Domesday Book) the king and members of the royal family held 17 per cent, bishoprics, priories and abbeys, of which there were about 100, 26 per cent; lay barons, of whom there were about 170, 49 per cent; and royal servants, officials and old English lords and their dependants 8 per cent.[2] In practice many manors were sub-infeudated, granted by their lords to lesser landholders, at the next stage down the social feudal ladder. How a particular manor fitted into these patterns produced different local experiences. It could be part of the great estate of a major baron or wealthy ecclesiastical body, just one of an array of manors spread over several counties. Or it could be part of a middling estate, held by a lesser tenant-in-chief, a less wealthy church body, or an important tenant of a great lord, again possibly extending over more than one county. Or it could be in the lordship of a rank-and-file military tenant, knightly or otherwise, whose sphere of influence probably extended no further than between one and three manors.

To live on a manor of one of the great magnates, William de Warenne, was to be part of holdings in Sussex (about half his land), Norfolk (about a quarter), Essex, Oxfordshire, Buckinghamshire, Bedfordshire, Huntingdonshire, Hampshire, Cambridgeshire, Suffolk, Lincolnshire, and the West Riding of Yorkshire. Most tenants would see little of such a lord, except in his favourite or strategically located holdings. In fact Warenne sub-infeudated most of his manors. In others most revenue came not from unfree peasant tenants owing services on his demesne lands, but from renders from freemen and sokemen. This applied particularly in the large Yorkshire manor of Conisborough, and in Norfolk and Bedfordshire, formerly parts of the Danelaw.[3] The varying patterns of Saxon landholding were not extinguished by Norman feudalism, even on the estates of one of the greatest new magnates. In yet other areas Warenne did hold manors run on the basis of directly exploited demesne lands, integrated within a common field system, and worked chiefly by peasant tenants. Rigid uniformity is not something the local historian should expect, despite the monolithic inflexibility suggested by some pictures of early medieval society.

Apart from locating a manor in the context of the lord's overall holdings it is important to know whether it was coterminous with a particular village and its fields. In such cases the life of the manor reflects that of the whole community in most basic respects. If, on the other hand, one settlement is divided between the jurisdictions of more than one manor, or a manor encompasses several settlements then the picture is less clear, or totally obscured. For example, Domesday Book is concerned only with the 'head place' of a manorial unit and may not mention other places existing within its area. Neither was the manor an exclusively rural phenomenon; some towns developed, or were developed by a manorial lord, without acquiring the distinctively urban, more independent form of borough government.

Despite the very considerable inequalities between lords and peasants the life of medieval manors required a necessary equilibrium between their interests. Lords exacted their rent in services, whether in kind, cash or labour, but enough had to remain in the peasant economy for the tenants and their households to subsist. The balance of resources had to be taken into account, whether varied by short-term misfortunes such as weather or disease in crops or cattle, or by more permanent shifts like those in population levels and the number of mouths to be fed. The land and its produce provided a shared concern. The manorial community was based on custom, often grounded in the recollections of local elders, rather than on royal jurisdiction or statute. Apart from a few twelfth-century surveys manorial documentation is available chiefly from the thirteenth and fourteenth centuries onwards. Written custumals record dues to be paid to the lord by unfree tenants. They included heriot or payment of the tenant's best beast on his death, and merchet, a money payment at the marriage of his daughter. On succeeding to a holding the new tenant had to pay an entry fine. Once in the holding the unfree tenant owed regular service in the form of compulsory labour on the lord's land in the manor. This involved both weekly work and extra days and numbers of people at peak times such as harvest. Such obligations came to be taken as a mark of unfree, villein tenure.

At its most basic then the medieval manor was about feudal lordship, about relationships of land holding in return for allegiance and services, and at a practical level about communal subsistence. The nature of the manor was epitomized by the manorial courts, through which the lord exercised his jurisdiction. Tenants, free and unfree, were obliged to attend, and to swear fealty to the lord. The courts operated on the basis of custom and it was there that the business of tenure and inheritance, of heriots, merchets and entry fines, of the regulation of communal agriculture, of some disputes between the lord and his representative, lord and tenant, and tenant and tenant was worked out. The courts of those manors with rights of criminal jurisdiction, through view of frankpledge, also dealt with minor misdemeanours. As local studies show the courts were by no means a one-way route for the handing down of seigneurial dictat. In many places the lord's rights were regularly infringed. It was the jury, made up of free and unfree tenants, which provided information, statements of custom and decisions in inter-tenant disputes.

All of these relationships were expressed in terms – villein, bordar, cottar, freeman, sokeman and others – which are alien to the twentieth-century reader in both form and concept. Local historians will find out what such terms meant in a particular place from written expressions of local custom, which are to be found in manorial court rolls, custumals and rentals, and in surveys made by central government such as the Hundred Rolls of the 1270s and inquisitions post mortem (see p. 77). Local variations are important, interesting and to be expected. It will prove fruitless to pursue some conveniently universal definition of, say, villeinage and expect it to apply in all areas at all stages of the Middle Ages, but neither is it wise merely to lump all local inhabitants together. Inevitably the question of tenure will have to be met and some general guidelines can be offered.

The majority of people was unfree. Of the rural population of

268,984 enumerated in Domesday Book 40.6 per cent were villeins, 32.4 per cent bordars or cottars (manorial tenants without land in the arable, common fields, but usually owing fewer services to the lord than villeins), and 10.5 per cent serfs. Only 13.7 per cent were sokemen or freemen.[4] However, what unfreedom meant varied over time and place. During Henry II's reign (1154–89) lawyers sought to define exactly who had the right to apply to the royal courts concerning rights of seisin, that is the right to hold land. The rights of an unfree, manorial tenant were determined solely by his lord, while a freeman could sue in the royal court. Three types of action in the king's courts were instituted at this time. The Writ of Right, the Assize of Novel Disseisin and the Assize of Mort d'ancestor allowed access to royal justice in cases of freehold property unjustly disseised, or where the rights of an heir were challenged. The definition of free and unfree thus mattered greatly and became more closely defined in legal theory than either in 1086 or in the later Middle Ages. By the thirteenth century what precisely the lord's reeve or bailiff could ask of a villein tenant was being more and more exactly defined and written down.

The villein's lot may seem burdensome. Yet it has been argued[5] that by precisely stating custom the tenant's position was known, protected and less easily worsened by increased demands from his lord. Restrictions on selling and willing holdings of unfree land may have helped to keep them intact, while the apparently better-off freemen on manors in areas like populous East Anglia were free to split their land amongst their families, which led to fragmented and less viable holdings. As Miller and Hatcher have written, 'there is no simple formula equating freedom with prosperity and villeinage with poverty, just as the lines lawyers drew between bond and free lose their sharpness when we subject them to scrutiny. It is not merely that there are many gradations between the fully bond and the fully free: everyday behaviour in the villages appears neglectful of these lines.'

Feudal lordship was a diminishing force in England from the late thirteenth century. Both military service and, more locally, labour service were being commuted to money payments and hired men used instead. The transition to a relationship between a landlord and a tenant on the basis of rent or lease was under way. The reality of villeinage was also changed in some manors by the lord's willingness to accept cash payments from villeins in return for them being free to sell land, move away, or send a son to school or into Holy Orders. The impact of manorial control also related to the degree of direct cultivation by the lord of his demesne, that is his land in arable, meadow and pasture. In some manors, especially those of lay lords, there was piecemeal leasing of demesne land by the late thirteenth century.

The social hierarchy in medieval England

Late eleventh century		Late thirteenth century		Late fifteenth century	
Landed/rural	**Urban**	**Landed/rural**	**Urban**	**Landed/rural**	**Urban**
Laity Tenants-in-chief [Earls, Barons] — *Clergy* Archbishops Bishops Abbots		*Laity* Earls, Barons — *Clergy* Archbishops Bishops Abbots		*Laity* Dukes Earls Barons — *Clergy* Archbishops Bishops Abbots	
Thegns/Knights, Lesser knights — Priests → →	Burgesses, Lesser burgesses	Knights, 'Lesser gentry' — Rectors, Vicars → Lesser clergy → →		Knights, Esquires, Gentlemen — Rectors, Vicars → Lesser clergy → →	Merchants
Freemen/sokemen, Villeins, Bordars, Cottars	Bordars	Franklins, Free, Villeins, Cottars [Unfree]		Yeomen, Husbandmen, Labourers	Master craftsmen, Journeymen, Labourers
Servi/serfs, Marginals	Marginals	Servants/famuli, Marginals		Servants, Marginals	Servants, Marginals

30. The social hierarchy in medieval England (after Dyer).

Manors had previously been operating in a climate of substantially increasing population, an increase sustained by more arable farming, and an overall extension of cultivated land and settlement. Formerly marginal land was brought under the plough and assarts cleared out of woodland. Demesne farming, directly involving the lord in producing crops for the market was generally at a high level. By the late thirteenth and early fourteenth centuries the situation had changed. The limits of sustainable expansion had been reached. Farming technology was insufficient to support intensive cultivation at earlier levels. Yields may have fallen and supplies of viable new land were exhausted. In many years, of which 1315–17 brought the most widespread disasters, famine conditions prevailed. Local studies frequently reveal signs of difficulty and decline in the manorial economy well before the impact of the Black Death.

Every aspect of local life was deeply affected by the drastic fall in population levels brought by the first epidemic of bubonic plague in 1348–9. The number of deaths has been much debated, with estimates varying from 20 to 50 per cent of the total population. This sudden relief of population pressure brought a change in the balance of power between lords and tenants. Market prices for produce fell. Tenants and labour were difficult to secure. The withdrawal from direct demesne farming, by both lay and church lords, was accelerated. More land was leased, and more was transferred from arable to pasture. Tenants were in a stronger position and became more mobile, both geographically and socially, despite attempts to impose restrictions like the Statute of Labourers, which pegged wages at pre-Black Death rates and sought to stop workers moving at will. It is often when 'norms' are changing that the most vigorous attempts are made by existing authorities to codify and enforce them. The various sumptuary laws passed in the fourteenth and fifteenth centuries are telling signs of such a preoccupation with indicating and defining status. They tried to ensure that the status of men and women could be recognized from their clothing. The length, cloth and cost of a man's coat separated labourer from gentleman. This was not enforceable legislation but its concerns are revealing.

The ties of villeinage were becoming a thing of the past. New designations like gentleman, yeoman and husbandman emerged as did new kinds of tenure. Copyhold entailed some payments to a manorial lord but no labour services; moreover it attached to the holding and not to the tenant, who had personal freedom. The social hierarchy to be found in England had shifted from a feudal pattern superimposed on strong pre-existing institutions, to an apparently more closely defined, still feudal framework, to a range of relative status which had much to do with economic and cultural position and very little to do with feudal, legal definitions.

Clues in the landscape

Many clues to the ebb and flow of a medieval community, its size and prosperity, and the influences which moulded it are to be found in the landscape. As in pre-Conquest local studies information and ideas drawn from documentary research, archaeology, historical geography, ecology and architectural studies will all be relevant. Only a very few late medieval maps, owing little to scientific surveying techniques, survive. The landscape picture has to be built up retrospectively from later maps, from surviving earthworks observed at ground level and from aerial photographs, from written surveys and terriers describing in words features such as field systems or parks, from the collection and plotting of field-names, from extant buildings or parts of buildings, and from the layout and plan of towns and villages and the plots, paths and roadways, and open spaces within them. Less frequently local archaeological excavations take place and add to the picture.

Saxon England, as we saw in the last chapter, was extensively settled and cleared of woodland. By the late Saxon period a pattern of small, relatively scattered groups of dwellings seems to have been giving way to larger settlements, recognizable as villages, in many parts of England. The appearance of these villages, and of the surrounding land on which they depended, was determined by a combination of three main factors. First, the physical environment of soil, climate, altitude and water supply; second, the economic context generated by agricultural capacity, subsistence needs and population size, and involvement with market transactions; and third, cultural factors involving lordship, custom, and jurisdictional and territorial interests. In large areas of the country the outcome was the landscape of the open-field village, often cited as the classic, medieval landscape. Here manor, church and the houses and surrounding tofts of the peasant cultivators were grouped at the centre of a field system with three essential elements – arable, meadow and pasture land. This produced the basic wherewithal of subsistence – bread, ale, some meat, animal feed and manure, the main means apart from fallowing of keeping the land in heart. Agriculture, and thus the landscape, was dominated by arable farming, carried out in two or three large, open fields. These fields were divided into strips, long and narrow rectangular pieces of ploughed land, themselves grouped into furlongs within each open field. The land of both the lord and the peasant tenants was held in strips scattered throughout these fields, the intensive cultivation and cropping of which was managed in common through the manorial court. Stock were important, but the capacity to maintain them in any numbers was limited. The regulation of access to the highly prized meadow land and to pasture, found on rougher land,

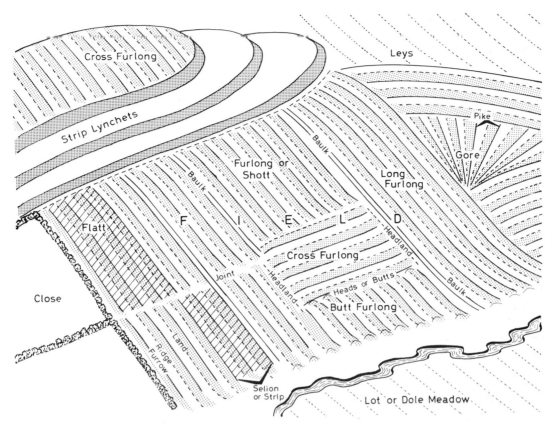

31. Medieval field systems: some terms illustrated.

Local dialect terms for similar features in arable fields varied from area to area. Amongst the names for the cultivated *strips* forming ridges of ploughland, were *ridge, land, selion* and *flatt.* Flatt could also be applied to a group of strips. Strips were sometimes held singly, sometimes in groups (as indicated by cross-hatching).

Baulks were unploughed strips, providing access to ploughed areas, while *headlands* were raised banks formed at right angles to the end of ploughed strips by the turning of the plough teams. Gentle reverse-S curves (see 'Long Furlong') reflect the line followed by the plough team between turns. *Strip lynchet* is an archaeological term for the terrace-like effect where strip cultivation was extended onto sloping ground.

Leys were grassland, sometimes laid on former arable land, and subsequently returned to the plough. Rich riverside *meadows* may retain earthwork divisions marking the annual allocation of portions, drawn by *lot,* to manorial tenants. Individually held land in the open-field system appears as *closes.*

on greens and verges, in woodland or in the arable field stubble after the harvest, was a major concern.

Given the ingredients of such landscapes it is not surprising that they, and the village communities associated with them, were concentrated chiefly in lowland areas, not in highland, moorland, marshland, or densely wooded areas, and also in the parts of the country where population levels were highest and local manorial control most intensively exercised. Thus the open-field zone extended from the north-east coast in Northumberland, down through Durham, Yorkshire and Lincolnshire into the Midlands and Southern Central England. This was not the typical landscape of the north and west, the West Country, East Anglia, and south-eastern England. For local historians the notion of general land-scape zones should always provoke caution. As we shall see from a Cumbrian case study, although clearly outside the open-field zone, lowland areas near the Cumbrian coast shared many of its features, while the uplands of the region developed a distinct kind of farming, landscape and society in their woodlands and fells. In such areas settlement was typically more dispersed, in farmsteads and hamlets, and where villages did develop they did so later. The north of England also suffered particular and lengthy political instability. The harrying of the North by the Normans and ongoing problems with the Scots affected landscape and settlement developments. In Durham, Yorkshire, Cumberland and Northum-berland the regular layout of villages and the systematic allocation of strip holdings in their fields seem to indicate a planned, imposed pattern which some historians link to 're-colonization' after the eventual Norman takeover. Contrasts are apparent with the less uniform, organically evolved village layouts more common in other areas. Certainly in the north of England manorialization was later and less intensive, with much larger manorial units.

The plans of towns and parts of towns also reveal contrasts between planned and organic growth. There may be varying patterns in the spectrum from planned to organic, ranging from towns planted from new by a sponsoring landlord, to those laid out over an existing settlement and its fields, to those focused on the formative presence of an institution like a castle or a monastery, to others which appear formless or polyfocal as they evolved to serve the economy of a surrounding area. Historical geographers have been active in identifying different types of plan and their methods of describing and analysing the physical form of a place can help local historians greatly in understanding the processes governing how and why a town, village or open landscape developed.

Woodland played an important part in medieval life and land-scapes. It was a valuable resource – for pasture, for timber, and for fuel. Its value was all the greater because of the extent of earlier clearance and the pressures for continued clearances in order to feed

32. Pannage: a valuable woodland grazing right (based on a late thirteenth-century manuscript).

33. The area between Cheddar and Draycott, Somerset (photographed in 1971), showing local landscape variations. In the centre is a medieval strip field system enclosed piecemeal and forming long thin fields, while the Mendip Hills (upper right) and the Levels (bottom left) show the larger rectilinear fields of later, comprehensive enclosures.

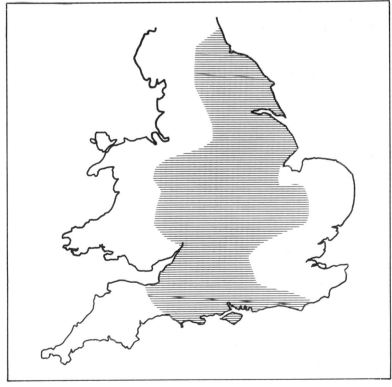

34. Extent of the open-field system (open-field area shaded).

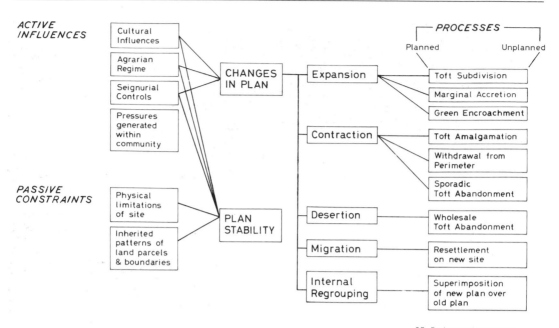

35. Factors and processes influencing village settlements and their evolution.

the growing population of early medieval England. Oliver Rackham has estimated that in 1086 about 15 per cent of England was woodland and that by 1350 this had shrunk to 10 per cent.[6] The need for access to woodland sometimes led to a manor including a portion of wood physically miles away, but bearing its name and with its boundaries demarcated by banks within a larger woodland. Similarly detached portions of meadow may be found, all part of the business of harnessing the landscape to meet current human requirements.

Forests were also of great importance in the medieval history of some localities. They should not be identified willy-nilly with woodland, for 'forest' had a specific meaning in this period. It was not necessarily applied to areas with trees but rather indicated that forest law applied. These by-laws were a useful way for the Crown or other lords to retain tighter control, exercised through forest courts, over the land and people than common law allowed elsewhere. Large parts of Essex, the east Midlands and south Derbyshire were thus forests, but in fact densely populated, with limited areas of woodland. Forests yielded grazing, hunting, deer, timber, and profits from their special court jurisdictions.

Another increasingly common landscape feature was the park. From 35 parks mentioned in Domesday Book the numbers boomed to around 3,200 by 1300. These enclosures offered separate grazing, timber, meat and social status. They were most numerous

BECKLEY

36. The diamond-shaped outline of the medieval park at Beckley, Oxfordshire, is still apparent in the centre of the picture. First mentioned in the Pipe Rolls of 1175–6, part of its circuit was being enclosed by a wall in the 1190s.

in wooded areas; Hertfordshire, with ninety known parks, had the greatest concentration. Medieval parks are traceable from surviving boundaries (often rectangular or rounded in shape, with banks for deer-proof fencing), from persistent field-names, and from contemporary documents, like the Close Rolls recording the necessary licence from the king to empark.

The evidence of medieval buildings is likely to be disappointingly sparse for many local historians. The local church is an obvious focus of interest and ways of 'reading' it are discussed in the following section on church and community. Other institutional buildings, for example monasteries, castles, hospitals and almshouses, have often fared less well, unless assured some continuity of use. This is often not their original one. Castles may figure as prisons, courts or seats of local government, and monasteries as parish churches or parts of private residences. Without such continuity the physical disappearance of major parts of the medieval local scene may be disconcertingly complete, as they fell victim to forces ranging from sixteenth-century religious change, to intensive quarrying for re-usable building materials, to nineteenth-century and other redevelopment schemes. At least such buildings, along with the major private houses that were beginning to be built later in the Middle Ages, will generally receive a good deal of space in printed sources of the kind described in Chapter One.

The form of other medieval buildings, the vast majority of domestic dwellings and farm and work buildings, is less well known. At manor house level enough examples survive to provide a definite general plan, centred around a 'public', communally used space, the hall, rising to the full height of the roof, and for most or all of the period heated by an open fire. There was an entrance directly into the hall, but screened from it, and this screens passage end of the hall was flanked by a cross-wing containing service rooms. Fire dangers meant the kitchen was often a separate building. At the opposite end of the hall to the screens passage was a dais where the head of the household presided and dined, with behind it doors to another cross-wing containing private space for the owner and his family in a solar and possibly a chapel. The manor house was the principal of a group of buildings, for servants and retainers, and also for practical farming, for this was also the centre of the demesne or 'home' farm.

37. Manor house, Chalgrove, Oxfordshire. A sympathetically restored example of a manorial house-plan, with hall, through passage, and cross wings. An upper floor to the hall and chimneys were added in the sixteenth century.

Southern English medieval houses of sub-manorial status, reconstructed at the Weald and Downland Open Air Museum, Sussex. Both had become part of later, larger buildings.

38. (LEFT) Timber-framed hall from Boarhunt, Hampshire, probably fifteenth-century and divided into a central hall, a screened storage area, and a separate, private room.

39. (ABOVE) Winkhurst Farm from Chiddingstone, Kent, was attached to other buildings, and consisted of a single room, the hall, one bay open to the roof and the smoke of an open hearth, and a second bay containing an upper room.

Peasant Cot

Hall-house

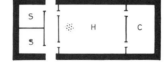

Long-house

Wealden house

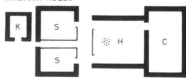

Peasant Farm

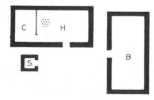

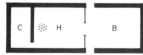

H   Hall or communal living area
C   Private chamber
S   Service rooms: buttery, pantry or store
B   Byre or barn
K   Kitchen
⁝   Hearth

40. Some types of medieval house-plan.

Below manor house level the domestic architecture of the peasant or townsman had not, with some late medieval exceptions at yeoman and merchant level, crossed the vernacular threshold, that is it had not yet reached that stage of development, permanence, sophistication and prosperity which would give it substantial and surviving form. In the sixteenth and seventeenth centuries most then surviving 'ordinary' houses were replaced or radically rebuilt as the vernacular building range expanded. The result has been that many ostensibly later houses in fact incorporate earlier, medieval dwellings, shrouded in subsequent fabric of periods from the sixteenth to the twentieth centuries. Local historians have much to contribute by careful observation and recording of buildings, as they stand or during modern building works. Roof construction, blackening of the inside of a roof (from the smoke of the fire of a medieval hall house?), hidden and exposed timber framing, inconsistent floor levels, the orientation and plot boundaries of a house are some of the factors worth considering. A number of medieval peasant houses have been physically unravelled from later buildings and reconstructed. To visit such houses, best seen at major open-air museums such as Singleton (Sussex), Avoncroft (Worcestershire), or St Fagans (South Glamorgan) is of great help in crossing the gulf of experience between ourselves and the dark, smoky atmosphere of the timber, wattle and daub, thatched and earthen-floored, one- and two-roomed houses of the majority of the medieval population. A revolution in comfort was to be made by the building and rebuilding of the late sixteenth century onwards, with ordinary houses acquiring such features as upper floors, fireplaces and chimneys, and window glass. Surviving medieval buildings show that some sub-manorial homes were edging towards greater permanence and comfort. These were largely built by those who benefited from the changed economic and social climate after the Black Death.

Signs of the contraction and depopulation taking place after 1348–9 can be seen in the landscape. The multidisciplinary study of landscape history, which grew up in the 1950s, paid particular attention to deserted medieval villages (DMVs). Clues from fieldwork, the humps and bumps of house platforms and hollow ways, or an isolated church which had long outstayed the community it was built to serve, were matched with references to settlements and their inhabitants in taxation and other documents from Domesday Book to nineteenth-century censuses, and with continuing use of place-names shown on large scale Ordnance Survey and earlier maps. The publications of the Deserted Medieval Villages Research Group, founded in 1952, plot the discovery of more and more 'lost' settlements. They also show that, with a handful of exceptions, medieval villages were not wiped out at a stroke by the plague of 1348–9. Rather their viability was gradually eroded, with the settlements most newly established under pressure of population growth in the twelfth and thirteenth centuries proving especially vulnerable. Few desertions had a single cause but related to the earlier size of the village (smaller places generally proving weaker), the nature of local soils and climate, altitude, and how close a village lay to other, more successful communities. It is always important to consider a particular place in relation to its neighbours. Many villagers, faced with reduced numbers, recurrent outbreaks of plague, increasing difficulty in winning a satisfactory livelihood, and growing options to move elsewhere, voted with their feet. Settlements dwindled. In localities where dominant landlords remained active in the fifteenth and early sixteenth centuries local historians may find a pattern of less gradual decline with a lord carrying out wholesale enclosure of land for increasingly profitable sheep pastures, thus causing rapid human depopulation. Research into village desertion has now produced evidence of some three thousand such sites.

In the course of this work the original DMVRG has significantly changed its name to the Medieval Sites Research Group (MSRG). It has become clear that deserted village settlements are only part of the picture and that local studies need to include both medieval hamlets and farmsteads and a close scrutiny of the villages and towns which survived late medieval recession but which changed in the process. Shifts and shrinkages within settlements were widespread and can be studied through the same mix of field observation, analysis of aerial photographs and maps, and documentary research that has been evolved in pursuit of England's deserted villages.

Church and community

The Church was ever present in English medieval local communities. As an institution it provided a universal ritual framework for individual lives from birth to death. Not only was the Church a spiritual focus but it intervened in matters of marriage, inheritance and personal behaviour through its own system of courts, it was a principal provider of education and charitable relief, and artistic endeavour was largely expressed in religious form. Church bodies – bishops, cathedral chapters and monasteries – owned and ran extensive manors and estates, created new market centres, and pursued commercial trading interests. Clerics were influential in royal government service and in the households of lay lords. The idioms of medieval English society were primarily religious. To date an event was to record it not only in relation to the year of the current sovereign's reign but also to an elaborate calendar of saints' days and festivals, for example a document might be dated the Monday after St Matthias 30 Edward I.

The local church building is often the most tangible evidence of this pervasive presence. It may well be the only surviving standing fabric of the Middle Ages. It was the central meeting place, not just for Sunday liturgy but throughout the week, its bell marking daily time and services. The church was a social centre – on the many feast days (some thirty or forty per year), and for public announcements, processions and games. These many roles mean that the church building, carefully read by the local historian, may mirror much of the fortunes of the local community at different stages during the Middle Ages. Surviving buildings reflect the emergence of a network of local churches set in defined parish units, the local involvement of lay and ecclesiastical lords, levels of economic prosperity, the balance of power between clergy and laity, and how that balance shifted before and after the fourteenth century. Whether a church has a rector or a vicar, the relative size and building dates of the nave and chancel, or the identity of those whose tombs are most prominent, will all help to explain local experience and aspirations, and to relate it to a wider, outside framework.

41. St Peter's Church, Hook Norton, Oxfordshire: the marked contrast between the simple Norman chancel and the later Decorated and Perpendicular nave reflects the process of appropriation. Recotorial rights, and responsibility for the chancel, passed to the appropriator, in this case to the Abbey of Oseney in 1129.

In 1066 English churches were still in a state of transition from the Anglo-Saxon system of large parishes served by teams of priests, operating from important central churches or minsters, to a pattern of local churches each with a resident priest. By the tenth century an increasing number of churches existed, often built as private chapels of local lords, but also used by local people. Some of these buildings were of sufficiently permanent materials to survive, and a handful, bypassed by later development, give us an idea of this early stage of construction. Most local churches were initially of wood but they were made more permanent in every sense by a major trend to build or re-build in stone, datable to c. 1050–c. 1150. These local churches did not fit into a ready made ecclesiastical hierarchy. Their emergence further eroded the old minster system. By the late twelfth century the pattern of local, community churches was widespread and it was at this stage that the Church formalized their position. The hierarchical mould hardened, to produce the carefully defined parish units with which English local historians are so concerned at every period until the nineteenth century.

English churches were, until the 1530s, part of the universal Church of Rome and subject to papal authority. Local historians must not be surprised to feel the repercussions of international power, both as a general influence and in specific disputes. For example, the formalizing in the twelfth century of the English parish and its place in a carefully graduated hierarchy of rural deanery, archdeaconry, and diocese, had much to do with the vigorous reforms of Pope Gregory and his concern to reverse the trend for spiritual property to rest in lay hands. The large number of seigneurial or estate churches in England obviously contravened this principle.

One corrective from the Church's point of view was the unprecedented number of grants of such property made in the twelfth and thirteenth centuries by lay lords, usually to monasteries. Parish priests were commonly supported by income drawn from three main sources – glebe lands (granted by the local lord for the priest's use); offerings from the congregation (including major feast days, at weddings and funerals); and chiefly by tithes. Tithes were a tenth part of the produce of the parish which the priest served. They were payable each year, and were divided into great tithes (on corn, hay, and wood) and lesser tithes (on other crops, young animals, and on the profits of such activities as milling or fisheries). The definition of the titheable area, the parish, was thus of great importance to the Church as a whole. Moreover when an English church was given by its patron, the local lord, to a religious institution the rights to collect the great tithes passed to that institution. It, as a corporate body, became the rector of the church, and usually took on the advowson, or right to present a priest to

42, 43. Many local places of worship, which subsequently became parish churches, began as private churches of manorial lords. Often manor house and church lie close beside each other, as here at East Quantoxhead, Somerset (ABOVE) and Asthall, Oxfordshire (LEFT).

the living and to be responsible for the souls of the local population. This priest was the vicar, or substitute, and the process is called appropriation. It brought a change from rector to vicar, and also meant that an outside (albeit religious) body became interested in the parish, collecting income from it, and being responsible for adequate clergy provision, and maintaining the chancel of the church building. By c. 1200 perhaps a fifth of English parishes had undergone appropriation; this proportion at least doubled by the end of the Middle Ages.[7]

This intensification of Church involvement was accompanied by a concern to establish minimum standards amongst the clergy serving parish churches. Priests were expected to instruct their flocks, ensure at least an annual confession and communion by all parishioners, to preach, to support the poor, maintain the fabric and hospitality of the parsonage, and protect the Church's rights in land, property and tithes. Clerical literacy and celibacy were enforced. The reforms also entailed a regular and more elaborate liturgy, in which an increased and separate status for the priest was stressed. This is reflected in the architecture of many English parish churches which at this period acquired larger, square-ended chancels. These accommodated the priest and his acolytes during the celebration of mass at a high altar now more distant from the congregation in the nave than in the characteristically smaller apsidal chancels of earlier churches, and flanked by the piscina and sedilia used in the rite.

The developments in local church architecture, and in religious life and organization tie in with a long-running tension between the authority of State and Church. The reforms of the twelfth century were the latest and most emphatic assertion of jurisdiction and influence by the Church. The first, post-Conquest Archbishop of Canterbury, Lanfranc, had succeeded in establishing, in 1072, a system of canon law and church courts which operated alongside royal and feudal jurisdictions. He also reformed diocesan boundaries, shifting cathedral centres to important towns such as Chichester (from Selsey), Salisbury (from Sherborne), Chester (from Lichfield), and Lincoln (from Dorchester-on-Thames). Both Church and State had strong networks of authority throughout the country. In contemporary constitutional theory medieval England was a harmoniously functioning whole, with different elements playing complementary roles. John of Salisbury, writing in c. 1160,[8] likened the State to a man's body, with the priests providing its soul, the king its head, the soldiers its hands, the peasants its feet, and the judges its eyes. When this balance was disturbed the results could be highly disruptive at a local level, as the civil wars of Stephen's reign (1135–54), the baronial wars of the 1260s and the Wars of the Roses in the fifteenth century, all amply demonstrated in the secular sphere. In matters of Church and State disharmony reached a peak in the twelfth and early thirteenth centuries when general, papally-led reforms were matched by overt clashes between king and archbishop in England. The constitutional focus of the quarrels between Henry II and Archbishop Thomas à Becket was the refusal of the Church to accept the Constitutions of Clarendon which required appeals to the papal court to be made only with the king's consent, and that clergy convicted in the church courts of crime be handed over to the royal courts for sentence. In 1205, under Henry's son John, a further trial of strength occurred when John refused to accept the pope's choice, Cardinal Stephen Langton, as Archbishop of Canterbury. England was placed under interdict by Pope Innocent III, John was excommunicated, and from 1208 to 1212 the liturgy was disrupted throughout the country; for example infant baptism could not take place in church and the sacrament was given only at the point of death. John eventually accepted papal authority, doing homage and promising an annual tax to Rome. A list of English churches paying papal tax in 1291 has been transcribed and printed,[9] a valuable source for local history which shows a clear pattern of parishes, set within a wider Church, whose spiritual drive, organizational strength, wealth, power and influence was at a peak, both nationally and locally.

By the early fourteenth century this authority and status were faltering. The papacy, now based in Avignon, was disrupted. Nearer home the Church figured poorly in a period of persistent misfortunes, whether from famine, disease, weather or war. It appeared more often in the guise of exactor of taxes, tithes, offerings and labour services, a large slice of a diminishing cake, than as the bringer of effective spiritual sustenance. The execution of Archbishop Sudbury of Canterbury in 1381 during the Peasants' Revolt, amongst whose leaders was John Ball, an excommunicate priest, is just one particularly well-known instance of anti-clericalism.

The Black Death exacerbated the situation. Many clergy died and available replacements were not always well-trained. Local communities were faced with a catastrophic plague and with a Church able to offer less effective pastoral care, and, as an institution, struggling to maintain itself by drawing on a gravely dislocated economic base. Yet this weakening of the Church's position did not mean that the English people moved away from religion. Indeed the local parish church building of the fourteenth and fifteenth centuries is often testimony to the very reverse. The lay community poured resources, and faith, into religious building and fittings. Instead of the earlier pattern of benefactions to large monastic houses the outlet was now more local. In the late Middle Ages the wills of individuals begin to survive. They show high levels of religious benefaction, endowing chantries (separate insti-

44. Anti-clerical feeling: bishop's mitre and cloven hooves (based on a drawing from the early fourteenth-century Luttrell Psalter).

tutions within local churches for the saying of masses for the dead, either named individuals, families, or groups like gilds and fraternities), obits (a more modest benefaction for a mass on the anniversary of a person's death), for lights before the statue of a favourite saint, or for the cost of whole or part of a building. Where religious orders were remembered it was frequently the friars who were chosen. The leading orders of friars – Dominican, Franciscan, Carmelite and Austin – were all well established in England by the mid-thirteenth century. A product of the energetic, reforming momentum in late-twelfth-century Italy, they brought popular, practical homilies offered in outdoor preaching and in their friary churches, which were based particularly in towns. Friars became favoured as confessors, and a share of their prayers was sought by lay people through confraternity links. The influence of the friars demonstrates both the vigour of late medieval church life and a shift away from the authority of the parish priest.

The search for religious truth in late medieval England also produced the first native heresy, Lollardy. This was a movement of the period between the 1350s and the 1520s, and in some ways pre-figured the Reformation. Lollards attacked the accumulated wealth of the Church, the involvement of clergy in government and lay affairs, and the heavy burdens imposed on the laity through the Church's own bureaucracy. They consistently argued against the subordination of the English church to Rome, and against clerical celibacy and monasticism. Lollardy challenged the necessity of confession to a priest, and of means such as pilgrimages and prayers for the dead in achieving salvation. They denied transubstantiation (the central doctrine of the actual presence of the body and blood of Christ in the changed bread and wine at the mass), and the efficacy of images, relics, and elaborate church fittings. Lollards emphasized the importance of preaching, and of direct access for all to the Bible. English translations of the Bible were made and were in circulation by the late fourteenth century.

In its early phases Lollardy attracted support at court and in parliament. After the movement became associated with potential political treason, through Sir John Oldcastle's rising of 1414, it persisted in the face of prosecution and with a less prominent following. Through the records of the church courts, wills, tax lists and other documents local studies show Lollardy to have been a movement including merchants, tradesmen, artisans and yeomen, many of them prosperous and well known in their communities. They risked public penance, imprisonment and execution by burning, yet Lollardy continued. Its particular strongholds lay in London, Essex and Kent, in the Chilterns and Thames Valley, in Bristol, in Norfolk, in Coventry, and in parts of Yorkshire and

Nottinghamshire. Discovering where and when Lollardy was strong or weak generates a series of questions typical of local history. Were there certain types of place where such beliefs flourished? Did they do so in settlements with an open and varied landholding pattern and thus greater freedom, or were they a reaction of communities with strong church authority or property ownership? Did Lollardy develop alongside particular economic and trading patterns or through direct contact with routes bringing travelling preachers and books? Were the same areas more receptive to religious dissent both then and later?

The presence of Lollardy represents a far cry from the early medieval religious scene. The role of the Church was transformed during the Middle Ages from that of a gradually growing number of small local churches, to a pattern of carefully defined parishes which were part of a highly organized ecclesiastical hierarchy and frequently owned by church institutions. Thus the local experience was of two authority systems, secular and ecclesiastical, sometimes in conflict, but both vigorous and pervasive in their influence. By the fourteenth and fifteenth centuries the balance of influence in both spheres was shifting, with greater emphasis on local and lay developments. As Dorothy Owen has written, 'the parish church had evolved from a territorial chapel dependent on a local land-owner, and controlled by him and his priest, into a shrine, meeting place, and possession of all the parishioners'.[10]

Crown and community

Every medieval community came into contact with the interests and influence of the Crown. This is reflected in the large part played in local historical accounts by information from the central records of royal government. Permanent written record of a wide range of transactions was first expanded by the Crown. Although others, including manorial lords, followed this trend later it is government records that are amongst the most varied, and until the late thirteenth century, the only consistently kept documentary pool for local historians.

The interests of the Crown, and the structures of government arising from them, ran along two parallel lines. First there was the king's feudal role as ultimate overlord, from whom all land was held. Secondly there was his relationship with all his subjects as a sovereign exercising rights (to taxation and allegiance) and obliga-tions (to provide justice, security within and for the realm, and to take counsel).

In the feudal context much of the business of government revolved around enforcing the obligations owed to the overlord in return for his guaranteeing rights to hold freehold land. (The

Crown did not concern itself with unfree land until the sixteenth century.) These obligations are called feudal incidents. They involved receiving oaths of homage and fealty, receiving aid (traditionally payments to help finance the knighting of the lord's eldest son, the marriage of his eldest daughter, and his own ransom, if imprisoned), receiving reliefs (payments by the tenant on inheriting a holding), exercising right of wardship (running and benefiting from an estate and arranging the heir's marriage when that heir was a minor), and exercising rights to escheats (taking over the lands of tenants who had died without heirs or whose lands were forfeit because of criminal conviction). A further element in the feudal relationship was the right to military service, originally the provision of armed and equipped knights and men but, by the reign of Henry I (1100–35), being commuted into a fixed money payment called scutage. Feudal incidents were obligations owed to the king by his direct tenants, and further down the chain by other tenants to their overlords.

FEUDAL INCIDENTS

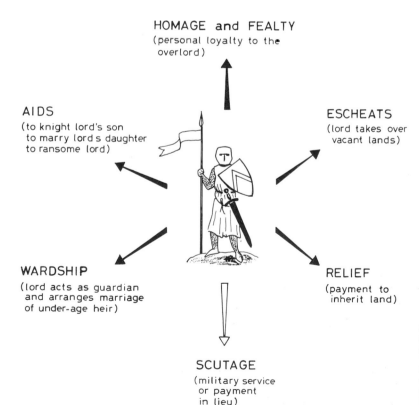

HOMAGE and FEALTY
(personal loyalty to the overlord)

AIDS
(to knight lord's son
to marry lord s daughter
to ransome lord)

ESCHEATS
(lord takes over
vacant lands)

WARDSHIP
(lord acts as guardian
and arranges marriage
of under-age heir)

RELIEF
(payment to
inherit land)

SCUTAGE
(military service
or payment
in lieu)

45. The right of the overlord to exact military service was the essence of the feudal system. This, and the five 'feudal incidents' shown, were often occasions for written recording of details of local lordship and landholding.

The Crown's concern to preserve its rights at all stages of this hierarchy generated many written records of great use in local history. Some were general accounts, most notably Domesday Book, which acted as a general catalogue of manorial holdings, referred to by those in royal government throughout the Middle Ages. Sadly there were no subsequent, nationwide surveys. The nearest equivalent, much richer in detail, is the Hundred Rolls of 1279–80. They give detailed descriptions, manor by manor, of the landholder, how the manor was held, the types of land and rights attached to the demesne, the free and unfree tenants and the services and rents they owed. This source offers great scope – for comparison with Domesday Book and with manorial surveys and custumals, for tentative estimates of local population size, and for analysing peasant tenure, social structure and land use. The Hundred Rolls also described towns, but unfortunately do not survive for all areas of the country.

They were drawn up in the reign of Edward I (1272–1307) in an active attempt to impose a vigorous administrative regime after the uncertain years of the baronial wars. Private jurisdictions were to be dealt with and royal authority to apply in all areas. The independent transfer of land, with the king's interests as feudal overlord being neglected, was especially to be stemmed. This weakening of feudal authority was inherent in the widespread practice of a sub-infeudation. For example, if A was a tenant-in-chief of the king, owing him military service of one knight, and sub-infeudated his holding to B, A then became B's overlord and not the king. A could negotiate services owed directly with B, and these might exceed the original knight's fee, giving A profits of which the king had no part. Or, should B die without heirs, the holding reverted not to the king, but to A. Middlemen were getting between the king and his rights. Edward I's response was to abolish sub-infeudation by the Statute of Quia Emptores of 1290. After that date all freehold tenants held direct of the king. A could still alienate land to B, but his personal overlordship over B disappeared, and the wording of charters or deeds changed with it. Loss of revenue and rights when subjects gave land to church bodies was also countered, by the Statute of Mortmain (1279), which forbade the alienation of land to the Church without royal licence. All this action, and the associated recording, of feudal incidents, licences and the Hundred Rolls, are the stuff of much medieval local history. It is useful to note how levels of vigour and development in royal government varied. Thus the influence of the Crown fluctuated in intensity. The reigns of William I, Henry II, Edward I and Edward III were all notable for expensive wars or energetic government following periods of instability. These kings had active policies, requiring spending and resulting in close concerns with rights, resources, and taxation. An effect of this was that they all produced particularly important local historical records, from Domesday Book to the Poll Taxes of 1377–81.

Apart from general responses, like the Hundred Rolls or Quia Emptores, the royal bureaucracy was alert to specific local cases involving feudal incidents. If a tenant of freehold land died the circumstances of the heir were investigated. These 'inquisitions post mortem' were compiled from the thirteenth until the seventeenth centuries. The process began in typical fashion. A writ from the king went to his officer, the sheriff or escheator in the relevant county, requiring to know what land the deceased held at his death, of whom it was held, its annual value, the services due from it, the identity of the heir, and proof of his or her age. On this basis a relief payment was required from any inheriting heir, the land was forfeit to the Crown in the absence of an heir, or the administration of the estate was taken over if the heir was a minor and subject to wardship. Often inquisitions post mortem included written 'extents', descriptions of the manor, its customs, tenants, and assets such as meadow, pasture, woodland, mills, gardens and dovecotes, a topographical, economic and social account of great potential, especially where it can be linked to the day-to-day detail revealed in any surviving manorial court rolls.

As sovereign of the nation, as opposed to feudal overlord, the king's business touched the localities in three main ways – justice, finance and administration. In all these aspects the reign of Henry II (1154–89) saw a transformation in royal government and the start of an abundance of records. The royal courts became increasingly important. As we have seen, processes were developed to speed up the hearing of cases dealing with rights to freehold land. The jurisdiction over these of the king's, rather than the lord's or county court, was established. This access was extensively used and many cases involving local land were recorded in the rolls of the curia regis and the eyres. Not only could the king, constantly on the move, dispense justice, but from the twelfth century pleas could be made to his justices, now sitting permanently in courts in London, and to the itinerant justices in eyre, on circuit throughout the country. The usefulness of these structures in civil matters is well illustrated by the development of the feet of fines procedure. When the ownership of land was determined in court a document called a final concord recorded the outcome in the form of a chirograph indenture. The transaction was written out twice on a piece of parchment which was then cut apart along a distinctive indentation. In any future dispute the validity of the document could be proved by matching the wording and indented edges across the join. From 1195, when such cases were recorded in the royal courts of Common Pleas or the Palatinates (covering Durham, Cheshire and Lancashire), a third copy, written at right-angles to the others, at the foot of the fine, was made and kept in the court records.

From the thirteenth century this procedure, couched in the form of a usually fictitious dispute in order to meet the forms of the court, was widely used to gain prestigious, written proof of local land transactions. Feet of fines are often quoted in medieval studies, and many have been published by record societies. They are a good example of the seemingly arcane character of many documents, which it is interesting and worthwhile to penetrate.

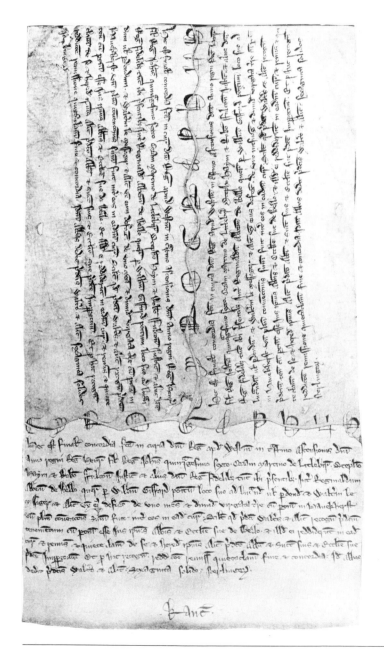

46. Royal courts used to record a local land transaction: a Kent foot of fine of 1272 (at bottom of the picture) together with the matching counterpart indentures intended to be given to the parties in the case.

The king's courts also dealt with criminal matters. They existed alongside two other court systems. First the earlier pattern, inherited from Anglo-Saxon England, of shire and hundred courts and tithings remained. The shire court met about every six weeks and was a meeting of the freeholders of the country, presided over by the sheriff, the king's 'viceroy' in the country. The hundred courts met every three to four weeks, while at the most local level the tithings were groups of ten men responsible for guaranteeing each other's good behaviour, and for pursuing a hue and cry and informing higher authority if a crime occurred. In addition there operated the feudal courts of the manor (covering both unfree and free tenants), and the honour, a larger area of overlordship. The king always reserved certain serious cases such as arson and homicide to his courts, and as we have seen they were also chosen by many to pursue civil matters. The royal courts gradually took on greater importance in both criminal and civil matters during the Middle Ages. This was at the expense of the older jurisdictions of shire and hundred, and of the authority of the sheriff. The creation of Justices of the Peace in the fourteenth century emphasized this trend. A new magistracy of landed gentry from the counties and of leading townsmen was set up, which worked with lawyers from the local area, and with justices and sergeants sent periodically from London. The JPs met in session at least four times a year (at Quarter Sessions) and, individually and collectively, were important figures of authority locally. They were charged with the suppression of disorder, seeking out and trying felonies and trespasses, indicting more serious crimes to go to the assize courts, and enforcing economic legislation, such as the Statute of Labourers. They became an intrinsic part of a structure of royal courts and judicial process which had begun to take shape under Henry II.

Royal finance required constant contact with the localities. Taxation was not a regular matter, and when taxes were assessed and collected the resulting lists are a major historical tool. Two much-used examples are the Lay Subsidy Rolls of 1290–1334, and the late-fourteenth-century Poll Taxes. The Lay Subsidies are sometimes called the tenths and the fifteenths from one levy at one-tenth of the personal property of tax-paying townsmen, and one-fifteenth in the case of country-dwellers. The resulting lists, for boroughs and vills, of named inhabitants and the tax they paid, link people and place, and indicate relative wealth within and between settlements. The Poll Taxes provide one of the best sources for population estimates after the Black Death. In 1377 a tax of 4d. per head was levied on all lay inhabitants aged fourteen and over, except regular beggars. Clergy paid one shilling. In 1379 payments were graded by rank, from 4d. to 6s. 8d. for earls, and clergy were exempt. Finally in 1381 all over fifteen were taxed except beggars. This was a controversial and changing tax, given new fame by debates over another poll tax in the 1980s. Tax resistance, and evasion, were also known in the 1380s and so local historians need to make some allowance in using such sources for the people whom the documents failed to 'catch'.

Year by year the king sorted out his financial relationship with the localities through the Exchequer, transactions which are recorded in the Pipe Rolls, described by W.B. Stephens as 'perhaps the most valuable of these [central government] records for the local historian'.[11] Pipe Rolls survive in a continuous series dating from the regnal year 1155–6 and many have been printed in the volumes of the Pipe Roll Society. Twice a year the sheriff of each county was summoned by writ to attend at the Exchequer at Westminster, which he did carrying coin, accounts and wooden tallies notched with grooves recording monies handled. Seated at the squared Exchequer board, facing the king's officials, he accounted for the profits and payments due to and from the king in his county. Money had to be collected in; this included scutage payments, rents and dues from royal land, feudal incidents producing reliefs or aids, and the profits of courts (fines or proceeds, like the sale of the goods of convicted criminals). A balance had to be struck with payments out, including grant of land, alms given, wages of royal employees, and the building or maintenance of castles or other royal properties. The resulting bargain was itemized in the Pipe Rolls, which may yield information on anything from wage rates to livestock prices, to building history.

Finally the work of royal administration should be remembered. Printed histories will be littered with references to Patent, Close, Charter and other Rolls. It was here that regular copies of communications from the king were kept from around 1200. Thus the Patent Rolls are the enrolments of open or 'patent' letters, issued open under the Great Seal, and dealing with matters such as land disputes, royal prerogatives, tax and revenue, grants of fairs, charters of incorporation, crown leases, and presentations of clergy to churches owned by the Crown. By the mid-fourteenth century the number of letters issued in the king's name by Chancery and other offices and courts was more than 100,000 per annum.

At the end of the Middle Ages there was more government and more record of it. During the fourteenth and fifteenth centuries the departments, like Chancery and Exchequer, became permanently fixed at Westminster, separated from the king's household, and increasingly staffed by laymen rather than clerics, by bureaucrats and lawyers. During this time the King's Council took permanent form, meeting in Star Chamber to give decisions and advice. By the 1340s Parliament had also acquired permanent form, as a representative assembly of two houses, Lords and Commons. Locally, as we have seen, the role of the sheriff was declining, and, instead of the irregular visits of the justices in eyre, a structure of

47. Orford Castle, Suffolk. The building of this Keep, and of a surrounding curtain wall with projecting towers which has now disappeared, are recorded in the Pipe Rolls between 1165 and 1173. During these years £1413 9s. 2d. was spent. The Rolls also record later maintenance and re-building work.

48. A Pipe Roll. Rolls are series of documents stitched together and rolled up. The Pipe Rolls were rolled around a rod or pipe. Like many other medieval records of royal government the existence of printed calendars and indexes eases the physical and intellectual task of unravelling this source.

JPs and regular assizes emerged. More lay and 'middling' people were involved in royal government, both centrally and locally. These important developments in the relations of Crown and locality took their place alongside the inheritance of Anglo-Saxon institutions and the products of Henry II's reformation of government.

Urban life

It has been estimated that there were some 540 towns in England in 1377.[12] That figure reflects a considerable growth in numbers of towns during the earlier Middle Ages, and measures the situation before the appreciable contraction in urban life which historians of some towns have suggested took place in later medieval England. The estimates of the late fourteenth-century situation are based on the Poll Tax returns of 1377 and reveal few towns of any great size, either by modern or contemporary medieval European standards. London had a population of 45,000–50,000, then there were four towns of between 8,000 and 15,000, eight between 5,000 and 8,000, and twenty-seven between 2,000 and 5,000. But the vast bulk of English towns, perhaps 500 of them, were local market centres of between 500 and 2,000 people. Collectively these small towns accounted for half England's total urban population, which was in turn about 5 per cent of the estimated total national population. Most people lived within a day's journey of an urban centre, although the greatest concentrations were in the most populous and prosperous east and south.

Many medieval towns may not seem immediately obvious to the modern eye. They were small, not densely built up, not busy throughout the week or year, they were closely linked to the surrounding countryside, and subject to royal governmental, ecclesiastical, and in some cases manorial jurisdictions, like their rural neighbours. How do local historians know they are dealing with a town? Richard Holt and Gervase Rosser offer a minimum definition of a medieval town, as '. . . a relatively dense and permanent concentration of residents engaged in a multiplicity of activities, a substantial proportion of which are non-agrarian'.[13] The key factor is not a particular size of population, nor a distinctive form of community government (although this may well arise from the economic communities of interest which grew up in towns), but the variety of occupations. Crafts and trades in textiles, leather and fur, victualling (both production and retailing), metal working, building, and luxury goods are likely to be found. Also many town dwellers were not natives, but immigrants from the countryside, a constant inflow needed not least because of high urban mortality rates. Although the unit of trade and industrial production in medieval towns remained the domestic household, and there were few big enterprises with large concentrations of potentially proletarian labourers, the town household was characteristically large, with high proportions of young, single people, living in as servants or apprentices. Thus, although the identity of many towns did indeed rest on their role as market centres for a surrounding rural area, they were distinctive entities within an overwhelmingly rural society.

Additional roles were important in the origins of some towns – in defence, as royal estate centres, as seats of civil or ecclesiastical administration, as religious places, as ports, or because of their place on long-distance trade routes. The development of a town may often be understood in terms of such functions. Geography and politics made some settlements natural focuses for urban development; a strategically-placed defensive site on a territorial border or a river crossing might offer security for trading, which then generated a permanent and broadly-based town community. Similarly a major institution such as a large monastic house could be the starting point, creating a demand for goods and services for itself and the visitors it attracted. Thus at the gates of the abbeys of Bury St Edmunds and Abingdon substantial towns grew. Their topography still reflects that orientation, but the towns developed a momentum of their own, sometimes producing tensions with the 'parent' influence in their initial formation. Thus fusion of functions in towns happened in the early Middle Ages and was largely complete by 1300.

The principal impetus in the history of some towns was simply that they were natural centres for marketing in a local region, accessible from a surrounding hinterland, and linked to road or river routes. Such towns grew organically, although they may subsequently have attracted additional importance, for example as administrative centres or the sites of monasteries. Yet other towns owe their origins to deliberate attempts to create a new town or to superimpose one onto a pre-existing village. There were considerable

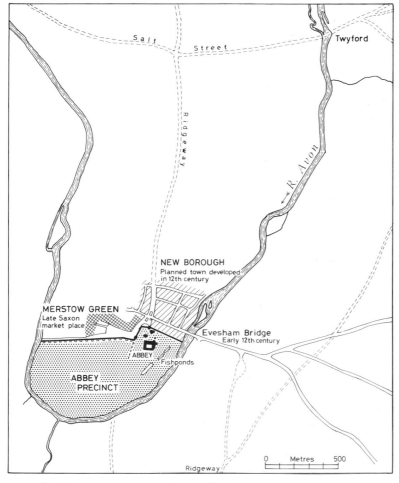

49. Evesham, Worcestershire: the Benedictine abbey, re-founded c. 975, was a formative influence on the establishment and growth of the town. Features include a late Saxon market place at the abbey gate, a planned town of the twelfth century, and the bridge built by the abbey and focusing routes on the 'new' town.

:::::: Ancient ridgeways & roads leading to Twyford crossing
===== Later roads aligned upon Evesham crossing
Abbey precinct walls: ——— Abbot Reginald, 1130-49 ▫▫▫▫ Abbot William de Cheriton, 1316-44

50. Chipping Norton, Oxfordshire: the old nucleus, with parish church and castle earthworks, lies (top left) beyond the borough created in the twelfth century by the Fitzalan family. This 'new' town has a large rectangular market place (with later encroachments), long, thin subdivided burgage plots stretching down to a back lane (right), and a road (still called 'New Street') bringing the main road into the market place (mid-left).

profits to be made from successful markets and annual fairs, from the dues and tolls charged to those trading there, from the granting of permanent property rights in the town, and from the jurisdiction of town courts which regulated trading, small debts and property transactions. Unsurprisingly many lay lords and ecclesiastical landholders, such as bishops and abbots, sought to create towns on their properties. New foundations reached a peak in the thirteenth century. Between 1200 and 1349 royal archives record several thousand grants of market rights by the Crown.

No new town, however influential its sponsor, was guaranteed commercial success. A locality needed, and could support, only so many markets. As Henry Bracton observed in the mid-thirteenth century, the necessary natural catchment area for a market was governed by the need for buyers and sellers to walk there and back in a day; this Bracton calculated as a radius of $6\frac{2}{3}$ miles. Given the rush of attempted town foundations at this time local historians finding reference to grants of markets or other urban rights should look for supporting evidence that either the grant confirmed existing urban activity, and was therefore not the date of the beginnings of the town, or that a planted town was actually an economic success and did assume urban form. Again topography can provide interesting clues of would-be market squares laid out, often with the tell-tale property boundaries of projected burgage tenements around them. But was the square a place of active trading, and were the tenements peopled by burgesses engaged in the crafts and trades which made for urban living? Did the distinctive settlement plan help to foster a commercially successful, increasingly self-conscious, self-governing town community?

Burgage tenure was a key feature of medieval towns. It meant that urban dwellers granted such holdings could freely alienate, that is sell, exchange or will property, unlike their contemporaries, the unfree manorial tenants. Such tenures, and the freedoms to trade that accompanied them, were the major incentive offered by town founders seeking to attract new settlers. Historians have long debated the freer and more independent communities this generated. Local historians will find a heavy emphasis in most town histories on the importance of the grant of a royal charter granting borough status as a necessary expression of the development of such urban status and identity.

51. The main street of Elmley Castle, Worcestershire, a would-be medieval market, which did not succeed despite the acquisition of a market charter by the Beauchamp family in 1254.

52. The Tchure, Deddington, Oxfordshire, with its long, narrow plot typical of a medieval burgage tenement. Although Deddington decayed as a borough and burgage tenure died out during the sixteenth and seventeenth centuries its layout is still that of a medieval borough. The Tchure stretches from New Street (first recorded in the early thirteenth century) to the Market Place and Church (in background of photograph). The later infill with small cottages is also typical.

With chartered borough status went free burgage tenure, rights to trade freely, to elect a council and officers, for the council as a perpetual corporation to hold and manage its own property, the right to hold a borough court (regulating the market, local trades and enrolling property deeds), and the right to account directly to the king for taxes and dues owed, rather than through his county sheriff. Nineteenth-century and later historians have been much exercised by the legal and constitutional niceties of town government, seeing it in itself as a proof of urban identity. The borough charter has been closely studied as it evolved in the twelfth and thirteenth centuries, drawing on the cumulative precedent of privileges granted to other towns. However it is now generally agreed that this formal definition of rights by the Crown expressed a pre-existent urban identity, to quote Holt and Rosser, 'a pre-legal, communal phase', during which independent, local governing groups had already emerged. A common focus for these self-governing aspirations was the gild merchant. Once formal borough status had been attained the role of the gild was likely to shift to primarily trade matters, although remaining an important mechanism for maintaining the authority of the ruling group in the town.

The importance of the formal charter in the minds of local historians must also be qualified by the fact that many undoubted towns never had royal borough charters. Many were the products of seigneurial foundation and retained a structure of manorial courts, but with clear concessions to the freedoms and status for tenants needed to produce a successful trading community. Salford, Stockport and Halesowen (the subject of a case-study later in this chapter) are just three examples of the seigneurial borough.

Alongside institutions of town government collective organizations of traders and craftsmen grew up, designed to define, protect and reinforce the identity and privileges of each group. As has already been suggested, in the twelfth century the gild was an independent body, within which the aspirations for self-government of mercantile élites could grow. With the development of borough government gilds tended to be less independent, and more tied to the ruling institutions of the town. In large towns there would be several gilds, strongest in the key crafts. From the mid-fourteenth century membership tended to become compulsory for anyone wishing to trade in that occupation. The gilds served the economic function of controlling the industrial workforce. They also had strong social, ritual and religious elements. In smaller towns there was often a single gild, also bringing together different roles, in economic regulation but also in public works and welfare, from poorhouse to bridge repairs, and from the building of a gildhall to maintaining a chapel or donating a stained glass window, portraying members' trades, in the local church. Late medieval gilds and fraternities were sometimes social, and not economic or craft-based. Such bodies might have out-of-town members, wore a badge or livery proclaiming affiliation, and stressed convivial solidarity through activities like annual feasts, funeral obsequies for members and chantries for the saying of masses for departed brethren. They have been likened to a proxy, extended family.

Urban lives were organized not only through councils, borough

53. The heavily restored church of St Mary, Wendover, Buckinghamshire. Late medieval wills reveal evidence both of lay piety and the appearance of churches. In 1510 John Legyngham, a local carpenter, made bequests to eight lights, the bells, and the 'sustentacyon of torches'. He also left 3s. 4d. 'to the makying of a window' in the now lost chapel of St John in the town of Wendover, which had developed to the west of the parish church by c. 1200.

courts and gilds or fraternities, but through parishes. Most towns had numbers of parish churches, possibly separate gild chapels, hospitals, and monastic foundations. Here much of the elaborate ritual of plays, processions and ceremonies which has been so much stressed by Charles Phythian-Adams[14] and others as an essential part of late medieval town life, was played out. In a mobile, and sometimes volatile society, the hierarchy of merchant élite, organized crafts and trades (from masters through journeymen to apprentices), traders, servants, the poor and vagrants was spelt out, sometimes with tension-letting reversals of status like the ritual of the boy bishop.

For all their distinctiveness medieval towns were not autonomous entities, but outgrowths of a largely rural and initially feudal society. Towns were dependent on succeeding as centres of exchange of rural produce for manufactured goods, some of them brought from or sent to distant markets. The decline in the fortunes of the rural agrarian economy after the Black Death has generally been assumed to have brought decline and contraction to the towns also. Certainly towns were highly vulnerable to the spread of the plague. They were already dependent on inflows of rural people to maintain their populations. Such migration continued but by 1400 many towns were contracting. Houses in some places disappeared, open spaces were left. Some towns, seeking to exploit such properties, pressed for charters of incorporation, which were still being granted in the fifteenth century. Markets dues tended to fall, as did the business of crafts and trades.

Not all towns were dependent primarily on local trading conditions, and long-range trade could mould their fortunes. Ports, fair towns and places with manufacturing specialities could counter a general trend to urban contraction. The best-known examples in late medieval England are obviously wool and cloth trading towns. From the fourteenth century the balance had shifted from large-scale, raw material exports of wool, to overseas trading in home-produced cloth. As we shall see from a case-study of Colchester, towns able to take advantage of export markets in cloth could prosper greatly, but they were also extremely vulnerable, because of their lack of diversity, to changing fashion or political developments which might disrupt their markets. Although wool and cloth dominated, other relevant sectors of trade influencing town histories may include timber, fish, wine, spices, salt and silk. England was linked by trade to the Low Countries, Italy, the

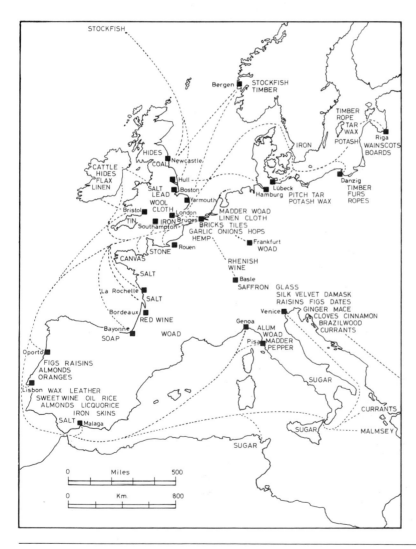

54. England's overseas trade contacts in the later Middle Ages.

Baltic, France and Iberia. The prosperity of Hull or Lynn fluctuated with the fortunes of the Hanseatic League, and that of South-ampton with the phases of the Hundred Years War. The import-ance of provincial towns was also affected by the influence of London, which increasingly dominated trade sectors, like luxury goods, and the organization of finance.

The picture of English towns in the later Middle Ages has tended to be a gloomy one of decline. Given their functions in the economy it will not be surprising if local historians find this to be so. They must, however, remember that some towns had marketing opportunities which made their experience very different, and that within individual towns a situation of fewer people pressing on available resources could mean considerable prosperity, at least for some of the townspeople.

Cases and places

The life of a classic, open-field manorial community is well represented by the Oxfordshire village of Cuxham. In 1271 the manor was given by Walter of Merton to his recently founded Merton College in Oxford. The College still owns property in Cuxham, and, through this continuity of corporate ownership (as opposed to the often more uncertain fluctuations of inheritance and purchase amongst lay families), full records were kept, and have survived. From these P.D.A. Harvey has produced a detailed picture of the period from 1240 to 1400 when the demesne lands of Cuxham were directly cultivated by its lords.

Harvey writes of a manor 'whose bounds were identical with the parish and the vill and which forms a single economic unit and social community'. The primary agricultural purpose was reflected in a village made up of peasant households, and surrounded by a landscape of three open arable fields. The lord did not live in the village, although the Warden, Fellows of the College, and their professional estate manager, the steward, visited from time to time. Merton's interests were represented on a day-to-day basis by the reeve or bailiff, usually a villein with his own landholding in the village. Judging from the manorial court rolls of Cuxham this could produce certain conflicts of interest. At the first court held after the annual audit of accounts in 1299, Robert the Reeve was in mercy, subject to fine by the court on charges which included his wife seeking hay in the lord's garden and in the pasture of Folewelle without permission, his wife entertaining the lord's *famuli* (paid estate workers) to beer on a working day and keeping them there when they should have been doing the lord's work, and Robert himself retaining a black horse belonging to the lord at his house for a month, and using the horse to harrow his land and to cart muck, so that the horse was much weakened, to the lord's serious loss. Behind most manorial tenants named in medieval documents was a working household, for whose members the tenant was responsible. Like the wife of Robert the Reeve, they too must be brought into any account of such communities.

The majority of the Cuxham villagers were customary tenants and their families. In 1279, described in the Hundred Rolls, there were eight villeins (compared with seven in 1086) and thirteen cottars (compared with four in 1086). There were also three freemen. The village population had grown and with it the number of customary holdings. Each villein had half a virgate of land. In Cuxham a virgate was thirty acres; the size of virgates or yardlands varied from region to region. For his fifteen acres each Cuxham villein paid yearly, to quote the Hundred Rolls,

> 1 quarter of wheat and a quarter of a bushel of wheat and half a quarter of oats.. Item, 3 chickens and 2 chickens and 1 cock, 2 white loaves or 6d. at the lord's choice, and one silver halfpenny, and he must work every second day throughout the year except on the Sabbath, feast days, the feast of the birth of (our) Lord, the feast of Easter and Pentecost. This service can be commuted at the lord's will for 5/-. Item, he must redeem his sons and daughters and must work at harvest with 5 men.

The villeins lived on the south side of the village street, nearest the ancient core of the settlement, where the church and manorial curia lay side-by-side. The curia contained not only the manor house, but its barns, byres, stables, dovecotes and granary. The cottars

55. Cuxham, Oxfordshire. Despite an unspectacular appearance it, like many places, has a rich local history, known particularly from medieval manorial records. On the left is one of the few houses with surviving probably medieval fabric, while on the right is the site of the manorial *curia,* with beyond it the modest church.

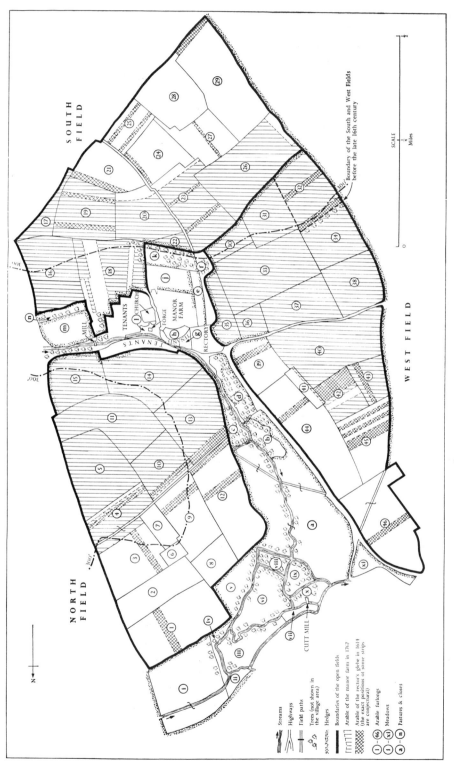

56. The fields of Cuxham in 1767 (based on the earliest suviving map of the village's open fields).

were the group which grew most in early medieval Cuxham. They
held no land in the arable fields. In 1279 not all of them owed the
same service to the lord for their cottages and surrounding plots.
Some paid two or three shillings a year, while others paid similar
amounts and owed six days work at harvest. Despite this modest
labour service the tenurial burdens on cottars were clearly much
lighter than those on villeins. Their presumably more recently
created holdings were located on the north side of the street and
along side turnings. The freemen owed suit of court, scutage
payments and small money sums. Cuxham had its miller, fuller,
blacksmith and brewer; dual or multiple occupation was the norm
then and long after, and these men appear also as tenant landholders. Finally there was the rector of the parish, whose rectory
lay on the opposite side of the manor house from the church, and
whose glebe lands were part of the open fields.

The landscape of Cuxham has been retrospectively reconstructed. The first fully detailed map of the village, which accompanied the tithe apportionment of 1848 (the year in which the
open fields were finally enclosed) together with the earliest map of
Cuxham, an estate survey of 1767, were used as a starting point to
link back through field and other names in the many intervening
documents to the Middle Ages. The positions of North, South and
West Fields, the furlongs within them, and of meadows, pastures
and closes can be fixed. Cuxham was a landscape designed to
exploit intensively the available resources, with meadows naturally
found along the stream through the centre of the village, and the
two mills at either end. The manorial economy was very much part
of a larger unit; Merton manors lay elsewhere in Oxfordshire, in
Northumberland and Durham, in Kent and Surrey. Cuxham
contributed to Merton's overall needs, mainly in cash. Produce was
also sent into Oxford. Commodities of which Cuxham was short,
notably hay and wood, were brought from other manors. Cuxham
was particularly linked with nearby Pyrton.

The fields of Cuxham were cultivated on a three-course rotation:
spring corn, winter corn, and fallow. Between the furlongs there
were balks and unploughed paths; boundaries between tenants'
land were marked by mere stones. Wheat occupied half the arable
available each year. For the demesne it was a cash crop, linking
Cuxham to Henley on the river Thames, the entrepot for shipping
of grain to the already demanding London market. Other corn
crops were oats (important as animal feed), barley and dredge. The
Cuxham cropping was not wholly monolithic; the manorial
accounts make it clear that nitrogen-fixing crops such as peas and
beans were being grown, in sections of the spring-corn field in the
thirteenth century. By 1339–48 they occupied 12.6 per cent of its
area.

The demesne's two plough teams were made up of twelve to

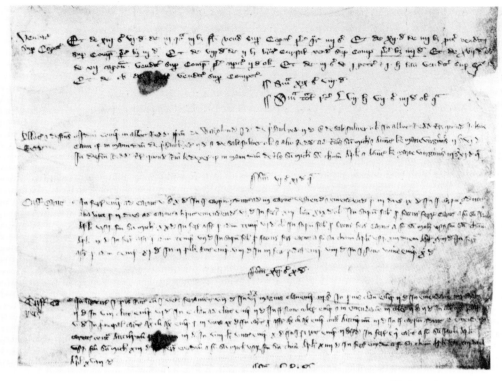

57. Manorial account for Cuxham, 1348–9, the year of the Black Death.

sixteen oxen and four ploughing horses. Sheep were not always kept at Cuxham and flock sizes never reached more than 150. Other 'stock', pigs and pigeons for example, were for the table. Some engaged in the consumption: in 1293–4 according to the accounts a cat ate a cheese! Overall the farming and the landscape were dominated by arable cultivation.

Developments at Cuxham throw light on several broad questions about medieval society. For example the decline of labour service. As early as 1240 hired hands (casual labour and the full-time estate workers, the *famuli*) did as much of the work carried out for the lord at harvest as did customary tenants. Nor was the common field lay-out immutable. The manorial court roll of 1355 refers to 'the lord's separate land', in the arable field, a clear case of convenient consolidation. The impact of the Black Death is also seen at Cuxham. It struck in the winter and spring of 1349. From payments of heriots, the death of reeves, disappearance of names, and unfilled tenancies Harvey estimates a fall in population of 60 per cent. By 1377 the Poll Tax return lists only thirty-eight inhabitants over fourteen, one-third of the probable population in 1348. By 1359 Merton's demesne was let to tenant farmers and the College was an absentee landlord. For some the changes were advantageous. The Grenes of Cuxham were already upwardly mobile. In 1279 they had held one of the freeholds in the village. By the early fourteenth century both free tenements were in the hands of Robert ate Grene, one of them right in the centre of the village, adjoining the manorial curia. By judicious marriage and patiently acquiring landholdings in scattered acres and half-acres in no fewer than seven adjoining parishes he built up an estate. Robert kept up to 100 sheep and paid about one-third as much tax again as any of the local villeins. At the Black Death his successor seized the opportunity to acquire more property in Cuxham. In the early fifteenth century the Grene 'estate' was sold and the name disappears from Cuxham, an interesting example of late medieval social and geographical mobility.

A valuable contrast to the lowland, manorial scenes of Cuxham is provided by Ian Kershaw's study, based on monastic accounts, of the estates of Bolton Priory in the West Riding of Yorkshire between 1286 and 1325. In 1324–5 the Augustinian Priory drew rents from no fewer than forty-five villages and hamlets in Wharfedale and Airedale. This clearly lies in the geographers' highland zone, a wet area of poor quality soils. It now presents an overwhelmingly pastoral landscape, yet in the thirteenth and early fourteenth centuries it must have looked very different. Subsistence required arable farming. Unlike lowland Cuxham oats (75–85 per cent of demesne output) not wheat dominated corn production. Crops were spring not winter sown. Some land was only temporarily cultivated. Like Merton College Bolton Priory was an energetic exploiter of demesne. Some was organized within manorialized villages but other areas were separate, ring-fenced establishments, outlying granges run directly from the overall centre of the estate as extra-manorial units.

The Priory's peak of estate expansion and direct management was in the 1290s and because it is their accounts rather than court rolls which survive, it is from the landlord's perspective that the picture has to be drawn. The canons had four main sources of income, the profits of lordship (rents, fines and dues), returns on extensive arable demesne, the fruits of appropriated churches, and above all profits from sales of wool. They sold the fleeces of their own flocks, at their biggest 3,578 animals, and were middlemen for other producers. The market was an international one, through east coast ports to Flanders, and to Italian merchants. The Priory borrowed against its wool sales from both the Peruzzi and the Frescobaldi. Cuxham and Malham or Appletreewick were each exploited for the lord's profit, but the intermeshed activities of the small, manorially controlled open-field community of wheat-producing Cuxham were very different from those of the upland sheep pastures where the Augustinians of Bolton were neighbours of the even bigger 'ranches' of the Cistercians of Fountains. On northern manors labour services were generally lighter than in places like Cuxham. This is borne out by the manorialized parts of the Bolton Priory estates. For example, in Harewood parish customary tenants owed twenty-two days work per year, and no weekly labour. Paid labour was much relied upon. It took two forms: the permanent staff of estate workers, *famuli*, including on the home farm, demesnes and granges, carters, oxherds and shepherds and casual workers, engaged particularly at times of peak activity, for reaping, mowing, threshing and winnowing. Paying for the *famuli* and the seasonal workers accounted for between 13 and 17 per cent of the Priory's costs.

Finally these dale and fell settlements provide ample evidence of the pre-Black Death agrarian crisis. The period from 1315 to 1320 was a catastrophic time. Torrential rains and wretched harvests in both 1315 and 1316 reduced grain yields on demesne and from tithes to about half normal levels. The Priory was buying wheat at prices five times the normal levels. In the same years sheep disease led to the loss of two-thirds of the Priory's flock of around 3,000 animals. In 1319–20 cattle mortality reduced their oxen and essential motive power, from 139 to 58. On top of this came violent Scottish raids. In 1318–19 the Scots, having marched through Northumberland and Durham into Yorkshire, turned westward through Airedale and Wharfedale, before returning north up the west side of the country. The Priory's tenants fled with their stock, crops and animals were taken by the Scots, buildings and property burnt. In 1319–23 the Patent Rolls record that the king took the Priory into his protection. After 1320 there was leasing of demesne lands at fixed rents, a fall in stock numbers, and a lapse in the collection of many tenants' rents. For the rest of Bolton Priory's history as a landlord in the area only land immediately around the Priory was directly farmed and when dissolution came in 1529, the estates were dispersed within four years into the hands of a variety of new lay owners.

Cumbrian cases bear out similar, contrasting experiences of adjacent lowland and upland places. The lowlands produced earlier established communities, organized through manors, and with a sizeable proportion of arable cultivation achieved through a core of permanently tilled fields sometimes supplemented by patches of outfield pasture, dug up and tilled in rotation (the so-called infield-outfield system). By contrast the upland woods and fells were settled later, used primarily for cattle, sheep and pig-grazing, were more distant from concentrations of seigneurial presence, and were only gradually organized into township and manorial units. Later and sparser settlement produced in many northern communities larger jurisdictional units, not only in manors, but also in parishes, frequently subdivided into ecclesiastical chapelries and civil townships. Angus Winchester sees, in medieval Cumbria,

58. (OPPOSITE) Lorton, Cumberland: contrasting medieval landscapes. Low Lorton lies in the valley of the River Cocker, which appears on the left of the map. In the modern landscape contrasts persist between larger, square fields based on nineteenth-century reorganization of strip fields in the valley and the irregular medieval assarts of the fellside settlements. (From A. Winchester, *Landscape and society in medieval Cumbria* (1987).)

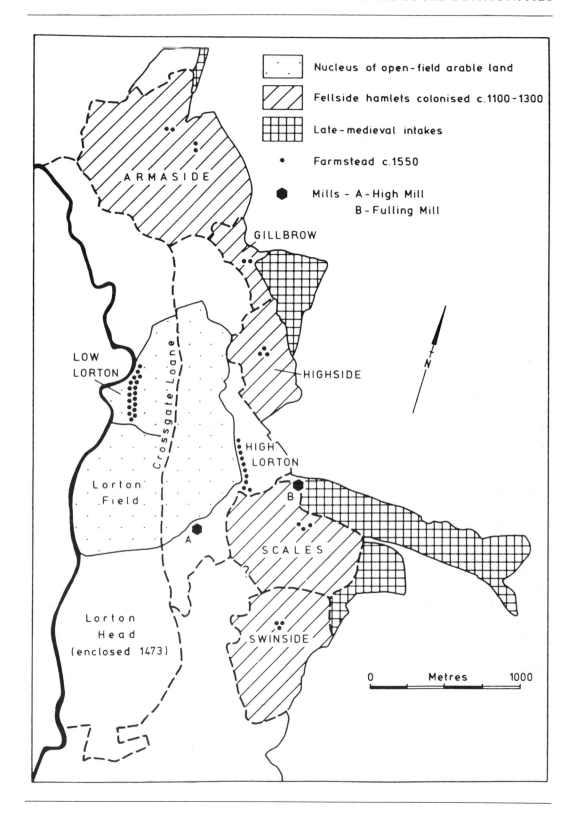

Nucleus of open-field arable land

Fellside hamlets colonised c.1100-1300

Late-medieval intakes

• Farmstead c.1550

Mills - A-High Mill
B-Fulling Mill

ARMASIDE

GILLBROW

LOW LORTON

Crossgate Loane

HIGHSIDE

HIGH LORTON

Lorton Field

B

A

SCALES

Lorton Head (enclosed 1473)

SWINSIDE

0   Metres   1000

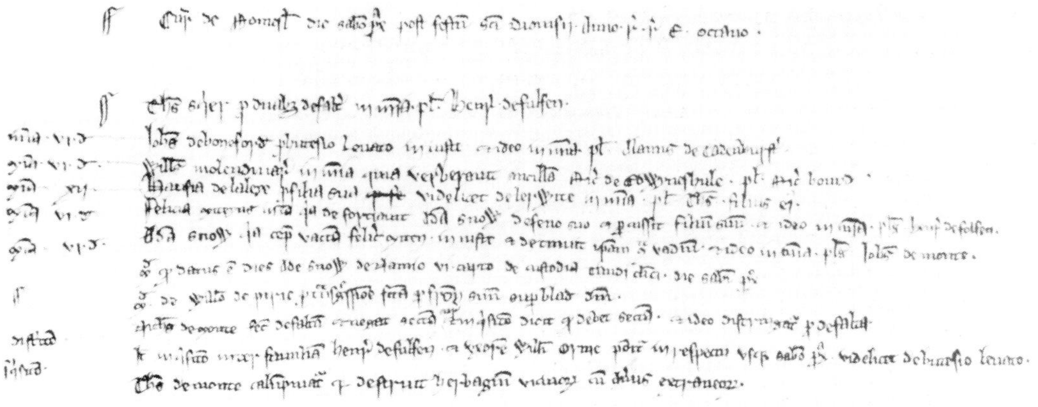

59. Proceedings of the court of Romsley from the court roll of the Manor of Hales (Halesowen, Worcs.) 1280–1.

contrasting developments in upland and lowlands with, by the sixteenth century, distinctive upland communities in which customary tenancies had taken on an hereditary nature, and local élites of 'nascent gentry families' had developed positions of considerable influence.

Two West Midlands studies, by ingenious use primarily of manorial documents, uncover something of the peasant's experience. Christopher Dyer begins with evidence from a variety of areas. By collating numbers of manorial surveys and the Hundred Rolls, he has calculated that an average of between 42 and 45 per cent of customary holdings were less than half a yardland or virgate (about fifteen acres) by the end of the thirteenth century. Only East Anglia is markedly different, with the average of small holdings rising to nearer 80 per cent. From this point, near the end of a phase of sustained population growth, Dyer reconstructs the budgets of the peasant tenants of Bishop's Cleeve in Gloucestershire. A detailed survey, carried out in 1299 for their lord, the Bishop of Worcester, shows the manor populated by four yardlanders, eleven half-yardlanders, twenty-seven cotlanders (with twelve acres each) and thirteen smallholders (with three acres). In addition a third of local landholders were freeholders. They farmed in a manor containing two villages and two hamlets, lying partly on lowland, clays of average quality for corn growing, and partly on the scarp edge of the Cotswolds. Dyer carefully balances six determinants of their annual fate. Income depended on the size of holding; the productivity of agriculture (for example, whether a two or three-field system applied made great differences to the proportion of his arable a tenant could actively employ); and on availability of other sources of income (from the produce of stock, from family working as hired labour for others). Consumption and expenditure revolved around family size; amounts of food needed for consumption by the household; and outgoings in rents and taxes, to manorial lord, king and church. If peasants kept accounts they have not survived and so information on, for example, yields per acre has to come from accounts of manorial demesne. Acknowledging some risks in making use of available sources Dyer concludes that a yardlander like Robert le Kyng of Cleeve village could look to a cash surplus in a normal year of farming his thirty acres of arable, exercising pasture rights for his thirty sheep, his two cows, two oxen, and a horse or two, and paying out his rent, tithes, amercements in the manorial courts, and any labour and equipment costs. However, the lot of his half-yardlander neighbours was increasingly marginal, having to rely on the produce of garden, poultry and family labour, and probably having to work for others themselves. The cotlanders, the three-acre men, and (despite lower rents and services) the freeholders of small acreages endured a precarious existence, even in normal years. They were, in the phrase of Zvi Razi, 'the harvest sensitive element in rural society'.

This is one conclusion of the most comprehensive attempt yet to reconstitute a medieval community. Zvi Razi has culled from a near-continuous sequence of court rolls for the manor of Hales-owen, Worcestershire, 3,435 named villagers (2,057 male and 1,378 females). From these he has reconstituted 677 families, and a further 364 with some hypothetical linkage. Halesowen was a large manor of some 10,000 acres, its population dispersed between a small market town and twelve rural settlements, and in the lordship

60. Numbers of children in Halesowen families reconstituted from the court rolls. There are marked contrasts between the poor, middling and rich, and between the pre- and post-Black Death periods (after Razi).

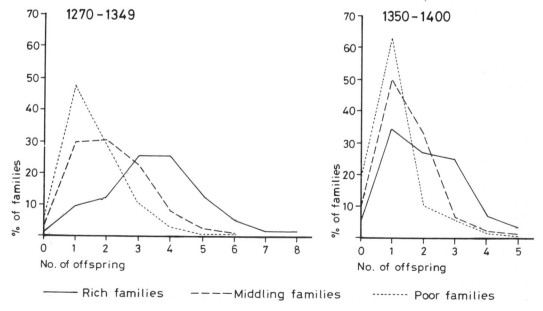

70 1270-1349

% of families

No. of offspring

70 1350-1400

% of families

No. of offspring

—— Rich families   – – – – Middling families   ········ Poor families

from 1217 of the Premonstratensian Abbey of Halesowen. In the pre-plague years Halesowen shared the experience of population growth, with 71 tenants in 1086 and at least 215 by 1313–15. By plotting numbers of tenant deaths, pleas of debt, and cases brought for misdemeanours such as illegal gleaning, Razi established recurrent levels of distress between the 1290s and 1348, with crises of famine level prices in 1293–5, increased deaths in 1310–12, and the famine of 1315–17 reflected in mortality rates of some 15 per cent amongst tenants in 1316–18. Inheritance by the eldest son applied and peasants married only when a property, however small, was available. Despite this most families in Halesowen manor had more than one son and daughter staying to settle there. In terms of better life expectancy and greater numbers of children over twelve the better-off tenants outdid their poorer neighbours.

About 43 per cent of tenants, rich and poor alike, died in the Black Death, yet the same amount of land remained in cultivation. The Abbey was leasing its demesne within two years. Vacant tenant holdings were also taken up, often by kin; Razi calculates that 63 per cent were taken on by rich families, 32 per cent by middling, and 5 per cent by poor. No appreciable recovery in population took place by 1400, although life would seem to be easier for those left behind. In fact plague recurred, and Razi argues that the age structure of the population had become older. Certainly there was more migration, almost half of sons over twelve are not recorded in the manor at the time of their father's death, compared with 27 per cent in 1270–1349. The step of getting married seems to have been easier with greater availability of land. In 1270–1349 illegitimacy rates were high, judged by no fewer than 117 lerwytes (fines for an unmarried woman's unchastity) as opposed to 220 merchets (tenant's dues for a daughter's marriage). After 1349 the number of lerwytes fell considerably, although this intriguing ratio cannot be pursed beyond 1386, for the significant reason that tenant resistance forced the Abbot to abandon collection of merchets. Halesowen was profoundly damaged by the plague, but survived, in changed form, to prosper.

The same tides of circumstance also produced failed communities. As many as 3,000 abandoned villages are now known in England. The most famous is Wharram Percy in East Yorkshire, under joint historical and archaeological investigation by Maurice Beresford and John Hurst since 1948. Here the total desertion of the site, apart from the church, has allowed a long-term excavation covering 6 per cent of the 40-acre site. This has been used with documentary research and landscape study of the 1,500-acre township and beyond. It seems that in the Saxon period the village was still a shifting group of up to six dwellings, one of several such groups in the township. These evolved, at an unknown date between the tenth and twelfth centuries, into a single, compact

61. (OPPOSITE) Plans of the excavated church at Wharram Percy, East Yorkshire, showing the different periods separately, starting with the small private tenth- and eleventh-century churches (I and II), followed by the large twelfth-century parochial church (III and IV), with aisles and chapels added (V–VII), and then the gradual reduction in size of the church (VIII–XII) as various settlements in the parish became deserted and population decreased.

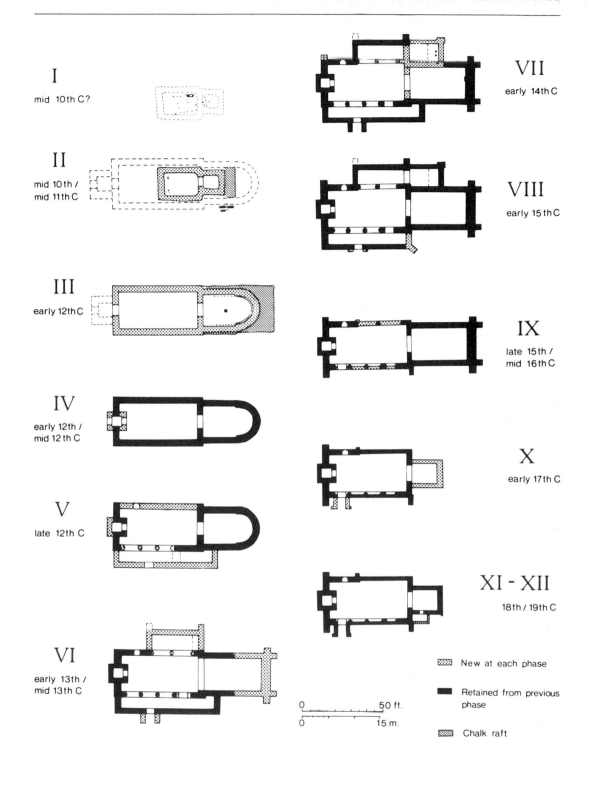

I
mid 10th C?

II
mid 10th /
mid 11th C

III
early 12th C

IV
early 12th /
mid 12th C

V
late 12th C

VI
early 13th /
mid 13th C

VII
early 14th C

VIII
early 15th C

IX
late 15th /
mid 16th C

X
early 17th C

XI - XII
18th / 19th C

New at each phase

Retained from previous
phase

Chalk raft

0   50 ft.

0   15 m.

community of thirty or so houses, with manor house, church, vicarage, and open fields. The peasant houses were arranged along three frontages. This, and the methodical distribution of lands within the open fields, suggest a possible planned layout.

Beneath the house sites known from grass-covered earthworks, were several other house foundations, homes progressing from timber to stone, but not always on the same alignment. The fluid nature of the plan at times in the village's history was also notably apparent in the case of a twelfth-century manor house, abandoned and built over by peasant houses, perhaps as part of a major re-planning. From excavations the plan of peasant houses is becoming known. At Wharram Percy the typical form between the fourteenth and sixteenth centuries was the longhouse or laithe, of stone and timber, combining human and animal housing. Further south plans with the animals separated from the people were evolving by this date.

The population of Wharram Percy after the Black Death was still high. Its houses continued to be built and repaired. Yet by the early sixteenth century the village was deserted. It is not known whether this was by a process of attrition or by an act of seigneurial policy to promote sheep pasture. In an area with lucrative opportunities to grow wool for the cloth industry Wharram Percy did become a place of sheep pastures. It was one of four of the six townships in the parish to be depopulated. In all of this the church building is a barometer of development and decline. From a tiny, two-cell late Saxon building discovered by excavation, it grew in the Norman period to a larger nave and apsidal chancel. To this were added a thirteenth-century, square-ended chancel, aisles and a side chapel, until it reached its fullest extent in the early fourteenth century. Thereafter it gradually shrank in size, with aisles lost and chancel shortened.

Wharram Percy is exceptional in the length and intensity of the research devoted to it. Most sites are known from non-excavational evidence. Such is Widford in Oxfordshire, a collection of humps and bumps in a grassy meadow alongside the river Windrush. Again an isolated church is the most obvious sign but unlike Wharram Percy it never developed with a growing community. At Widford the very simplicity of the simple nave and chancel confirm that this village was never large or prosperous. In 1086 there were four villeins, three bordars, and four serfs at Widford. In 1327 four taxpayers paid the Lay Subsidy and in the more comprehensive Poll Tax of 1381 thirteen people in ten households paid. By 1524 there were only three payers of that year's subsidy. Widford was always a small place, near to the flood level of the river, bounded by Wychwood Forest to the north, and close to the substantial village of Swinbrook in the east and the prospering market town of Burford in the west. In the fifteenth century it seems to have

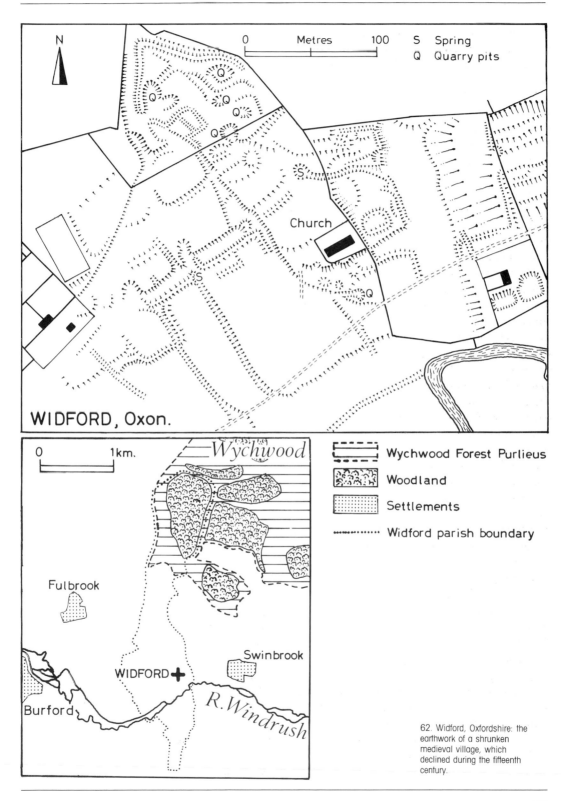

WIDFORD, Oxon.

S Spring
Q Quarry pits

Church

Wychwood

0   1km.

Wychwood Forest Purlieus

Woodland

Settlements

Widford parish boundary

Fulbrook

Swinbrook

WIDFORD ✚

Burford

R. Windrush

62. Widford, Oxfordshire: the
earthwork of a shrunken
medieval village, which
declined during the fifteenth
century.

63. The now isolated church of St Oswald, Widford. Its modest size and architecture reflect the village it originally served.

dwindled, leaving its 'unimproved' church, the mill and a farmstead.

The towns most studied and about which most is available in print have tended to be the larger, chartered boroughs, well provided with charters of foundation, grants of privilege, rentals, property deeds (for some places enrolled in the borough's own registry), court records, and the statutes and records of chantries and gilds. Yet, as we have already seen, the great majority of English medieval towns were smaller and not always chartered. Brief case studies of two of these, Halesowen (with a population of about 600 in 1300), and Colchester (with 3,000 to 4,000 inhabitants at the same period) have been included here, while references to studies of larger towns will be found in the section 'Further reading'.

Halesowen we already know as a manor, covering twelve rural settlements and a small town, from which the manor took its name. The town was the product of a late-thirteenth-century foundation by the local lord, the Premonstratensian Abbey of Halesowen. It was one of the hundreds of smaller market towns founded or sponsored by lords, both lay and ecclesiastical, in the thirteenth century in what Rodney Hilton has called 'an epoch of seigneurial euphoria'. He calculates that 85 per cent of towns in the West Midlands were owned by such lords. Halesowen was small but successful. It had trading connections with the already developing Birmingham area, and was conveniently placed in terms of routes in the Severn and Stour valleys, and between major towns, Coventry and Worcester, via Bromsgrove and Droitwich. It crossed the dividing line between large market village and small town by developing a diverse and somewhat specialized range of non-agricultural occupations and certain institutional features. This happened without Halesowen ceasing to be part of a manor or acquiring a royal charter.

The affairs of the town were run through the manor or hundred court (Halesowen claimed separate hundred status), records of which survive from 1272 until the early sixteenth century. Hilton has used these to reconstitute details of the economy and families of the town. The results are inevitably less comprehensive than Zvi Razi's study of the rural parts of the manor; customary tenure did not apply and peasant inheritance, marriage and death are therefore not recorded in the same way. Nevertheless Hilton finds the activities of 311 people recorded between 1272 and 1282, and 1,716 between 1299 and 1349. Around 40 to 50 per cent of these were residents in the town. The town grew because the Abbey granted privileges to attract people there. In the late 1260s a formal grant of the same privileges as those of the burgesses of Hereford was made. People came to the new town, in particular from the rural part of the surrounding manor. Land was held with burgage tenure, giving toll-free access to buy and sell in the market. Others, without land, paid to trade and for the liberty of the town. Goods traded were grain (particularly oats), malt, livestock, woollen and linen cloth, bread, ale, meat, fish and vegetables. Occupations included bakers, cooks, brewers, craftsmen in textiles, leather, metal and wood. Trade and manufacture was carried on in household units, often with more than one occupation. Hilton comments on the high proportion of female immigrants to the town, and their work, including brewing, baking and stallholding.

The borough court met monthly, and twice a year for minor criminal cases, arising from its frankpledge jurisdiction. Between sessions disputes arising from markets and fairs were dealt with by occasional 'pie powder courts'. Regular business included debts, contracts, the quality of bread and ale, grants of burgage tenure, and the sanitary (or insanitary) consequences of trades such as dyeing and butchery. In the early years of this seigneurial borough, up to *c.* 1320, there were tensions between lord and town, with spasmodic demands for labour services, payments from incomers marrying women with burgage tenure, and heriots. Thereafter relations seem to have settled down, unlike other towns with similar constitutions. For example, in the famous case of Cirencester the townsmen established a gild merchant in 1403, only for it to be abolished by the Abbey in 1418. No such gild merchant emerged in Halesowen, although the Hereford grant of privileges would have allowed it. Hilton finds, however, that by the early fourteenth century established families, perhaps one hundred of them, had become settled in the town, and were forming an élite, identifiable by their presence as jurors in the borough court. The town had a modest version of the characteristic medieval urban hierarchy of merchant élite, organized crafts with masters, journeymen and apprentices, trades and food processors, and a shifting group of servants and marginals. The separateness of the town from the manor was not registered by outside authority; for example, it was taxed and dealt with by the justices in eyre as a single manorial unit, a frustration for later historians trying to unravel the two. Yet, as Hilton argues, Halesowen town developed sufficient economic momentum and independent social identity to continue successfully into the post-Black Death period, a time when over half the village markets in the West Midlands failed to survive.

R.H. Britnell's study of Colchester takes the urban story on into the later Middle Ages. He, too, uses court rolls, linked to a monastic cartulary, calendars of government records, and feet of fines. The fortunes of the Essex town are followed from 1300 to 1525. In the early fourteenth century Colchester was a market town of some 3,000 to 4,000 people, existing as the marketing centre for a large, agricultural hinterland. A century later its population had probably doubled, and the town was a centre of textile manufacture, producing distinctive russet cloths primarily for export, with its chief markets in Gascony (with wine as a return cargo), and the Baltic, particularly Prussia. Britnell ties this economic success to a flexible structure within the town, limited regulation of producers and the expansion of credit allowed through the town's court. Successful traders concentrated their efforts in the town and, at a time of agricultural depression, were not diverted into the countryside by the lure of prestigious land purchases. Britnell's study belies previous generalizations that later medieval English towns were inevitably drawn into decline by the depressed nature of an agrarian economy of which they were an adjunct. In fact some towns could, and did, prosper. However, there were dangers of a different kind when an urban community depended for its prosperity on a single source, in Colchester's case overseas cloth exports. Between 1415 and 1425 these markets were depressed; Colchester merchants tried to retrieve the situation by switching to higher quality cloths. Britnell finds that this move also produced a more oligarchic, regulated pattern of production and marketing. When the Prussian and Gascon markets collapsed in the 1440s relative stagnation turned to contraction. The fifty years to 1525 saw the disappearance of a distinctive Colchester cloth, the restrictive regulation of the smaller traders and craftsmen, and a trend for the big men of the town to look outside to land purchase. By the early sixteenth century Colchester's population was one third below its former peak. Halesowen and Colchester form useful contrasts between

English towns at different stages of their development, and during different periods. In both cases economic functions and fortunes were pre-eminent in determining their medieval histories, and their government and institutions evolved to reflect this.

This section has drawn on the work of P.D.A. Harvey, *A medieval Oxfordshire village – Cuxham 1240–1400* (1965); Ian Kershaw, *Bolton Priory. The economy of a northern monastery 1286–1325* (1973); Angus Winchester, *Landscape and society in medieval Cumbria* (1987); Christopher Dyer, *Standards of living in the later Middle Ages. Social change in England c. 1200–1520* (1989); Zvi Razi, *Life, marriage and death in a medieval parish. Economy, society and demography in Halesowen 1270–1400* (1980); Maurice Beresford and John Hurst, *Wharram Percy, deserted medieval village* (1990); R.H. Hilton, 'Small town society in England before the Black Death', reprinted in R. Holt and G. Rosser, *The medieval town 1200–1540* (1990); and R.H. Britnell, *Growth and decline in Colchester 1300–1525* (1986).

The main sources demonstrated in use in their work are:

* manorial court rolls, accounts, terriers, custumals, rentals, deeds
* central administrative records of lords, e.g. Bolton Priory's account book
* monastic cartularies, tithe accounts
* borough court records, grants of privilege
* Hundred Rolls, subsidy assessments, Poll Tax returns
* printed texts and calendars of central government rolls series, inquisitions post mortem, legal records such as Feet of Fines
* post-medieval maps and surveys
* archaeological excavation, earthwork survey (involving aerial photography, ground survey, map analysis, documentary research).

Sources

More evidence is available for the Middle Ages than most local historians expect. However, it can certainly seem daunting – mostly documents, largely written in Latin (until the very end of the period when some English appears), in unfamiliar handwriting, and using many alien concepts; feet of fines, villeinage and seisin are just some of these. Local historians should not despair but adopt the rule of always trying to use first in their researches the great numbers of printed texts and particularly calendars. A calendar contains summaries, in English, of original documents, and many of central government records, at once some of the most potentially useful but the most difficult sources for local historians, are available in this form. From these calendars and their indexes local references can be culled. A useful preliminary to hunting down these volumes in the nearest major reference library is to scan the references to local volumes of the VCH and the English Place-Names Society. These will give a good introduction to the records in which local material has already been identified. The standard reference work, which lists texts and calendars printed by both the PRO and other national bodies and local societies, is E.C. Mullins, *Texts and calendars* (published by the Royal Historical Society, vol. 1 to 1957 (1958), vol. 2, 1957–1982 (1983)). This includes summaries of the content of each volume listed.

Having used calendars and printed English texts to the full it will inevitably be necessary to turn to Latin texts or original documents to answer certain questions. Here, too, help is at hand. Medieval Latin is hardly of classical complexity or purity, and many sources employ a relatively restricted vocabulary. Armed with Eileen Gooder's *Latin for local history: an introduction* (second edition, paperback, 1978), and perhaps fortified by working in a local group or adult education class, many local historians have cracked the code. The common form of many documents, the familiar order of elements, and regular use of the same sequences of words is also an encouragement.

Given the opportunities for using printed sources, examples in this section of documents in their original form are restricted to two basic cases, first, the text of an entry in the best-known of all medieval documents, Domesday Book, showing the processes of transcription and translation, and second, probably the most commonly occurring document type, the charter or deed, showing its highly standardized format. The chapter will end with a checklist of the principal sources for medieval local history.

Domesday Book

Domesday Book, so-called for its judgemental and intensive enquiry, began with William I's directive, made at his Christmas Council of 1085 when, according to the Peterborough Chronicle, the King had

> very deep speech with his wise men about this land, how it was peopled and by what sort of men. Then he sent his men into every shire all over England and caused it to be found out how many hundred hides were in the shire and what land the king had, and what stock on the land, and what dues he ought to have each year from the shire. Also he caused it to be written how much land his archbishops, bishops, abbots, and earls had, and, though I may be somewhat tedious in my account, what and how much each landholder in England had in land or in stock, and how much money it might be worth. So minutely did he cause it to be searched out that there was not one hide or yard of land, nor even

(it is shameful to write of it, but he thought it not shameful to do it) an ox, or a cow, or a swine that was not set down in his writ. And all the writings were brought to him afterwards.

The questions asked survive in a draft copy of the survey for Cambridgeshire:

What is the manor called? Who held it in the time of King Edward? Who holds it now? How many hides? How many ploughs on the demesne? How many men? How many villeins? How many cottars? How many slaves? How many free men? How many socmen? How much wood? How much meadow? How much pasture? How many mills? How many fish ponds? How much has been added or taken away? How much, taken together, was it worth and how much now. How much each free man or socman had or has. All this at three dates, to wit, in the time of King Edward and when King William gave it and as it is now. And if it is possible for more to be had than is had.

Commissioners were sent into each county to collect this information. Each hundred or wapentake made a return of landholding to the county court, and within each hundred the priest, reeve and six men in each manor were responsible for checking the information. The returns were collated by county, and within county by landholder and manor. Landholders were listed under each county beginning with the king, then tenants-in-chief (usually starting with archbishops, bishops, religious houses and lay magnates), and finally minor tenants. This mighty job of transcription was done by royal scribes at Winchester and it is amazing how seldom they needed to insert a marginal note of 'R' ('requiret'), indicating missing information.

Their abbreviated transcriptions of the full, original surveys are bound into two volumes. Great Domesday covers all the counties of England, except Northumberland, Durham, Cumberland, Westmorland and Lancashire. Parts of the last three counties are covered under Lancashire and Cheshire. Neither does Great Domesday cover Essex, Norfolk and Suffolk, the richest parts of the kingdom, which are listed in greater detail and appear in the separate Little Domesday. A number of 'satellite' or later surveys also survive; the Exon Domesday refers to Wiltshire, Dorset, Somerset, Devon and Cornwall, the Winton Domesday (1107–28) to Winchester, the Boldon Book to the Palatinate of Durham (1183), and there are 'Inquests' for Ely and Cambridgeshire.

There are three printed English translations of Domesday Book available to local historians, in the relevant county VCH, in the lavish facsimile and accompanying county essays, indexes and translations of the Alecto edition of Domesday begun in 1986, and in the paperback Phillimore series, edited by the late John Morris, with its sometimes controversial modern translations. Because

TERRA ALANI COMITIS.

A	TERRA ALANI COMITIS	
D	The land of Count Alan	

2

3 In Waltham

4 h̅b Radulf' ſtalre .

	2	3	4
A	M	In WALTHAM	h'b Radulf' ſtalre .
B	Manerium	In Waltham	habuit Radulfus Stalre .
C	Estate	In Waltham	had Ralph (the) Staller
D	Estate	In Waltham Ralph the Staller had	

5 vi. car' t're ad g'ld'. **6** T'ra ad . xii . car'. **7** Ibi h't n'c comes alan' .iiij. car'.

	5	6	7
A	vi. car' t're ad g'ld'.	T'ra ad . xii . car'.	Ibi h't n'c comes alan' .iiij. car'.
B	vi.carucatas ad geldum. terrae	Terra ad . xii .carucas.Ibi habet nunc comes Alanus .iiij .carucas	
C	6. carucates to the of land geld	Land for 12 ploughs.Here has now Count Alan 4 ploughs	
D	6 carucates of land to the geld	There is land for 12 ploughs.	Now Count Alan has there 4 ploughs (in demesne)

8 7 xii.uill. **9** 7 i. bord. **10** 7 x viij. ſoch

	8	9	10
A	7 xii . vill'	7 i. bord'.	7 x viij .ſoch'
B	et xii villanos	et i bordarium	et xviii sochemannos
C	and 12 villeins	and 1 bordar	and 18 sokemen
D	and 12 villeins and 1 bordar and 18 sokemen		

11 h'ntes. ix.car' 7 dimid. **12** Ibi eccl̅a 7 p̅b̅r. **13** 7 lx. viij. ac' p̅ti.

	11	12	13
A	h'nteſ . ix .car' 7 dimid'	Ibi eccl'a 7 p'b'r.	7 ix . viij. ac' p'ti.
B	habentes ix.carucas et dimidim	Ibi ecclesia et presbyter.	et lxviii. acre prati.
C	having 9 ploughs and a half.	There is a church and a priest and 64	acres meadow
D	having 9½ ploughs	There is a church and a priest and 64 acres of meadow	

14 T.R.E. uat xx. lib. **15** m̅ xl.v.lib. **16** Tailla.xv.lib.

	14	15	16
A	T.R.E. val' xx . lib'.	m' xl . v . lib'.	Tailla . xv .lib'.
B	Tempore valuit xx libras Regis Edwardi	modo xlv libras	Tailla xv libras
C	In the time valued 20 pounds of King Edward	now 45 pounds	Tallage 15 pounds
D	In the time of King Edward it was valued at £20, now it is worth £45. Tallage £15.		

there are facsimiles and translations available, and for most areas of
the country, Domesday is an easy text for the local historians to
take and follow through the stages from the abbreviated Latin in
the hand of the Winchester scribe, to the extended version with
Latin words in full, to a literal and finally a clear English version.
This is just what Geoffrey Bryant, studying Domesday with a
group from the local branch of the Workers' Educational Association (WEA) did with the entry for Waltham, Lincolnshire. The
transcription and translation of this typical entry are reproduced
here, by kind permission, from his *Domesday Book, how to read it and
what it means* (1985).

In just fifty-seven words we are told the present holder of the
manor (Count Alan, a cousin of the Conqueror, who 'had some
442 manors in Yorkshire, Lincolnshire, Cambridgeshire, Norfolk,
Suffolk, Essex, Hertfordshire, Nottinghamshire, Hampshire and
Dorset'), the previous incumbent under Edward the Confessor, the
extent of the demesne arable, the numbers and status of tenant
landholders, the amount of arable they held, the local meadow, the
existence of a church with a priest, and the value of the manor
before 1066, in 1086, and of its annual manorial tax (tallage). From
these bare bones, and in relation to other entries, much can be said
about Waltham. The study also shows how transcription and
translation may be made manageable.

A medieval charter

A charter was a grant of land or rights. Such documents existed in
Anglo-Saxon England, as we have seen, but became much more
common in the Middle Ages. Charters were made by the king, to a
lay individual or spiritual body, but also by such parties themselves
to individuals or other institutions. This type of document therefore turns up in many archives, in estate and family papers, in
monastic cartularies (or registers of charters) and in borough
records, as well as governmental rolls series.

The transmission of property had originally involved the physical handing over of a clod of earth from the land involved or some
symbolic object like a key or a knife before witnesses. Only
gradually, especially in the twelfth century did the written record,
in the form of a charter, become a regular part of the deed. Charters
continued to record the transfer in the past tense ('I have given and
granted . . .'). They have certain standard and distinct parts.

64. (OPPOSITE) The Domesday
Book entry for Waltham,
Lincolnshire as transcribed,
extended and translated by
Geoffrey Bryant in the study
discussed here.

65 A typical private charter of the late thirteenth century: grant and quitclaim by Robert Wyton of Broughton to Thomas prior of Mottisfont, post 1290 (Hampshire Record Office, ref. 13 M 63 / 127).

The opening words *Omnibus Christi fidelibus* followed by the name of the grantor and *salutem in Domino* are standard for this type of transaction, which is a grant and quitclaim (*me ... quietum clamasse*) of one acre of Robert's land with appurtenances in Broughton, lying between the land of Mottisfont Priory and the land of John de Gussyche, and abutting southwards on land called Osmershulle. The reference to lords of the fee (*dominis feodi*) in the *habendam et tenendam* clause, which describes the tenure of the property granted, reflects changes introduced by the statute *Quia Emptores* in 1290, which curbed the practice of subinfeudation by stipulating that tenure of land in fee simple and associated services were owed to 'chief lords of the fee' (the ultimate of whom of course was the Crown) rather than to named donors who themselves owed service to a lord.

Thomas, Prior of Mottisfont, and three of the witnesses named here also appear in a charter from the same collection (13 M 63 / 128) which is dated the feast of St John the Baptist 22 Edward I (1294).

Palaeographically the charter uses standard abbreviation symbols and letter forms for the late thirteenth century. The original deed was authenticated by a wax seal attached to a tongue threaded through the fold at the foot of the document.

Principal sources for medieval local history

★ *manorial records*

These are often found amongst the estate records of later, post-medieval owners. The most important categories are:

- accounts, for individual manors or compiled centrally for a larger estate
- manorial court rolls
- written surveys
- rentals
- custumals
- deeds or charters

★ *records of royal government*

- Domesday Book
- Hundred Rolls
- Lay Subsidy Rolls
- Poll Tax returns
- administrative or Chancery records. These include incoming correspondence and inquisitions post mortem. Relevant series are the Charter, Patent, Close, and Liberate Rolls
- Records of justice, particularly of the Courts of Common Pleas (including Feet of Fines), King's Bench (including Coroner's rolls), Exchequer, and Parliament (including petitions). The king's locally-delivered justice is recorded under the General Eyres (*c* 1166–1348), Assizes (from *c* 1250), Goal Delivery, and Oyer and Terminer
- financial records of the Exchequer, notably the Pipe Rolls

★ *ecclesiastical records*

- papal, for example calendars of papal letters
- diocesan, including visitations, registers, and court books. Wills, some of them written in English by the fourteenth century, fell within this jurisdiction
- parish. A few late medieval survivals, including fifteenth-century churchwardens' accounts
- monastic, particularly cartularies, or registers of documents relating to a monastic house's properties, including appropriated churches

★ *town records*

- royal charters
- grants of privilege
- borough court rolls
- borough ordinances

- rentals
- property deeds
- gild or fraternity ordinances, deeds

★ *literary and personal records*

- wills (see ecclesiastical records)
- letters. They survive in rare cases in the fourteenth and fifteenth centuries. The best known examples are the Paston letters
- chronicles
- literature in English. Two fourteenth-century examples are Chaucer's *Canterbury Tales* and William Langland's *Piers Plowman*

★ *landscape and buildings*

- earthwork evidence, for example of ridge and furrow in open fields, or of DMVs
- aerial photographs
- maps. In most cases post-medieval estate and Ordnance Survey maps have to be used retrospectively, and in conjunction with documents
- place- and field-names
- botanical evidence, for example hedgerow studies, or 'indicator species' for ancient woodland
- the form of settlement plans
- surviving buildings
- artefacts, fixtures and fittings, such as monuments, stained glass, wood- and stonework.

References

1 J. Ravensdale, *The Domesday inheritance* (1986).
2 E. Miller and J. Hatcher, *Medieval England. Rural society and economic change 1086–1349* (1978), p. 16.
3 ——, op. cit., pp. 17–18.
4 H.C. Darby, *Domesday England* (1977), Appendices 2 and 3: Categories of rural population by Domesday counties, pp. 337–45.
5 e.g. Miller and Hatcher, op.cit., pp. 128–33.
6 O. Rackham, *The history of the countryside* (1986), p. 88.
7 J.H. Bettey, *Church and parish* (1978), suggests that a quarter of English parish churches were appropriated by monastic houses before 1200, but see R.A.R. Hartridge, *A history of vicarages in the Middle Ages* (1930), pp. 77–89; and R.N. Swanson, 'Universities, graduates and benefices in later medieval England', in *Past and Present*, no. 106 (1985), p. 36.
8 Policraticus of John of Salisbury, quoted in D.C. Douglas and

G.W. Greenaway (eds.) *English historical documents 1042–1189* (2nd edn., 1981), pp. 837 et seq.

9   *Taxatio ecclesiastica Angliae et Walliae auctoritate Papae Nicholai IV, circa 1291*, Record Commission (1802).

10 D. Owen, *Church and society in medieval Lincolnshire.* (History of Lincolnshire, vol. 5, 1971), p. 142.

11 W.B. Stephens, *Sources for English local history* (1981 edn.), p. 71.

12 R.H. Hilton, 'Towns in English medieval society' in R. Holt and G. Rosser, *The medieval town 1200–1540* (1990), p. 22.

13 R. Holt and G. Rosser, op. cit., p. 4.

14 C.V. Phythian-Adams, *Desolation of a city; Coventry and the urban crisis of the later Middle Ages* (1979).

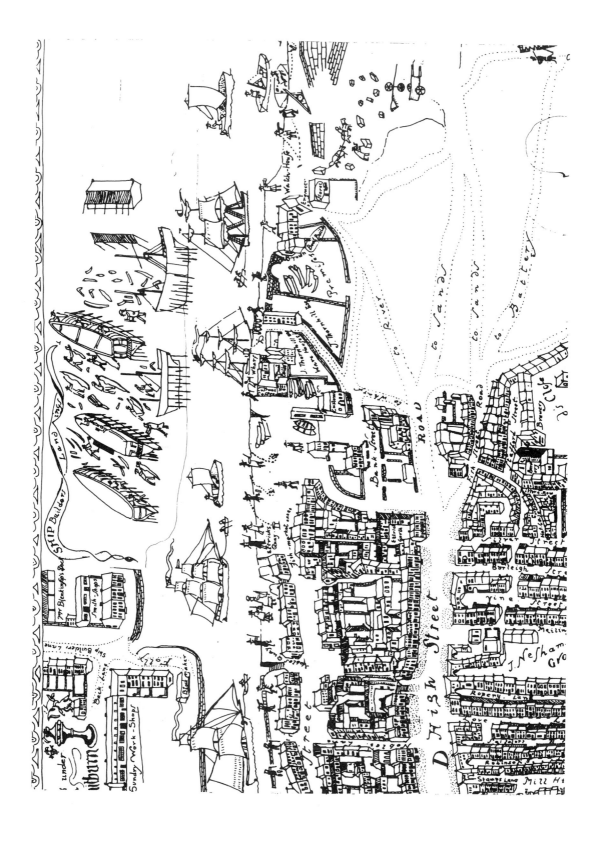

CHAPTER FOUR

Degree, Priority and Place: Early Modern Communities, *c. 1530–c. 1750*

> The heavens themselves, the planets, and this centre
> Observe degree, priority, and place,
> . . . . but when the planets
> In evil mixture to disorder wander,
> What plagues, and what portents, what mutiny,
> What raging of the sea, shaking of earth,
> Commotion in the winds, frights, changes, horrors,
> Divert and crack, rend and deracinate
> The unity and married calm of states
> Quite from their fixture! . . .
> Take but degree away, untune that string,
> And, hark! what discord follows; each thing meets
> In mere oppugnancy . . .

Shakespeare, *Troilus and Cressida*, Act I, iii

These words of Shakespeare, spoken by Ulysses in *Troilus and Cressida*, have been much quoted to convey the sense of unsettlement, of change, and the fear of the consequences of change, which was characteristic of late sixteenth-century England. Shifting degree, priority and place are certainly apparent to the local historian, who will commonly find at this time different individuals, groups and institutions taking central positions in manor and parish, town, village or church.

Many major historical developments were under way during this period, among them the break with Rome, the dissolution of the monasteries, the Protestant Reformation, the creation of an established state church, the growth of royal government and the making of the parish system of local government, the rise of a new gentry, the emergence of yeomen, husbandmen and a growing number of landless labourers, the return of rapid population rises

66. (OPPOSITE) Detail from *Rain's Eye Plan of Sunderland,* 1785. This tableau records a community already transformed by trade and industrial activity in the early modern period. Sunderland Keels bring coal from collieries along the River Wear for shipping in larger vessels. Shipbuilding yards, block and rope makers, smiths' shops and warehousing have all sprung up along the riverside.

after a period of sustained stagnation, price inflation, agricultural changes which some historians see as amounting to an agricultural revolution, and increased levels of poverty, vagrancy and migration. Some of these developments, although generated centrally, had a universal impact locally, as in the case of the setting up of the Church of England and of parish government. Others, such as population growth, with all its economic and social consequences, were largely the sum of local changes. Yet other events, such as the dissolution of the monasteries, and the changes in lordship and landowning which followed, applied in many but not all localities. However, taken together the changes experienced in mid-sixteenth-century England amount to the greatest upheaval undergone before the transformations of urbanization and industrialization between 1760 and 1850. All were worked out, to a greater or lesser degree in actual communities. Observing and assessing this process makes this a key period for the local historian. This chapter outlines patterns of experience to look out for, before going on to a variety of case studies, and a review of the growing range of sources available.

Manor and parish

The manor had been a dominant organizing element in local life in the Middle Ages. As an institution it continued into the post-medieval period but how far it remained influential varied from place to place, and according to circumstances such as whether a manor covered the whole settlement or was one of several amongst which jurisdiction was divided. If there was still a communal field system in which the lord had a direct stake then he might be concerned to regulate it actively through his manorial court. The relative importance of the post-medieval manor did not only depend on local circumstances. The Tudor monarchs, as part of their assertion of central power, sought for a local unit through which to transmit their authority uniformly to grass-roots level. They chose not the manor but the one organizational mechanism consistently present throughout the country and which could be readily linked through existing chains of command to higher authority – this was the parish.

From the 1530s until the 1830s the parish was the basic unit of civil local government in England. In both country areas and in towns, where the built-up area could include several parishes, it was invested with a comprehensive range of responsibilities. In 1538 the parish, in the combined shape of the parson and churchwarden, was directed to register the vital rites of passage in the lives of everyone in the community – their baptisms, marriages and burials. The parish constable was to report regularly to Quarter

67. The royal arms, emblem of Church–State links, appeared in many local churches after the Reformation and became compulsory after the Restoration of 1660. A pre-1707 Stuart royal arms in Hook Norton Church, Oxfordshire.

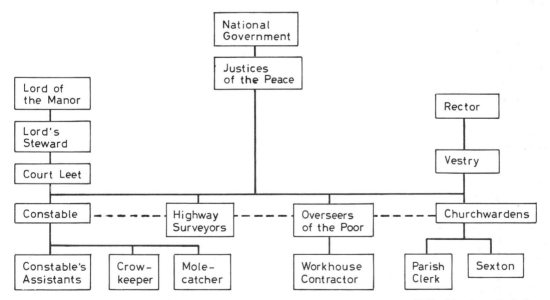

68. Parallel systems of authority and government through parish and manor were a feature of some post-medieval communities, as at Wigginton, Oxfordshire (after F.D. Price, *Wigginton Constables' Book 1691–1836* (1971)).

Sessions on public nuisances, sedition, recusancy, disaffection to the dynasty, blasphemy, drunkenness, gambling, injuries, homicides, robberies, thefts, riots, tumults and suicides – a formidable catalogue showing the inextricable links between religious conformity and loyal citizenship, and the dual civil and ecclesiastical nature of the parish system of local government. The parish was also increasingly charged with the relief and control of poverty. After the passage of the Elizabethan Poor Laws in 1601 this responsibility was specifically laid upon an additional official, the overseer of the poor. They, usually two per parish, were to distribute in relief poor rates voted by the parish vestry. Like other parish officers these men were ordinary parishioners elected by their peers to serve for a year at a time, without payment. Of all the duties those of overseer generally proved the most onerous. The parish was also charged under the Highways Act of 1555 with certain road maintenance, to be overseen by yet another elected official, the Surveyor of the Highways. In addition to this the parish not only collected local rates but was used to gather in county and national taxes. Last but not least, in areas where manor courts had ceased to fulfil this role, the vestry oversaw community regulation of the open fields. The parish was further tied into hierarchies of authority by the churchwardens' obligations to report, usually twice a year, to the archdeacon concerning the state of the church fabric, the conduct, or lack of it, of the parson, the attendance at church of all parishioners, their behaviour in and out of church, the conduct of ale-houses, and sexual mores, including adultery, sodomy and illegitimacy. Offences were then subject to trial in the church courts, and these procedures were rigorously used in many communities in the sixteenth and seventeenth

69. A rare surviving church court in St Nicholas, King's Lynn, Norfolk.

70. Parish government touched on virtually every aspect of local life before the 1830s. An early eighteenth-century fire engine and communal thatch hook, for pulling down burning roofs, in Hook Norton Church, Oxfordshire.

centuries. As will be apparent, any area which a local historian studies will be part of a number of jurisdictions. The archdeacon and bishop, the county or borough through Quarter Sessions, a town corporation, or the sovereign may all have business with local people or property. However, it is the parish which is most often central to local research.

Only in the nineteenth century did any large-scale diminution of the parish's role come with the growth of modern central government. Until then the parish, as reflected in the multitude of records its government generated, was the arena in which most aspects of people's lives were played out.

Community and social structure

What kinds of community did the parish structures created or adopted by the Tudors serve? The vast majority of people, over 75 per cent, still lived in the countryside, but in a setting subject to major pressures, important among them population growth. After the decimation of the Black Death there had been no rapid recovery in numbers. That changed in the early modern period. Between 1520 and 1700 the population of England doubled. Growth was particularly rapid in the years 1560 to 1640. The consequence of this for local communities was direct. The price of all commodities, but especially of foodstuffs rose. Inflation set in. For those with access to land, especially larger landholders, this meant opportunities for high returns on produce. The sixteenth and seventeenth centuries were a time of improvements in agricultural methods and of increased yields. Locally this could involve the appearance of new

71. The 'great rebuilding' of provincial England in the late sixteenth and seventeenth centuries marks the increased prosperity of a widening range of local people. New and remodelled houses were still firmly in vernacular style, built for and by local people, using local materials and local money, rather than observing external notions of 'polite' architecture. The Reeve's Cottage, Hook Norton is a typical product of this change.

crops, increased use of grasses and pulses, more flexible rotations within sub-divisions of the old open-field systems, the keeping of more stock, specialization of products, and enclosure or consolidation of individual holdings. Those able to take advantage of agricultural change and market prices prospered, as is clearly reflected in the high levels of building activity found in much of provincial England at this time. In many villages, especially in open-field England, it is from the Elizabethan and early Stuart periods that many vernacular houses date. Not only aristocrats and gentry were improving or building anew, but also yeomen, husbandmen and craftsmen. The 'great rebuilding' is an important area for local studies, providing the chance both to record and interpret surviving buildings, and to link them to economic change and social aspirations in a particular community.

What was good news for some was bad news for others in the very same places. Those who had small or no landholdings led economically marginal lives. If they had to buy all or most of their food, at the price levels reached in the later sixteenth century they were in severe trouble. Poverty and vagrancy increased markedly. The sense of fear and unsettlement this produced is clear from contemporary accounts and literature. 'Sturdy beggars' and 'masterless men' were a present threat as people were on the move in search of better chances. In some areas the Reformation disrupted established mechanisms of charitable provision. The problem of poverty grew. In the 1590s a combination of acute factors, a string of bad harvests, severe epidemics, discontent and opposition to enclosure, triggered the first comprehensive national legislation for the relief of the poor. Its deterrent terms speak loudly of the mood of the times. Able-bodied poor were to be returned to their home parish, or if that was unknown to their last place of abode, after having been whipped. If they became destitute in their own place then they were to receive aid only after having been put to work in a 'house of correction'. How individual communities actually treated their poorer members is revealing to local historians. Poverty, and how to respond to it, loom large in many parish records. Dual motivations, of moral concern and Christian charity on the one hand, and of fear, suspicion, resentment and a desire to control on the other, may well emerge. This is an area of local life where the distribution of wealth and power and the position and attitudes of individuals and groups can be seen. What exactly 'community' meant, its strengths and strains may be discerned. An unusually direct testimony from a member of a mid-eighteenth-century vestry illustrates the tension. The voting of parish rates, for the maintenance of the church, for the highways, and above all the relief of the poor, was always a testing point. Thomas Turner, the thirty-five-year old shopkeeper of East Hoathly, Sussex, was a conscientious parish officer, serving on several occasions as churchwarden and overseer. On 24 March 1763 he wrote in his diary:

We stayed till near 1 o'clock quarrelling and bickering about nothing and in the end hardly did any business. The design of our meeting was to have made a poor rate in which . . . everyone might pay his just quota (in proportion to his rent) of the money expended in maintaining and keeping the poor. But how do I blush to say what artifice and deceit, cunning and knavery there was used by some (who would think it cruel and unjust to be called dishonest) to conceal their rents, and who yet would pretend the justness of an equal taxation was their desire. But however great their outward zeal for justice appeared, that cankerworm of self-interest lay so corroding in their hearts that it sullied the outward beauties of their would-be honesty. I say 'would-be'

72. For the less fortunate: the poor-box at Abbey Dore, Herefordshire, 1639.

honesty because I look upon that man, be him who will, that endeavours to evade the payment of his just share of taxes to be a-robbing every other member of the community that contributes his quota, and also withholding from the poor what is their just right, and above all sinning against a positive command of our Saviour of doing to others as we would be done unto . . .[1]

Historians approaching the early modern period from such perspectives have produced a different view from older, nationally and politically oriented studies. For W.G. Hoskins the first half of the sixteenth century was 'an age of plunder' by successful 'political adventurers and predators'. For Keith Wrightson in his survey of the century 1580 to 1680, it was a time of polarization, producing new gulfs between the prospering and a growing class of landless, wage-labourers at the bottom. As Margaret Spufford's study[2] of local communities in Cambridgeshire has shown, many people were already in such a position; in her three villages 2:5 were landless labourers in the 1520s and 3:5 by the 1690s. The trend is clear, although it advanced more slowly in northern and western areas, as our local case studies will show.

Population: growth and stagnation

We have seen how in the case of prices, prosperity and poverty general and rapid rises in numbers of people were a major catalyst in legislative action, personal fears and animosities, increased geographical mobility and social polarization, in the late sixteenth and first half of the seventeenth century. Sometimes population variation could directly cause change, for example in producing price inflation or even dearth of essential food supplies in an agricultural system still with limited technological capacity for expansion. Sometimes population fluctuations show the result rather than the cause of events, for example in places deserted because of the local landowner's actions in converting land to pasture or parkland, thus removing the *raison d'être* of the previous settlement. Population variations may mirror the most fundamental facts of local life in other ways, reflecting major changes of behaviour on the part of many ordinary individuals. Parish register studies suggest that in the late seventeenth century, after a period of considerable growth and the crises and tensions that went with it, people in English communities were getting married later, at 28 for men and 26 for women, compared with $26\frac{1}{2}$ and $23\frac{1}{2}$ respectively for Elizabethan and Jacobean bridegrooms and brides studied by Peter Laslett, and with the 25 for men and 23 for women found in the early nineteenth century. Also between 1640 and 1720 a lower proportion of the population was marrying at all. These choices were the principal reason for falling numbers of births, while death rates were rising or stable. The result was a period of static if not declining populations.

Every local historian needs to turn a keen eye on the demography of her or his community, looking at its essential components of births, marriages and deaths (or in the demographers' terminology, fertility, nuptiality and mortality), together with that other main ingredient, migration. Since 1981 we have to guide us E.A. Wrigley and R.S. Schofield's *magnum opus, The Population history of England 1541–1871: a reconstruction*. This offers the local historian many things. The three main areas are a critical view of the strengths and weakness of that core local history source, the parish registers, 1538–1837, and an assessment of how these can be used; secondly, the best picture yet of the population history to which any local study should be related; thirdly, Wrigley and Schofield provide a series of stylized models of the interaction of various factors and processes, such as nuptiality, fertility, mortality and migration, with food prices, real wage levels, the demand for labour and for goods, and the proportions of rural and urban dwellers. Their analysis shows that there were three major phases of experience. First, between 1540 and 1640 births, deaths and marriages all rose strongly, births more than deaths. Population grew. Second, between 1640 and 1710 births and marriages first fell and then oscillated until 1710 when they began to rise. Deaths rose until 1680 and then flattened out. Growth was halted, or sometimes reversed. Thirdly, between 1710 and 1870 births and marriages rose. Deaths rose until 1750, mainly because of high mortality in the 1720s and early 1740s, and then declined. Population growth took off in a major way, driven chiefly by increased fertility rather than falling mortality.

Wrigley and Schofield conclude that until 1800 English population was governed by a continuing precarious balance between numbers of people and available resources, a 'catch 22' of increasing population having to be pegged back by checks. In the local population history of English parishes between 1540 and the late eighteenth century they see such checks at work: there is the long-term self-regulating check of delayed marriage and thus reduced fertility, as was operating between 1640 and 1710; there are the sudden and drastic checks imposed by epidemic disease (Wrigley and Schofield identify national and local crisis periods discernible from mortality rates in the registers); there are the less abrupt but still acute crises of subsistence, experienced in times of harvest failure and high prices. Sometimes dearth and disease hit together, for poor nourishment increased vulnerability to some diseases; for example, typhus is notorious as a disease for its association with poor conditions.

Finally, in addition to occasional experiences of short-term

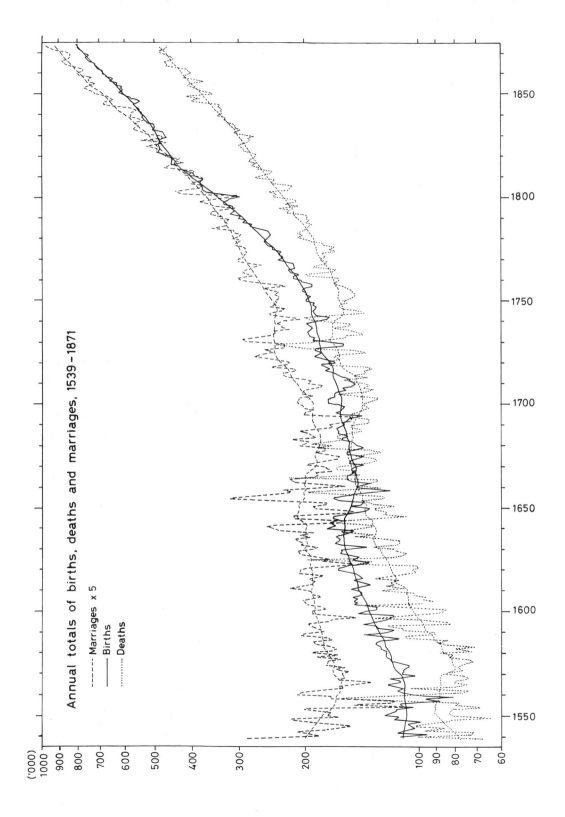

Annual totals of births, deaths and marriages, 1539 – 1871

----- Marriages x 5
——— Births
········· Deaths

The demographic crisis in Halifax 1585–8

Quarters	1585		1586				1587				1588			
	3	4	1	2	3	4	1	2	3	4	1	2	3	4
Conceptions	69	72	82	55	70	39	32	40	49	57	72	99	92	69
Burials	42	54	87	47	41	49	87	81	97	271	283	130	63	60

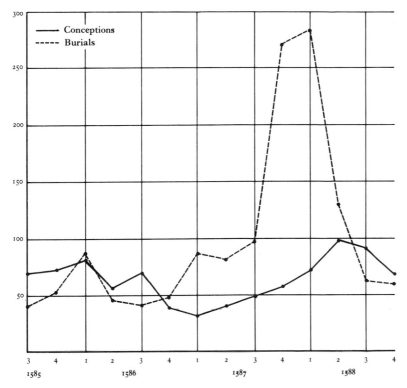

74. A local crisis, revealed in the register of Halifax parish, West Yorkshire for 1585–8. The fall in conceptions in 1586, followed by a rise in burials, together with other references to bad harvests in 1586, to high prices, and a depression in the Yorkshire cloth industry, suggest a crisis of subsistence leading to high mortality. (Conceptions are calculated from the number of baptisms nine months later.)

upheaval the registers reveal regular seasonal variations. Baptisms consistently show a peak in March, suggesting most conceptions in late spring and early summer, always excepting first babies which were usually conceived shortly after the wedding, if not before – yet another aspect of behaviour revealed in the registers. Burials are most numerous in March/April, and least so in July. Marriages are most numerous in early summer, after the prohibited period of Lent, and in late autumn after the hay and corn harvests when life was relatively less busy, and harvest earnings and annual hirings made prospects more secure. Only in the nineteenth century did these rhythms, determined by a predominantly agrarian way of life, begin to break down. By then the Malthusian population regime of checks to growth which seems to have so affected the fortunes of individuals, families and communities was also a thing of the past. Rural labourers were now most often wage labourers with no tie to a landholding or motivation to wait for marriage until they came into such a holding. Rather youth and individual

73. (OPPOSITE) Individual behaviour and wider community fortunes frequently relate to population trends. The overall phases already described are apparent in this data, aggregated from 404 parishes. The 'smoothed' line is a moving average (after Wrigley and Schofield).

earning capacity were an advantage and non-agricultural earning opportunities were growing. With these changes, as we shall see in the next chapter, came growing but changing rural communities, and a broader shift from rural to urban, from agrarian to industrial, from subsistence to market, and from traditional to modern.

The urban scene

What part did towns play in the local life of early modern England? In 1500 about one-tenth of the population lived in towns of some size, by contemporary standards those with over 1,000 inhabitants. By 1700 the proportion was one-fifth. Yet this was not a period of great expansion for most provincial towns. Firstly, London accounted for the lion's share of this increase in urban living; its population rose from some 60,000 to 575,000 during the period, or to look at it another way, from 1.5 per cent of a national population of around 2.3 million in the 1520s to 11.5 per cent of a national population of 5.06 million in 1700. Secondly, the growing prosperity experienced by some towns in the later sixteenth century was generated more by increasingly commercial farming and the success of the rural cloth industry than by town-based activities.

The local historian, whether interested in London itself, in a provincial town or in a rural area, will frequently find evidence of the capital's emphatic growth of dominance at this period. That growth contributed to the relative stagnation of other communities, as was the case of provincial ports overtaken by London's share of two-thirds of all exports of native products and 80 per cent of national imports by 1699–1701. This role meant that many places all over England had active commercial links with London. These ties, and provincial dependence on London for financial facilities, were reinforced by the development there of banking systems in the later seventeenth century. London's pull as the centre of trade nationally was expressed in an expanding and increasingly regularized network of routes, for road and river traffic, for people, goods and public posts, focused on the capital. Foodstuffs and manufactured goods produced in the provinces might go via London, while the city's own expanding population exercised a voracious demand for food and goods which was felt all over England and into Wales, Scotland and Ireland. Thus the local historian may find London tradesmen investing in a seventeenth-century enclosure agreement, aimed at increasing cattle production in a country area many miles from London, but intended to supply its market. Product specialization rather than locally-orientated subsistence growing received a major boost from the 'London factor'. It could change a local landscape and open up a community to outside influences and fluctuations of fortune. This comes across,

75. Connections with London were widespread and important. This monument to Robert Gray in St Mary Magdelene's Church, Taunton, Somerset records that, 'Taunton bore him London bred him . . . / Taunton blest him London blest him / This thankful town that mindful city / Share his piety and his pity'. In 1636 Gray founded almshouses in Taunton for ten poor women, six poor men and the teaching of ten poor children.

for example, in the anxious letter written by Elizabeth Purefoy, lady of the manor of the small village of Shalstone on the northern borders of Buckinghamshire and Northamptonshire, in January 1745. She is writing to Mr Robotham, innkeeper 'at the King's Head near London' and the Purefoys' agent in London:

> . . . . I am sorry to hear there is such bad distemper amongst your cows. I thank God we have not one cow amiss at Shalstone nor within twenty miles of us. . . . Our parishioners have sent a certificate to London that our cattle of all sorts are in good health, so our butter and everything we send to Town . . . [3]

The coal industry of the north-east, expanding greatly at this time, is another example of local life geared to production for London.

London also 'ate' people. There was a constant movement from all over the kingdom to and from London, but particularly to the metropolis. Given that its burials consistently outstripped its baptisms, the only way the city's rapid growth could be sustained was by massive in-migration. This was such that between 1625 and 1775, but particularly in the late seventeenth century, the effect was to supress national population levels. For some, called 'betterment' migrants, the move improved their chances. Apprentices are the best-known example of this. For others, men and women, the move to London was much more a push, precipitated by hard times in their home communities. These are the 'subsistence' migrants. Migrants made for a shifting population with many single, young people. Finally in appreciating the significance of London for local history, its overshadowing political and social role is likely to be felt. During the early modern period the central importance of the capital for parliamentary and political life, for legal matters, for Society (including the marriage market), and culturally became firmly established. Ruling members of many localities spent a great deal of time there. The Home Counties saw a new intensity of estate purchase and country house building by those anxious to be near the hub of things. Emulation, in patterns of consumption, architecture, ideas, and social forms, like coffee houses and assemblies, all became apparent in provincial life.

What then of the provincial towns? Recent English urban history has suggested a clear hierarchy amongst them. At the top were the 'regional capitals' such as Norwich, Bristol, Exeter, York and Newcastle-upon-Tyne. These cities had populations of perhaps 7,000 in the 1520s. They were small compared with major continental European towns, which were not overshadowed by a capital so dominant as London, but served as ports, distributive centres and commercial focuses for large hinterlands. They were economically diverse and sophisticated, had shops and crafts and social facilities serving a wealthy élite (including surrounding landed gentry who might have town houses there), and they were places of civil and ecclesiastical administration. Lesser towns, as well as rural areas, looked to them.

Then there was the middle tier or 'county' centres. By 1700 there were some 120 such towns with populations of 2,000 plus. They were less economically sophisticated than the regional capitals but offered a range of permanent shops, professional services including doctors and lawyers, had major markets, were the scene of important administrative events like assizes and county sessions, and offered rich patrons facilities such as assembly rooms, large hotels, cock fighting and horse racing.

The most numerous type of early modern town was the country

76. The growing importance of some provincial towns as social centres is seen in their architectural emulation, particularly of London. The Mansion House, Doncaster, Yorkshire, completed in 1748, was claimed to be one of three in the country, along with London and York.

market town. All towns were country towns still in terms of their topography and activities, with open country nearby, animals, orchards, gardens, farms and open fields. The basic unit of life was the household, in which trade, craft production and business were carried on as well as domestic life. Even allowing for these broad differences from our later image of town life, many country market towns may seem difficult to recognize as urban. As in the Middle Ages they remained small, with 500 to 2,000 inhabitants, and numerous, over 500, with most in the south and east of England. Their chief function was as a place of local marketing and exchange. Unlike the regional and middle-tier towns they were not always incorporated. They had no luxury, social or major administrative role nor any mass industry. Local studies suggest that on average they had 25 or less distinct occupations, compared with 50–100 in middle-tier towns, or 171 for Norwich in the early seventeenth century. Peter Clark and Paul Slack[4] have proposed four main criteria of urban character between 1500 and 1700: first, size and concentration of population; second, sophisticated political structures and forms of government; third, specialized economic functions with a significant proportion of people in non-agricultural occupations; and fourth, that the community has an importance beyond its own bounds. The country market town may have only two or three of these attributes and demonstrate a distinctly rural feel, especially on non-market days. By contrast the other types of town will have all four characteristics.

They will also often be corporate boroughs. The period 1500 to 1760 saw a new rash of borough creations, around 160, most in the south and east. Rather than being a flowering of urban independence many were associated with gentry influence and political aspirations. Both old and new boroughs were liable at this time to be drawn into the mesh of gentry and aristocratic patronage. The old forms of town government persisted, with freemen, and tiers of representative bodies variously titled, for example a common council and a small inner council of aldermen and mayor. As with parish vestries it is fascinating to discover, from corporation and trade records, from monuments and benefactions, just who the influential and powerful were, and whether the town's corporate life retained the independence and vigour so often observed to be lacking by 1700.

One key to this may be how far a town was attracting new blood in the form of in-migrants. Despite the exceptional magnetism of London other towns, especially the larger ones, had also drawn their newcomers, betterment and subsistence, in the sixteenth century. Did this flow decline? It has been argued that this indeed happened, partly because the push factor of distress was less acute in many areas after 1660, but also because enterprising migrants were attracted less to old-established towns with their closed ruling and trade groups, and more to the newly growing urban centres, the dockyard towns and the spas, or to the country areas where there was land and economic space to gain a foothold. Such places included the textile/farming areas of Lancashire and Yorkshire, the coalfields of the Tyneside countryside, or, as we shall see, the woodpasture terrain of north-west Shropshire as exemplified by Myddle. These places may prove to have been a healthier prospect in every sense than a town.

Local historians will find it well worthwhile to assess their town in relation to other towns in the area, or their village in relation to a town or towns. Local urban fortunes and pecking order were not static. Changes in a town's fortunes or functions can have wider repercussions, as John Chandler's comparison of Salisbury's sphere of influence in 1377, 1642 and 1811 shows. If your village had prospered from sending produce to a nearby town and from being on the route of travellers to that place, only for the town to decline, or conversely if your town, like Halifax in the early eighteenth century, became the focus for a far-flung domestic woollen industry on the surrounding moorlands, then fluctuating urban fortunes will loom large in your local history.

77. (OPPOSITE) The close relationship which may exist between the fortunes of towns and surrounding rural communities is seen in the higher concentrations of population around Salisbury and Wilton in the 1370s, in rentrenchment during the less prosperous seventeenth century, and in returned expansion for a wide area round the towns in the nineteenth century (after Chandler).

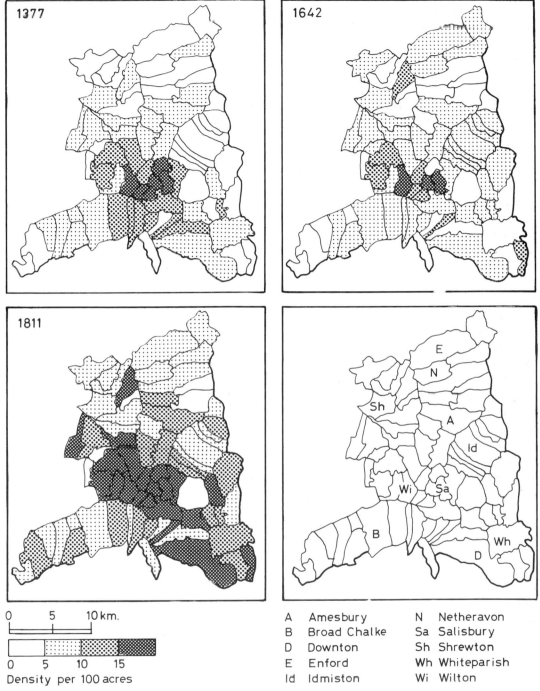

1377

1642

1811

0   5   10 km.

0   5   10   15
Density per 100 acres

A	Amesbury	N	Netheravon
B	Broad Chalke	Sa	Salisbury
D	Downton	Sh	Shrewton
E	Enford	Wh	Whiteparish
Id	Idmiston	Wi	Wilton

Population density in south-east Wiltshire

Beliefs and institutions: the role of religion

Religion played a major part, both directly and indirectly, in local experiences in the sixteenth and seventeenth centuries. The greatest apparent change came between 1530 and 1570 when England was severed from the international community of the Church of Rome and religion became a matter of state. The sacred and secular became inextricable. The central institutions of national and local life were dislocated. In particular the monastic presence – as landlord, owner of local advowsons and tithes, as a source of education and of lay employment – disappeared. More gradually forms of worship and the hearts and minds of ordinary people were affected by successive waves of change, in ritual observances, and also in theology and doctrine. These ideas moulded not only attitudes to the next world but behaviour in the present, often in such a way as to alter the tenor of local life. Reformation thinking brought questioning of justification by works, and for some meant rejecting indulgences, pilgrimages, confession, private masses, and all the means to salvation acquired by material works, and chan-nelled through the mechanisms of the institutional church. In its place was put the individual's personal search for salvation and a subsequent state of grace. The doctrinal debates are complex but the shift in thinking they represented profoundly affected local experiences. Some of the consequences will be found in the increased accessibility of liturgy, with an official English Bible and Book of Common Prayer. In church buildings wall-paintings were whitewashed over, images removed, rood screens dismantled, and stone altars replaced. What in Protestant eyes were symbols of superstitious belief in the sacrificial nature of the sacrament were superseded by wooden communion tables. These were placed away from the east end of the chancel and communicants gathered round them to share in a commemorative rite, the Lord's Supper. Such were the more tangible changes.

Part of the shift was very clearly to do with alterations imposed by the Crown from above, rather than generated within local communities. Henry VIII's Reformation was essentially an institu-tional affair of state and, in the case of the dissolution of the monasteries, of pressing financial need. Only in Edward VI's reign did state dictats extend to radical doctrinal changes, the trans-formation of church interiors, and the introduction of compulsory texts. The reversal of much of this in Mary's reign must have been bewildering in the extreme for local people and was a matter on which they were required to take immediate action, as payments in churchwardens' accounts for successive dismantlings and re-erections of roods and images and lights show. The accession of Elizabeth I in 1558 saw an immediate search for a religious settlement as an essential part of political stability. The Act of

78. The Lord's Supper, celebrated in Puritan style with communicants gathered around a communion table, not separated by a rail from an altar in the chancel.

Supremacy restored the sovereign as head of the English Church after the papal resurgence of the previous reign, while the Act of Uniformity sought to establish 'religion by state ordained', in the form of a moderate Protestantism. It became a matter of statute, not just of canon law, that all citizens should attend church. Stability and comprehensiveness were the aim. The Elizabethan church settlement strove to find the middle way theologically and liturgically, although strong Puritan influences may have influenced the tenor of the 1559 Act more than the pragmatic Elizabeth is believed to have wanted.

Religious nonconformity was not legally defined as being outside the Established Church until the 1660s but the striving of different shades of religious thinking within the church is one of the recurrent themes of English local history at this time. The Puritan approach was moulded by a Calvinist belief in predestination, that only those divinely ordained would achieve salvation. These 'elect' were predestined for heaven, while the rest of the population were consigned, by original sin, to damnation. Far from generating a passively self-confident approach to life in those who believed themselves to be amongst the 'godly', Puritans felt that they must look everywhere around them in everyday life for evidence of God's opinion of them. The actions and thoughts of themselves, their families, neighbours and fellow townsmen or villagers were all of deep significance. Moreover, because Puritans believed that the actions and authority of civil government, local and national, should proceed from the truths and authority of the church of the godly, rather than vice versa, they felt that their views should guide the behaviour of all, not just in church, but at work and play, in school and ale-house, between parents and children, and between husband and wife. The religious climate, whether produced by acts of state or individual conscience, played a persistent and dynamic part in individual and collective experiences.

79. The Quaker meeting house, Jordans, Buckinghamshire, built in 1688, the year before Protestant dissenters attained legal toleration of their worship, although not in civil matters, such as public office-holding. The isolated situation of Jordans, and its meeting house keeper's cottage and stables, suggest the hostile climate of the years 1660–89 and the 'gathered' nature of a congregation travelling to worship from a wide area.

The tensions generated by the struggle to make the Established Church a comprehensive one were a major factor in the outbreak of civil war in 1642, and were only partly resolved by the legal exclusion of Protestant Nonconformists in the 1660s. This recognition of their separateness (as recusants or adherents of Roman Catholicism had also been set apart since 1558) excluded them from full citizenship. Only in 1689 did any measure of tolerance for Protestant dissent come, and its adherents continued to be excluded from public office until the 1820s. After the intense ferment of religious ideas in the England of the 1640s and 1650s, and the time of active persecution of dissenters up to 1689, the heat went out of this aspect of local life. The Established Church in the late seventeenth and eighteenth centuries was secure in its role as a prop and adjunct of a state dominated by an oligarchy of landed aristocrats, underpinned by a patronage system of which church preferments became more and more part. The old dissenting denominations which emerged out of the seventeenth century, the Quakers, the Independents or Congregationalists, the Baptists and the Unitarians now had freedom to worship and, despite continuing legal disabilities, played a stable role in many communities at least until the period of evangelical revival, which belongs to our next chapter.

80. Anglican communion, *c.* 1700.

Changing lordship

One of the 'religious' changes of the sixteenth century that had greatest impact on local experiences was the dissolution of the monasteries. This involved the physical and institutional dismantling of some five hundred and sixty houses, great and small, between 1536 and 1539. In addition to the spiritual and cultural impact of this dispossession of what must have seemed an immutable part of many towns and rural areas, the enormous estates of the monastic houses meant that their seizure produced a change of lord and/or rector and tithe owner in many places. The land and rights passed temporarily into the hands of the Crown.

As one longstanding 'outside' influence in many localities was disappearing so another, the centralizing and integrating influence of an assertive, monarchical state was making itself felt. In sustaining this role, both at home and abroad, Henry VIII and his successors suffered a perennial problem – lack of money. For a monarch who was still expected to live of his own and for whom the collection of taxes was not a regular and automatic annual process, this was a major difficulty. Some historians have interpreted the tensions between Henry and his successors and those who voted the taxes in Parliament as a clash between central, increasingly London-based interests and those of the provincial localities, specifically the county communities of newly prosperous and powerful gentry. Also contentious were the alternative sources of cash the Crown sought, for example the maximum possible exploitation of Crown lands and offices through the mechanisms of prerogative courts such as Star Chamber, Wards and Augmentations. Here were other seeds of overt conflict which eventually germinated in civil war in the next century. More immediately most of the vast ex-monastic lands had to be sold or leased on for quick returns in the mid-sixteenth century. The records of royal government for this period are rich in surveys of many localities. It is interesting to speculate what would have been the historical consequences if the Crown had not divested itself of these vast holdings.

That it did so meant that new lay lords and tithe owners appear centre stage in many local manors in the mid-sixteenth century. Many who took advantage of this buoyant land market were new kinds of lords, members of the rising gentry so beloved of modern-day historians of Tudor England. Some had made money in trade and were keen to translate it into landownership, which was still the chief source of status and influence. Others had risen through the professions, particularly law, and through the expanding area of royal service. Some had been directly involved in implementing the Reformation changes. Those who

81. Forde Abbey, Dorset. The cloister and chapter house of the Cistercian Abbey incorporated by post-Dissolution lay owners, notably Edmund Prideaux in the 1650s.

did not prosper on the whole at this time were the lay aristocracy of medieval origin. The over-mighty lords of the later Middle Ages, with great followings, amounting to private armies, were unacceptable to the Tudor monarchs, especially those with the misfortune to be in any way related to the royal house, and thus a possible dynastic threat. Other aristocratic lines had perished by military misfortune or biological chance. Thus local historians are very likely to find major changes in their local structures of landownership and community control at this time. We turn now to look at some specific case studies of this and other factors at work in local history.

Cases and places

Contrasting communities: agrarian roots

In 1688 some three-quarters of the English population lived in the countryside, but there was no universally typical form of agricultural settlement and related community life. Local studies have shown the need to look for varied social structures. The communities of arable and fielden areas, fells and moorland, fens, forests, heathlands, pastoral vales, wolds and downs have all been claimed as distinctive types.

Take the chill and barren terrain of the fells and moors of Yorkshire and Lancashire, in places like Rossendale or the vast parish of Halifax. There the soils are acid, the climate cold and wet. The landscape was dominated by poor grassland, grazed by hardy livestock, cattle on the lower slopes and sheep higher up. Arable acreages were relatively small. The common field management around which the life of many lowland communities revolved was inappropriate. The existence of generous common grazing rights was more important. The chief crops were oats (this was an oatcake not a loaf society), barley and rye. They were grown on a household need rather than a market basis. This was primarily a pastoral, chiefly a cattle-based economy. Fodder was therefore vital. It came from meadows in the valley floors and from adjacent lowland areas. These local economies were formative influences but not rigidly closed entities. Thus, as well as fodder being brought in, stock was sold to lowlanders in the autumn, and longer-range links were felt when cattle were driven through or from the area, on their way by drove roads to the ever more magnetic London market.

In the households of the fell and moorland regions by-employments boosted hard-earned farming income. There was mining and quarrying and there was spinning, weaving and knitting. It was in this local household economy that the leading

82. An eighteenth-century Pennine home, the setting for both work and family, production and reproduction. It was in such domestic and rural contexts that many leading sectors of the industrial revolution developed.

83. Angelzarke, a Lancashire moorland landscape.

sectors of the industrial revolution, wool and cotton production, had their beginnings, and through which production continued to be organized in some sectors of work into the early nineteenth century.

These communities were characterized by secure tenure, weak manorial control, dispersed settlement rather than carefully monitored nucleated villages, and great degrees of personal freedom, including that to alienate land freely. Sub-letting, partible inheritance (splitting a holding between heirs) and early enclosure of land by agreement were a consequence of such regimes. In such areas the trend was for the number of holdings to increase; in Rossendale in 1507 there were 72 copyholders, in 1608 there were 200, while in 1662 there were 314. With such small holdings (2 1/2 to 6 1/2 acres) it was possible to make a living and for younger sons to stay locally and set up on their own account. Survival was increasingly related to the additional support given by industrial employments, so that by 1750 many locals were craft producers with a sideline in farming, rather than the other way round. Increased specialization produced greater local diversity, yet tied local economies more and more to outside markets.

The typical experience of a community in a different kind of area between 1530 and 1750 could be radically different. This is very clear from Margaret Spufford's study of three contrasting villages in Cambridgeshire. They are Willingham in the fens, Orwell on the clay and Chippenham on the chalk. The Willingham fenlands produced a stock-farming and dairying regime, nearest in character to the upland moors just described. In Willingham, too, small holdings not only survived but there was fragmentation to produce more numerous holdings of two to sixteen acres. Manorial control was weak, arable land was relatively less important, and a family's wealth and status were determined more by their access to common grazing and numbers of stock. The community could retain its younger sons. It experienced high mortality.

By contrast the chalkland terrain at Chippenham had a more arable-orientated agriculture. Between 1560 and 1636 the old medieval holdings of yardlands and half-yardlands disappeared. In their place emerged a village society in which more people were holding big shares of land (over fifty acres) and there were more cottagers, with tiny or no arable open-field holdings. This engrossing, or accumulation of land in fewer hands did not come from seigneurial initiative by the lord, rather it was associated with prospering yeomen taking the opportunity to buy land from their less fortunate neighbours, in particular during the hard and inflationary years of poor harvests and high mortality of the 1590s. It is likely that these circumstances also forced younger sons to leave Chippenham. The causes Spufford sees as primarily economic rather than lordly or legal.

Finally Orwell, in the Cambridgeshire claylands, also saw a fall in the number of customary yardlanders and half-yardlanders, accompanied by a rise in bigger holdings and in cottagers, now

84. Natural boundaries and soil types, a significant factor in the contrasting histories of the Cambridgeshire villages of Willingham, Chippenham and Orwell.

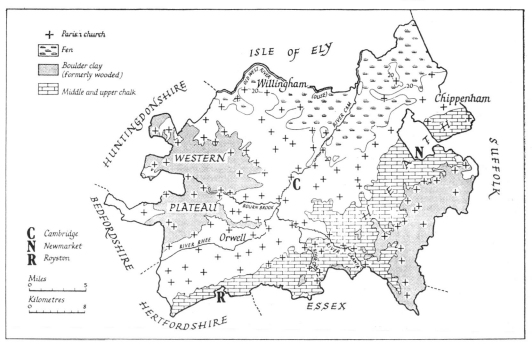

more and more dependent on wage labour to survive. Unlike Chippenham manorial influence played an important part here, with demesne land expanded to take in arable and common. Since Orwell's custom was impartible inheritance, the land going to a single heir, other members of the family had to look elsewhere for a livelihood. In fact contemporary wills show efforts to provide for them out of the family estate, sometimes placing finances under great stress.

Not only do studies like those of Spufford give us valuable ideas as to how local variables, of topography, soil, settlement pattern, manorial strength, tenure and inheritance customs or alternative employments, may act upon the life of a community, but they offer important new evidence in major historical debates. The disappearance of the small landholder has long been a focus of attention. This process has been seen as a key to the transformation of English society from one of close-knit, consensual traditional communities, to modern class-based settlements in which wealth, influence, prosperity and poverty are unequally distributed and collective interests and feelings have been lost. This change used to be widely associated with the parliamentary enclosure of common field systems between 1760 and 1830, but local studies increasingly show small landholders in the open-field villages that were most affected by parliamentary enclosure to have been declining in number since at least the late sixteenth century. By contrast circumstances in pastoral areas, like Rossendale or Willingham, could encourage small landholders to support, or even initiate, enclosure by agreement.

This section is based on Margaret Spufford, *Contrasting communities. English villagers in the sixteenth and seventeenth centuries* (1974), and Joan Thirsk (ed.), *The agrarian history of England and Wales*, vol. 4 1500–1640 (1967). The sources demonstrated by these studies include:

* *manorial records*, including court rolls, rentals, surveys and leases for evidence of custom, inheritance, terms of tenure, changes in size and occupiers of holdings, seigneurial policy or lack of it

* *parish registers* for aggregative analysis and reconstitution (see below), helping to answer questions like, 'Were the 1590s bad in these places?' or, 'Do younger sons seem to have migrated away?'

* *wills and inventories* for levels of wealth and landholding, nature of farming, social status, attitudes to inheritance, family, the poor

* *national taxation records*, the lay subsidies of 1524–5, and the hearth taxes of the 1660s. Spufford finds that in Cambridgeshire in the 1520s a quarter to a third of the rural population were

already wage labourers, rather than property owners. She uses the hearth taxes in conjunction with 150 probate records for her villages to establish the social hierarchy. For example, yeomen had an average holding of 92 acres and wealth of £180; husbandmen had 21 to 40 acres and £30; craftsmen were worth £40 on average and some were also landholders; labourers, of whom over half were landless, were worth £15

No. of hearths	House style	Median wealth
One hearth	Hearth in the hall	£25
Two hearths	No bedroom fires	£60
Three hearths	Ave. no. of rooms 6–8	£141
Four hearths	Ave. no. of rooms 6–14	£360

★ *central court records*, Exchequer and Chancery, for contentious issues, additional details of status, property.

Urban lives: households and occupations

Local historians will find ample advice about how to reconstruct a community and its patterns of life, but less often will they find this task carried through. This is particularly the case for towns, which, with their larger and more mobile populations, and more complex economic and institutional ways of life, have always been a challenge to local historians.

One piece of micro-history that has successfully tackled the challenges of community reconstruction and urban life is Mary Prior's study of Fisher Row, Oxford, and the fishermen, bargemen and canal boatmen who lived there between 1500 and 1900. At first sight this may look like a disproportionately big book on a seemingly small subject, for Fisher Row is a short stretch of riverside now crammed between the railway station and the city centre. At its peak of population, between the 1790s and the 1840s, it contained 3,000 to 4,000 people. However, reading about Fisher Row reinforces the sense of satisfaction and understanding given by local history when it really gets inside the lives and behaviour of actual people in specific places and real circumstances. Because the study is successful at that level, it also provides insights into a whole range of wider concerns – occupational communities, inland river and canal trade, the history of the family, genealogy, economic change, how to reconstruct a community, and the history of Oxford.

To take just one of these, the history of the family and household is a key part of any local historian's understanding of a particular place. Dr Prior finds that the particularity of Fisher Row lay in its complex family patterns, and that these in turn reflected the occupations that moulded the lives of everyone who lived there. Many words have been expended on debating whether the basic family unit in England

85. Fisher Row. Opposite the mound of Oxford Castle and on the right-hand bank of the river lies Lower Fisher Row, below it and above the bridge Middle Fisher Row, and beyond the bridge Upper Fisher Row (from David Loggan's map of Oxford, 1675).

was the nuclear, two-generation family (a constant or modern, post-industrial phenomenon?), or the extended, multi-generational family (characteristically pre-industrial?). In Fisher Row we can see how it actually was in one community in the pre-industrial and industrial periods. The answer is that family patterns varied according to occupation, so that the two main types of inhabitant of the Row before the coming of the canal, the fishermen and the bargemen, had very different family patterns.

> Fishing exploited a limited resource, whilst barging was a service industry which, whilst trade was buoyant, might well seem almost limitless. If fishing was like farming, barging was more like running a chain of stores like Mothercare or C & A Modes. Wherever there was a town of suitable size and position there was a demand to be met. In each generation only one of the fisherman's sons could normally expect to become a fisherman . . . the successful bargemaster, however, could provide openings for all his sons.

Thus fishing families were characteristically nuclear and barging families extended, and both were found in Fisher Row. Dr Prior goes on to show how extended family patterns also appeared in the nineteenth century, among a third, new occupational group, the canal boatmen. With the men away on the canal boats a society of extended families and kinship networks grew up in the Row, where the most important factors were the pubs, the women and the family. By avoiding any dogmatic 'either/or' of family type, and by venturing into the 'dense thickets of genealogy', family reconstitution and house repopulation before attempting conclusions, this study gets us thinking about the multiple perspectives we need to adopt as local historians. We can see the individuals, their work, the composition of the households in which they lived, but also how kinship and shared work interests produced 'a sort of large household under many adjacent roof-trees'. They must be seen together as well as separately.

Looking at separate families enabled Dr Prior to consider another perennial local history question – how much did people move around, and did this have a destabilizing effect on any sense of community? There was a good deal of movement into and out of a riverside trading place like the Row. However, the reconstitution points to stayers as well as movers. The stayers were well-established families with trading interests in the Row and on the river, the 'core' families of the community, while the movers were more often young, single people with little social or economic investment in the place. Overall local life was stable rather than shifting. This was the general pattern in Fisher Row until the railways undermined its trade in the mid-nineteenth century. Until then the Row was a secure home base for successive generations of

86. 'A sort of large household under many adjacent roof-trees.' Middle Fisher Row, Oxford, photographed in 1885.

family dynasties like the Bossoms, Beesleys and Tawneys, despite their connections with another, far-reaching network, the linear community along the Thames and beyond.

The sources used by Mary Prior in *Fisher Row. Fishermen, bargemen, and canal boatmen in Oxford, 1500–1900* (1982) include:

★ *city records*, chiefly for Oxford. Amongst these were Council minute books, freemen's registers, apprenticeship records, property leases, ale-house licences, Quarter Sessions minutes, and seventeenth-century poll tax lists

★ *parish papers*, with registers for family reconstitution playing a part, and some use of poor law papers, churchwardens' accounts

★ *court records*, in addition to city Quarter Sessions, including deposition books of ecclesiastical courts from the seventeenth century

★ *wills and inventories*, particularly for the different patterns of family inheritance

★ *private property records*, including leases and rentals, terriers and other estate papers, for house repopulation. Such records came from Oxford colleges, the University and a brewery as well as the city authorities

★ *maps*, including the fortunate survivals of sixteenth-, seventeenth- and eighteenth-century town maps, and a more detailed plan of the Row, drawn up in connection with a law suit

* *antiquarians' collections*, particularly Anthony Wood and Thomas Hearne

* *central government records*, for court proceedings in Courts of Chancery and Requests, Exchequer records for sixteenth-century lay subsidies and seventeenth-century hearth taxes, Prerogative Court of Canterbury wills, canal papers in British Transport Historical Commission

* *records of the Thames Navigation*, Thames Commissioners, accounts of the canal company.

All places lie in more than one jurisdiction and require local historians to look at several types of source. The Fisher Row study shows how a town can have a particularly wide range, city or corporation, institutions like colleges or gilds, businesses, several parishes, as well as the usual range of county and national references.

Mary Prior's maxim in tackling all of this should stand any local historian in good stead – to inject the maximum of imagination into the questions posed but to exclude it from the answers.

Poverty, piety and power

Religious change was one of the major ingredients of local experience in the sixteenth and seventeenth centuries. No individual or place could escape the attempts to enforce conformity of the successive Henrician, Edwardian, Marian, Elizabethan, Laudian and Carolingian religious settlements, nor the often acute unsettlement of the Civil War and Interregnum. Many sought an active part in such changes, and far from being passive victims of outside ideas and authority, strove from a religious base to remould the secular as well as the spiritual life of their communities.

This was clearly the case in the rural parish of Terling in Essex, which has been the subject of intensive scrutiny by Keith Wrightson and David Levine. Despite Terling's subsequent reputation for high Protestant zeal, here, as elsewhere, the impact of the Henrician and Edwardian reformations was institutional rather than theological. The local Trinity gild and the parish chantry were both dissolved. The church interior and the liturgy observed there were altered; statues, lights and the rood disappeared, wall-paintings were whitewashed over, royal arms displayed, and the vernacular Bible and Book of Common Prayer brought into use. Yet local studies, including that of Terling, suggest that it is only in the 1580s that a more fundamental change in internal, individual beliefs emerged. A

Protestantism of conviction and of Calvinist complexion had taken root. This shows up in the phrasing of wills, whether that of the testators themselves or scribes. The eloquent and individualistic phrasing of some suggests the will-maker's own words. The wording varied but the trend was clear; it changed from predominantly Catholic, for example entrusting his or her soul to 'Almighty God, the Blessed Virgin Mary, and the whole company of Heaven', to a Puritan reliance on redemption through Christ alone, as for example a soul bequeathed to 'Almighty God and his only Son our Lord Jesus Christ, by whose precious blood and passion I hope only to be saved'. The last 'Catholic' will in Terling dated from 1562. By the 1580s the Puritan bent of local religious life was also clear in the increased number of prosecutions in church courts for non-attendance at church and for failing to take the sacrament. Most offenders were labourers. Cases were also brought against Sunday working, sports or drinking in the ale-house.

87. The alehouse (from a seventeenth-century chapbook).

88. Jacobean church furnishings of distinctly non-Puritan elaboration at Croscombe, Somerset, including a pulpit (dated 1616), readers' desk, box pews, rood and parclose screens.

89. A parish church, High Wycombe, Bucks., before its nineteenth-century restoration. Worship in this post-Reformation interior focused on the lofty pulpit in the nave, which was separated from the chancel by the massive Carington family pew, the royal arms and texts of the ten commandments.

By the 1620s and 1630s Wrightson and Levine can identify in Terling a ruling élite of like-minded co-religionists. Their wills were noticeably Puritan. They were drawn from the higher levels of village society, the yeomen. They held the chief offices in the local parish government, and, together with a zealously Puritan vicar, they dominated local life. This power was challenged during the 1630s by Archbishop Laud's efforts to enforce religious conformity in matters of liturgy (for example, the placing of the communion table at the east end of the chancel behind the communion rail, the wearing of surplices by the clergy, the making of the sign of the cross at baptism), and in terms of episcopal and ecclesiastical authority over clergy and laity. The battle was a fierce one, but in Terling in the 1640s Laudian Arminianism was rejected. This was clear from the weekday lectures in the church, the rejection of Prayer Book forms, the insistence on taking the sacrament standing and around an unrailed communion table no longer in the chancel, and with the minister without a surplice. During the Civil War period the Puritans, confident in their identity as God's elect and in their mission to govern the rest of the community in their day-to-day lives according to divine revelation, set out to guide Terling. As the vicar John Stalham wrote in 1647,

> some competent number of you have fallen in with me in a time of Publique Reformation, to witnesse against Popery, Prelacy, Superstition, Schisme, Heresie, Prophanesse and Formality and have helped towards their Extirpation according to Covenant.

90. A 'godly minister' (from a seventeenth-century chapbook).

This was a congregational church, but run by an élite operating, as Wrightson and Levine have put it, 'the cultural aggression of the godly'.

Such fervour bred schism and individualistic tendencies which throve in the years between 1642 and 1660, when all forms of authority were under challenge. Puritan unity disintegrated in Terling. When at the Restoration an Anglican uniformity was reimposed it was impossible in Terling and many other places that the Church of England could any longer be the sole, comprehensive church which it had attempted so uncomfortably to be since 1529. Stalham, the vicar, was ejected in 1662 for failing to comply with the Act of Uniformity. The separatists were now legally defined as nonconformists, and communities with strong Puritan traditions like Terling were deeply divided in the following penal period of persecution of dissenters. Seventy-five villagers were prosecuted for failure to conform between 1662 and 1685. They were neither labourers nor gentry, but of the middling sort, influential members of the community. It is striking that over one-third of churchwardens in Terling in the reigns of Charles II and James II had been in trouble with the Quarter Sessions, Assizes or church courts for nonconformity. The former vicar, Stalham, became a minister of the Congregational church in Terling. Parallel if unequal religious systems were now in being in the village.

Other separations and polarizations were happening. Careful interpretation of two very full national taxation lists, the lay subsidies of 1524–5 and the hearth tax of 1671, enabled Wrightson and Levine to see changes in the wealth and social structure of Terling. In the 1520s there were seventy-six resident taxpayers. Their assessments showed nine to be gentry or very large farmers, with a further twenty-eight yeomen, substantial husbandmen and craftsmen. Another eighteen were husbandmen and craftsmen, and twenty-one labourers or cottagers. Wage earners were already over a third of Terling's male tax-payers. The village was a prosperous one, in a prosperous county, Essex. By 1671 the picture had changed, with a rise in households to 122, and no less than forty (32.8 per cent) of these having to be exempted from paying tax because of poverty. The size of the upper echelons of Terling society had stayed much the same – ten gentry and large farming households, twenty-nine of yeomen and wealthy craftsmen, twenty-one husbandmen and craftsmen, but with a great increase in labourers and poor families to sixty-two households. Terling's experience was not an isolated one, for the Essex county average for householders excused tax because of poverty was 38 per cent, with an interesting variation between the south of the county (which benefited from the demand of the London market) with 23.2 per cent, and the north of Essex (where weaving as a source of earnings was declining) with 53.2 per cent.

Myddle, in the woodpasture lands of north-west Shropshire, is uniquely open to our scrutiny because in 1701–2 Richard Gough, a yeoman farmer born and bred in the parish and then sixty-six years old, wrote an exceptional insider's view of his own community. The way in which he chose to arrange it is telling. The *dramatis personae* of Myddle life in the seventeenth century are visualized in terms of their family and household units and associated landholdings, while their wider, parish identity is represented by their places in the hierarchy of pews in the parish church. Unlike Terling, by 1701 the people of Myddle did still generally adhere to the same church, and their attendance there on Sundays, drawn in from the dispersed dwellings of this 4,691-acre parish with its seven townships, was effectively the only occasion and place when the whole community came together, not just for worship but for social contact and business, to see and be seen. According to Gough Myddle, despite its scattered geography, was very much a coherent community of interests (and gossip) at the beginning of the eighteenth century. David Hey has built on Gough's testimony and enables us to contrast piety, poverty and power here with life in Essex or Cambridgeshire or Rossendale.

Terling had no dominant lord because the parish was divided between manors. Neither did Myddle, for there the lord was absent, but manorial courts continued to be held on his behalf. The authority of the Church also seems to have been relatively intact in Myddle as the presence of gentry, yeoman and husbandman farmers, tradesmen and craftsmen, labourers and servants at services suggests. Myddle had not been immune from clerical upheaval (a royalist rector had been evicted in 1646 and a Puritan ejected in 1662), but the subsequent low levels of nonconformity suggest that religious controversy and division had made little lasting mark.

This difference in experience between Myddle and Terling is not perhaps surprising. General and local historians of the Reformation in England have pointed to the high incidence of early and continuing Protestantism in London, in eastern England, and in port areas, including Bristol. All of these were accessible to strong continental influences, quite apart from Lollard precedents or internal local factors making for independent thinking in religious or other matters. Thus London, Kent, Essex, Norfolk, Suffolk and Cambridgeshire yield strong evidence of early and powerful Protestant adherence while Lancashire, Yorkshire, Lincolnshire, Staffordshire, Devon, Cornwall, Somerset, the Welsh Marches, Hampshire and, perhaps surprisingly, Sussex appear more conservative. Every such generalization begs examination; for example if you had lived in several Yorkshire towns before 1558, amongst them Beverley, Rotherham or Halifax, as opposed to the countryside, you would have encountered significant Protestantism. With such provisos in mind the south and east of England, into which Terling fell, was generally earliest and most strongly Protestant, and the north and west, including Myddle, less radical in religion and in politics, as its stronger royalist adherence in the Civil War may be taken to show.

91. In some families and some places private, as well as public, behaviour was deeply affected by religion (from a seventeenth-century chapbook entitled, 'An Hundred Devout Admonitions left by a Dying Mother to her children').

In other ways Myddle shared the experiences of Terling. It too saw large population increases and a higher proportion of its people at the lower end of the social spectrum. Between 1563 and 1672 the total number of people rose from about 270 to around 450. Because local incumbents conveniently noted the status of adult males in the parish registers we know that from 1541 to 1570 labourers formed only 7.1 per cent of adult males mentioned; by 1631 to 1660 it was 31.2 per cent. However, only 16.5 per cent of the inhabitants of Pimhill Hundred in which Myddle lay had to be exempted from paying the hearth tax in 1672 because of poverty – a radically different experience from that of Terling only the previous year. Why so? Large numbers of poor immigrants had been coming into Myddle parish in search of labouring work and a cottage holding. There was sufficient space, geographically and economically, for the parish to absorb them without the severe problems found elsewhere. Between the late fifteenth and the early seventeenth centuries drainage of meres and woodland clearance enabled the farmed land of Myddle to be increased by 1,000 acres. There were extensive areas of waste where incomers could squat and acquire cottage holdings. There was access to common land. In the context of Myddle cottagers were not the poverty-stricken landless labourers increasingly found in Essex. Their growth as a proportion of the community did, however, inevitably broaden the base of its social structure. At the top, and in the prized front pews of the parish church, were the relatively few gentry and prosperous farmers and their families who occupied the twelve major farms of the parish, varying between 100 and 650 acres. For all their wealth they were not the most stable of Myddle society. Hey concludes that they had a 50:50 chance of retaining their property for three generations or more. Myddle's urban links were particularly with Shrewsbury and the parish's leading families included prosperous town tradesmen buying into land. The continuity in Myddle society was supplied by the families occupying the forty-eight smallholding tenements, a quarter of them by freehold and the rest by leases for three lives, as was common in Shropshire. These families worked ten to ninety acres and concentrated on stock-raising and increasingly dairying. They formed large, stable, kin networks, with younger sons often staying in the parish, perhaps earning through supplementary crafts such as gloving and weaving. From this group came the core families of the parish. As we have seen, by the late seventeenth century the picture was modified by some one-third of the population being labourers, a relatively rare state in Myddle in the 1520s. In general trends Terling and Myddle seem alike, but in terms of the consequences of change, something which can only be fully understood through local studies, the realities were very different.

The sources used by Wrightson and Levine in K. Wrightson and D. Levine, *Poverty and piety in an English village: Terling, 1525–1700* (1979) and by Hey in D. Hey, *An English rural community: Myddle under the Tudors and Stuarts* (1974) will by now be familiar as those to which local historians working between 1530 and 1750 regularly turn. The main ones used here are:

* *Quarter Sessions rolls*, order books, presentments and wage assessments

* *ecclesiastical court records*, especially depositions

* *central government records*, especially sixteenth-century lay subsidies, seventeenth-century hearth taxes, chantry certificates

* *parish registers*, churchwardens' and overseers' accounts and settlement papers

* *manorial and estate papers* including rentals, court books and rolls, surveys and (available for the first time during this period) maps

* *wills and probate inventories.*

Sources

In reviewing the sources available to a local historian interested in the period *c.* 1530–*c.* 1750 we repeatedly find that a type of evidence appears for the first time ever or in any quantity. This is true of parish registers, poor law records, wills and inventories, vernacular buildings, maps with local detail, estate and quarter session records, and the personal evidence of letters and diaries. Not only was more evidence produced from the sixteenth century, but more of it survives, both written and in the form of buildings. The nature of the sources also changed. More than ever before was generated by local people rather than at the centre, was written in English, dealt with individuals and families rather than mentioning them only incidentally in the records of institutions, and covers a much wider social spread. For the first time we have extensive records of the poor as well as the rich and middling, of women and children as well as male family heads. Rather than struggling to exploit to the full typically scanty evidence, as in the Middle Ages, the 'problem' now becomes deciding priorities amongst available materials. Content, survival, present location, language and handwriting will all need to be considered. Out of this there are certain sources which are most generally available, useful and manageable. This section begins with an overall checklist of types of evidence, and then goes on to show in more detail the nature of, and ways to use two of the most basic. This is *not* to say that you should ignore the others. For example, the records of the central courts, particularly Chancery, deal with all manner of local detail, especially in the verbatim depositions of witnesses' evidence. They are however of vast extent, lack a topographical index, and are kept in the Public Record Office. All of this means that it is only sensible for the local historian to delve into what one writer has called this 'great bran tub' when he or she has got to know more obvious local sources, and through them picked up local names or references to enclosures of land or disputes over property which may offer a way into the indexes.

The checklist is organized according to which institution, group of people or person produced the evidence. This is also the basis of where the evidence will be located archivally. In practice the business involved frequently cut across divides. For example, parish poor law concerns were constantly involving magistrates, sometimes at Quarter Sessions, while punishments handed down by ecclesiastical courts were enforced by secular courts if necessary. For the categories referred to only briefly in the checklist information on where to find out more appears in 'Further reading'. Examples of their use also occur in the section 'Cases and places' and in illustrations.

★ central government records	– taxation lists e.g. 1524–5 lay subsidies, 1660s hearth taxes
	– muster rolls
	– Protestation Returns of 1641–2
	– Calendars of State Papers Domestic
	– central courts of equity, e.g. Exchequer, Chancery
	– prerogative courts to 1640, e.g. Star Chamber, Requests and Augmentations

* ecclesiastical records of diocese and archdeaconry
  - courts (including churchwardens' presentments, depositions)
  - visitations queries and answers
  - glebe terriers
  - faculty papers
  - probate records

* Quarter Sessions

* parish registers

* other parish records
  - vestry minutes
  - churchwardens' accounts
  - papers of overseers of the poor including rate assessment lists, accounts (showing relief paid), settlement certificates and examinations, removal orders, bastardy examinations, bonds and orders, apprenticeship indentures
  - accounts of surveyors of the highways
  - constables' books
  - militia papers

* town records
  - Council minutes, in incorporated boroughs
  - freemen's register, also in incorporated boroughs
  - accounts, of property, market tolls, festivities, charities
  - courts
  - charity and education

* estate records
  - court rolls
  - custumals
  - surveys
  - accounts
  - rentals
  - leases
  - deeds
  - mortgages, bargain and sale, conveyances, final concords
  - plans and maps
  - correspondence

* maps
* buildings
* diaries and letters

Three contrasting types of early modern source – probate inventories, surviving vernacular buildings, and parish registers – will be amongst those most useful to local historians. It is worth considering them in greater detail.

Probate inventories

This is the probate inventory of Richard Kimble, a clothier of Newbury, Berkshire, who died in 1627. From it we know that, based in a four-roomed house in the town, Kimble was involved in cloth-making in all its stages, from 'raw' wool to yarn, to woven cloth, to the finishing processes of burling and shearing. He had no looms in his shop or living rooms so must have been engaged in trading in raw materials and then in finishing and selling cloth which had actually been produced by outworkers, spinning and weaving in their own homes. Kimble's £108. 10s. 0d. of debts owed, against 'goods, chattels and howshold stuffe' valued at only £93. 9s. 0d. suggests that trade was not good, as does the modest nature of the furniture and linen in his one-hearth home. Unlike many contemporaries there is no evidence that Kimble had a dual

92. (CONTINUED OVERLEAF) The probate inventory (1627) of Richard Kimble, clothier, of Newbury, Berkshire.

It: Brott wooll one Cod & half   0 — 14 — 0

It: Abirt wooll 20 Cod   24 — 0 — 0

It: Blew wooll one Cod   1 — 8 — 0

It: watchett wooll 10 pound   0 — 8 — 4

It: yearne for 2 clothes   12 — 0 — 0

It: 4 broad clothes ½ wrought   32 — 0 — 0

It: Eight yeards of narrow clothe   0 — 16 — 0

It: 10 pound of yeaven   0 — 8 — 0

It: Rape Oyle   0 — 8 — 0

It: a hundred of Rodwood   1 — 0 — 0

In the Shopp and barkeside

Imprii: 20 tourst of handels   1 — 0 — 0

It: 9 Speares   1 — 2 — 0

It: a sheareboard, yplancke, a frame
2: past boardes. 2. Breelinge stooles
3 Brushes. 4. cuttinge boardes. 6.
Leaden waughtes. 10 Breelinge prones
with other Instruments   } 0 — 12 —

It: a Earte, freyeare, forme, & Rope   1 — 0 — 4

It: 2 dozen of Hurdles   0 — 8 — 0

It: a parcell of Forkes   1 — 1 — 4

It: 3 storkyardinge framed with tardes 0 — 3 — 0

It: 2 Beames. 2 paire of Scailes
& 14 pound waightes a pound waight } 0 — 4 — 0

It: a beatinge Hurdell, with Cubbs
and other Lumber   } 0 — 5 — 0

It: Wood in the Barkesyde   0 — 7 — 0

It: a Marte   0 — 13 — 4

It: Roses & greene wooll

In the Butterie

Imprim one Brasse pott two
kettels, and Posner skillet   } 0 — 10 — 0

It: 7 peeces of pewter   0 — 8 — 0

It: A Byble/ —————————— 0 - 2 - 0

In the Hale

Impri: one foynt Table. 3. stooles
three Chaires & a dollbode } 0 — 18 — 0

It: 2: paire off Andirons, one
Ayre shovell, and tonges. 2. rotteribbs } 0 — 4 — 0
2. pott hookes and. 2. Spittes ————

In the Chamber

Impri. 2. foynt Bedsteades, one
fflock Bedd and Boulster And } 2 — 0 — 0
other thinges Apertainynge

It: Seaven Sheetes ————— 0 — 10 — 0

It. 2. Table Clothes, one dozen
off Napkins. 1. paire off pillotie } 0 — 4 — 4
And twoe other Napkins ————

It. one Chest. 2. Cofferes, 2 Boxes
And a smale Table Board } 0 — 6 — 0

It. His wearinge Apparrill And
the Money in his howse ————— } 1 — 10 — 0

Summa tot — 93 — 9

Debts which he oweth.

Imp. to Thomas Merriman ————— 34 — 0 — 0

It. to Henry Baron ————— 26 — 0 — 0

It. to Smyth. ————— 11 — 0 — 0

It. to Barby ————— 8 — 0 — 0

It. To mr Stampt ————— 10 — 0 — 0

It. to widdow Sollons ————— 10 — 0 — 0

It. to widdow Choulton ————— 1 — 10 — 0

It. to mr Bowater ————— 8 — 0 — 0

Richard william
Derow & Cotton   Summa tot. — 108 — 10 — 0.
william Pier

occupation in farming. General historical accounts tell us that the cloth trade in towns, as opposed to the countryside, was declining at this period; the survival of Kimble's inventory and of those of many contemporaries enables the local historian to test such generalizations, for both individuals and communities.

Our Newbury inventory is amongst tens of thousands which had to be produced to ecclesiastical courts all over the country as part of proof of probate. Until 1858 the courts of the Church of England had a monopoly of probate matters. It is in their records that a range of papers, the most useful being wills and inventories, are now to be found. The two are complementary: wills deal with real estate, the property holdings, if any, of the dead person, and his personal bequests, while the inventory lists and values all his moveable goods, and credits. The form of inventories was codified by an act of 1529, which also required that they should be praised by at least two men, usually relatives or neighbours, within three months of the death. Kimble had four praisers, perhaps because of the complexities of his stock-in-trade. They included debts owed by Kimble, which technically belong in a separate account. This 'mistake' emphasizes that these documents were not produced by court bureaucrats but by those who directly knew the people and place recorded. This led, particularly between *c.* 1530 and *c.* 1730, to most richly detailed pictures of domestic circumstances and livelihoods. After that time inventories become more scanty and standardized.

Not everybody left a will and/or inventory. It is not accurate to say, as is sometimes claimed, that only people with goods over the value of £5 made wills. You will find labourers and shoemakers alongside the yeomen, gentlemen or clergymen, although not proportionately represented. Another under-represented group are women, because of the legal exclusion of married women from property ownership. The wills and inventories of widows do occur however, while the rich evidence of the homes described in inventories, with their cooking, brewing, cheese- and butter-making, spinning, caring for the pig and the hens, not to mention the men and children, suggests the central role women had in maintaining the household economy.

The location of documents may vary. There were three levels of ecclesiastical court: the most local was the archdeacon's, which dealt with testators whose property lay in one archdeaconry; for those with holdings in more than one parish, straddling archdeaconry bounds, it was necessary to go to the bishop's consistory court; at the top of the tree, for those whose property lay in more than one diocese, or for some seeking the status of a higher jurisdiction, there were the two provincial Prerogative Courts of Canterbury and York. Today these PCC wills, most likely to cover 'top' people, are found in the PRO, while the more numerous wills and inventories of the archidiaconal and episcopal jurisdictions are found together in Diocesan Record Offices, usually coterminous with the County Record Office. Again the local historian needs to discover in which diocese her or his place lies or lay (beware sixteenth- and nineteenth-century changes in diocesan boundaries), or if it may just have been in the jurisdiction of an ecclesiastical peculiar, as we found at Monks Risborough. There are easy guides to these exceptions.

For what should the local historian look in wills and inventories? Both will help to pin-point what status, wealth and lifestyle were attached, say, to being a gentleman as opposed to a yeoman or a husbandman. You may find that this varies over time, for example that the designation yeoman fades in some areas after the mid-seventeenth century and that more people aspired to be gentlemen, or were for the first time called farmers. Wills indicate who were owner occupiers and who tenants. Their wording may show a Catholic or Puritan religious preference and a changing emphasis in charitable bequests. Do we see here evidence for the decline in charitable giving often claimed for the post-Reformation period? Bequests in wills give valuable evidence of family relationships, and perhaps of the attitudes underlying them, for example a shift from concentrating on preserving the inheritance through the elder son to more bequests to younger siblings, including better provision for the girls. This is an intriguing area, although beware assuming dramatic rifts from bequests when a son may have received his share during father's lifetime or a daughter already be dowried and well set-up rather than cut out of the will.

Inventories, as well as enabling us to build a picture of relative levels of wealth and social status, are a key to understanding the vernacular architecture of the period. They usually identify occupied rooms, of which the contents indicate the use. We can work out the number and location of hearths and (from the hearth furniture) likely chimneys. This and the order of rooms can, when related to local building styles, yield a likely building plan. However you will be extremely lucky to find enough supporting evidence to tie a surviving house firmly to an inventory. House contents in inventories show increasing or declining fortunes. The well-off of the late sixteenth century sport more joined chairs and tables, as opposed to stools, benches and trestles, they begin to have glass in their windows (initially listed in its frame as a moveable good), and the really well-off may be picked out by their silver spoons or clocks.

As with Richard Kimble much wealth was commonly tied up in stock-in-trade. From this we can understand processes, organization of work and levels of prosperity. It is largely the evidence of probate inventories which has led agricultural historians to argue for an 'agricultural revolution' in the late 1500s and 1600s. This may be traced through mention of new crops, grasses and pulses, indicating improved rotation systems, more fodder, less fallow and improved yields. Linked to this may be increased numbers of stock, evidence of more fodder, more manure (a key commodity) and perhaps of market specialization in local farming. Are new kinds of implements listed, do corn crops shift from rye to wheat (indicating a change from black to white loaves), do four-wheeled waggons for larger harvest loads begin to supersede the previously dominant two-wheeled carts?

To use wills and inventories, and other early modern records, you will need to be able to read the characteristic secretary hand in which Richard Kimble's inventory is written. This employs a standard alphabet, which will soon become familiar from booklet guides. Also try working through a document using a modern transcript, and familiarizing yourself with the common form which it, like so many sources, takes. It is extremely satisfying to decode this hand, as you will soon be able to do. With the minor exceptions of formal legal passages such as the court's endorsement on the bottom of probate documents, it is written in English, not Latin.

Finally, wills and inventories are a prime example of the universal local historical rule never to use a single source in isolation. Not only do wills link to inventories, but numbers of them may be compared by place, by time and occupation as well as family name, and linked to other evidence, the main instances being:

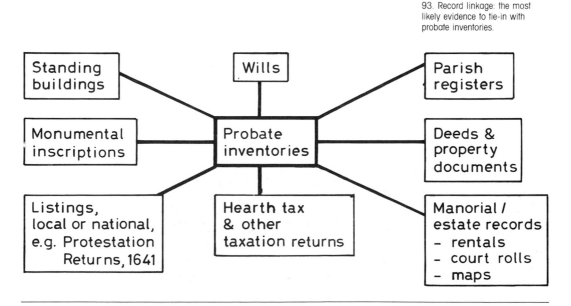

93. Record linkage: the most likely evidence to tie-in with probate inventories.

Buildings

The early modern period was the heyday of vernacular architecture. These were the homes and farm buildings built for local people, by local craftsmen, and using local resources – of materials, money and style. This was the time when people in local communities first had a sufficient share of wealth and resources to build or substantially rebuild in permanent form and in significant numbers. After this period local building was overtaken by encroaching outside influences, of imported materials and uniform ideas of style; the vernacular was overtaken by the polite.

The 'great rebuilding' of provincial England has been an important area of local studies, both at the level of structural minutiae, and on the broader front of how it relates to the economy and society of the community producing the buildings. Bob Machin has shown[5] how, in the dairying parish of Yetminster in Dorset, yeoman farmers had sufficient wealth from a lucrative local agriculture to build or rebuild in substantial stone, two-storied, chimneyed houses with a variety of rooms with distinct functions and a measure of privacy. In a parish divided between four manors they also had sufficient freedom and security to make it worthwhile to build. Here the great rebuilding took place between 1550 and 1650 and was clearly related to capital formation and investment decisions. In Saddleworth on the Lancashire Pennines the same factors produced a different outcome because of local conditions. There the injection of prosperity and security came with the growth of the family-based cloth industry. Building in stone came only in the seventeenth century, with most activity after 1650. There were no entrance halls, passages and separate rooms as in Yetminster but homes centred on two or three rooms and a single hearth. These

94. Yetminster, Dorset. The 'great rebuilding' at prosperous yeoman level is clear from the many substantial houses like this, built in the late sixteenth and early seventeenth centuries.

homes and workplaces then grew gradually and incrementally as industry took over from farming.

It is such homes that are going to be the focus of local building studies between 1550 and 1750. Churches had formerly been the barometer of local society, but now few were built, and many decayed, a situation on which nineteenth-century restorers were to seize. Perhaps the chief building activity in local churches was the erection of elaborate monuments or whole funerary chapels to important families. This assertion of wealth and patronage is seen in the other main areas of building activity, country houses, and such lubricants of influence as almshouses and town halls donated by increasingly dominant ruling families.

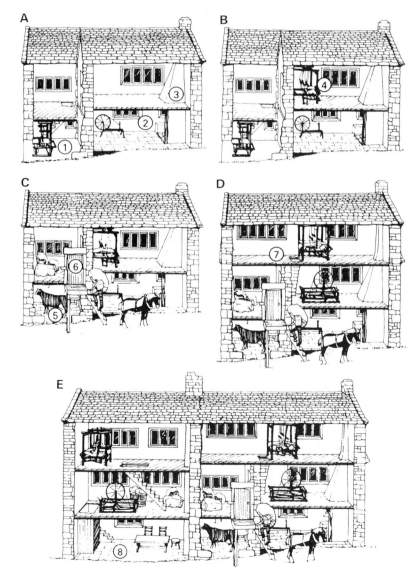

95. The development of Pinfold Farm, Saddleworth. A: It started with an inner room (1) shown with a loom, and a firehouse (2) shown with a spinning wheel. The smoke from the fire escapes through a hood (3) and there are lofts in the upper storey. B: Next, the upper storey is raised to form a loom shop (4). C: Then the house is extended to provide a slaughter-house (5) and given a taking-in door (6). D: The next stage adds a third storey (7). E: In the final stage, a complete new house of three storeys (8) is added on the left-hand side. (From A. Quiney, *House and home* (1986)).

96. Patronage and influence expressed in public building. Sir William Drake's almshouses, Amersham, Bucks., established 1657.

97. Town Hall, Brackley, Northants., built by the first Duke of Bridgewater, 1706.

Parish registers

These are the single most continuous, most generally available and most comprehensive source. Registers began in 1538 and continue to the present day. They had to be kept in each of over ten thousand ancient parishes and, sometimes separately, for chapelries within parishes. Unlike most sources they cover everybody from the lord of the manor and the parson, provided they were resident, to the humblest labourer, bastard child or itinerant.

98. Anglican Baptism, c. 1700.

This comprehensiveness may need qualifying in practice. In fact only 10 per cent of registers survive from 1538. Others are flawed by gaps. Common ones relate to periods of political upheaval, including Mary I's reign and the Civil War and Commonwealth period. Others reflect local factors, particularly clerical neglect or incapacity. Although the registers were supposed to form a complete record of baptisms, marriages and burials some areas suffered from under-registration because of nonconformity, or by the late eighteenth century because of an increasing inability to cope with larger and more mobile populations. Infant mortality rates were high and, since infants who had not been publicly baptised went unregistered, such births are missing from the record. Local historians commonly use baptismal entries as proxies for numbers of births but must remember that the ideal of baptism within three months of birth was not always attained, by parents who were either indifferent to or dissented from, the Anglican monopoly of this rite.

This catalogue of cautions may seem off-putting. However, so extensively used have parish registers been that there is ample guidance on spotting snags and how to allow for them (see Further reading). We are still left with thousands of pieces of information about local people, many of whom would otherwise be hidden from view.

Since the Parochial Records Measure of 1978 most parish registers, except the most recent ones, will be deposited in the Diocesan (usually also County) Record Office. Sometimes they will be most readily available in printed or typed transcript, largely thanks to family historians who have used them so intensively. This is a help, provided the transcript is accurate and complete, for registers can include a lot more than the names of individuals, and provided you can refer back to the original document, or microfilm of it, if necessary.

Parish registers tend to have common patterns. Six principal dates help to explain these:

* 1538   – Thomas Cromwell, Henry VIII's chief minister, ordered that every parson, vicar or curate was to enter in a book every wedding, christening and burial. The entries were to name the parties and were

to be made each Sunday. The book was to be kept in a 'sure coffer', with one key kept by the parson and the other by the churchwardens.

⋆ 1598 — Registers were ordered to be copied on parchment in a book. Some surviving registers begin at this date, while others originate at this time but with entries since 1538 or the first year of Elizabeth's reign, 1558, transcribed into them, usually obvious from the handwriting. It was decreed that the parish chest containing the registers should have a third lock, one for each warden, and that the wardens should observe the entries being made. It was at this time that bishop's transcripts (BT) were first required, an annual copy of all the previous year's entries to be sent to the bishop a month after Easter. Where parish registers are damaged or missing BTs can be a valuable proxy, provided they themselves have survived. The verdict of a review of the state of Oxford diocese's BTs in 1883 will wring the withers of every local historian and archivist for they presented 'a lamentable picture of episcopal negligence, parochial parsimony, and official rapacity'.

⋆ 1653–60 — During the Interregnum civil registration was introduced. Research indicates resistance to these new procedures. As far as the parish registers go there may be entries but they are likely to be patchy. The period of disrupted recording may stretch back into the Civil War years.

⋆ 1753 — Hardwicke's Marriage Act required full records of banns and of marriages in a proper book. The form of entry was laid down and it is here that we encounter the first printed forms in registers, a sure sign of standardization. A Hardwicke register has four entries per page and parties were required to sign. The Act provided that all except Jews and Quakers must marry according to Anglican rites. It has been observed that the marriage registers always tended to be best kept because of their importance as proof of legitimacy and rights of inheritance. Hardwicke's Act was concerned to tighten up marriage procedures because of just such upper-class concerns with clandestine marriages, not at local churches with due notice. Hardwicke registers offer local historians rare evidence on literacy because of their requirement for signatures.

99. Entries in a Hardwicke marriage register (Watlington, Oxfordshire, 1775–7).

* 1812 — Rose's Act required that three separate registers be kept. Some parishes, especially small ones, had entered all events into one book. These new registers followed a centrally-produced printed layout which included for baptisms the names, abode and description/occupation of the parents, and for burials the age and abode of the dead person.

* 1837 — Civil registration was introduced. The record became that of births, marriages and deaths and the Registrar-General was in charge of the system. Although Anglican parish registers continue, 1837 or 1851, with the first fully-developed census enumerator's returns, is usually the end of historical studies, for the source now loses its claim to be a comprehensive record of the vital events of people's lives.

One characteristic of parish registers between 1538 and 1837 is that generally the later you get the fuller is the information offered, for example naming both father and mother at the christening of a baby. This partly reflects the result of government direction and partly the expansion of the idea of written record. Local historians will also see the impact of particular incumbents. Some were neglectful; others used the registers to record additional information such as the causes of death, as they understood them, in the burial registers.

Others were less consistent but provided revealing insights. The vicar of North Aston, Oxon. noted the circumstances of that always poignant event, the death of an unknown, unacknowledged person:

> June 7 1627 A poor little infant being a manchild was by an unnatural hore the supposed mother left in an outbarn and forsaken redy & subject to have been devoured by hoggs or otherwise to have perished had it not been fownd in tyme. . . . . and dyed and was buried

Surviving superstitions emerge in the same register: 'December 5 1633 Androsse Sibil wife of Anthony died in childbed & was buried by candle in the Myste . . . '. Later the Reverend William Vaughan used the register book to note how the parish had been enclosed in Elizabeth's reign by the lord of the manor, how the vicarial tithes had been settled, and how the thirty-seven cow pasture commons in North Aston's cow pasture were currently, 1714, allocated.

In the registers of a small town, Burford, we find sudden death – 23 January 1617 William Hall 'Kilde with a pott at the Bull'; youthful misfortune – 12 January 1626 'Thomas Silvester drownd in his mothers well'; and extreme old age – 30 January 1626 'Innocent Grinnowaie being 105 years old'. The impact of great events is clear with, in June 1665, 'Great Pestilence in London dying nere 100000', while nearer home the impact of Civil War is apparent, including the execution of the Leveller rebels in May 1649, 'three soldiers shot to death in Burford Churchyard'.

For a majority of local people the registers are the central source of information, and sometimes their epitaph. This was the case for John Smith, citizen and labourer of Swinbrook, Oxon. of whom the parson wrote on his death at the age of 74 in 1809, 'NB he was an honest and very industrious man. He brought up a large family without any parochial assistance', a verdict as revealing of the clergyman's preoccupations as of John's character.

Amidst this wealth of individual detail lies a cumulative picture of some of the principal realities, rhythms and determinants of local and national life in pre-industrial England. There are two main methods of exploiting the registers in this way – aggregative analysis and family reconstitution. Aggregative analysis involves using every entry in a register to construct monthly, annual and decennial totals of baptisms, burials and marriages. A graph of these totals gives you a broad indication of whether the population of your parish (or chapelry or group of parishes) was experiencing natural increase or decrease, as shown in the balance of baptisms against burials. It was data such as this, drawn from the aggregative analyses of 404 parish registers that revealed the distinct phases of population experience graphed and analysed by Wrigley and Schofield with age at marriage and proportions of people never marrying being identified as primary causes of change. Local historians for the parishes not yet considered in this way can do much interesting analysis and relate it to known patterns elsewhere.

Besides the trends of experience revealed by aggregative analysis the graphs of events will clearly show acute episodes when numbers of burials rose to meet, or suddenly peak above, baptisms. Here are the crises of epidemic disease and of subsistence that had such a profound effect upon families and whole settlements. Their cause may often be deduced by looking at the time of year, length of onset, and duration, age of the victims, and other contemporary sources.

Particular strands of information may be drawn from the registers:

* crude birth and death rates (events have to be related to an estimate of total population)

* crude rate of increase or decrease

* sex ratio (nos. of males per 1,000 females)

* fertility rates (based on the ratio of marriages: baptisms over time)

* infant mortality (burials of children under one year: total baptisms)

* nuptiality (proportion of women buried who were wives or widows)

* age at marriage (linking a baptism to a marriage entry, but a difficult measure as it has been estimated that in at least 20 per cent of marriages one partner was not marrying for the first time)

* seasonality (the month in which events took place)

* illegitimacy and pre-nuptial pregnancy (the latter when the bride was pregnant at the altar as revealed by the time between the wedding and the first child's baptism)

* literacy (as revealed by signing of names in post-Hardwicke marriage registers)

* marriage horizons (using the abodes of partners in marriage registers to see the proportion of marriages involving outsiders, from how far away these outsiders came and in what geographical spread).

The second major method of analysing a parish register is by family reconstitution (FR). This involves a time-consuming historical jigsaw puzzle, using every mention of every individual in a register to attempt to describe all or some of the community's families over time. This is a long-established approach, extended and systematized by CAMPOP. At its most basic it involves making a record slip or index card every time an individual is mentioned as involved in a baptism, marriage or burial. Two slips will be needed when a woman marries, one recording her in her maiden or widowed name and another in her new, married name. All slips for a surname are then assembled, sorted chronologically and by baptism, marriage or burial. Then, starting with the marriages, the story of each couple is traced as far as possible. Once marriages are established then baptisms of children may be related, and then burials. Links between each of these family generations may emerge. Sometimes the exact nature of a link may require every scrap of information to be invoked. A common example might be that, since weddings usually took place in the bride's home parish, if the couple did not come from the same place and they then went to live in the groom's home place, the marriage will have to be deduced from the baptismal entries for their children in the register of the groom's parish. A death may be deduced from a change in the name of the wife in subsequent baptisms, or a reference to 'widow'. All the links must be tested carefully, and on occasion defeat or uncertainty admitted. All the frustrations of inconsistent spelling of names (is it the same surname, or is Maria the same person as Mary?), and of loyal adherence to the same christian names generation after generation will be met. These problems local and demographic historians share with family historians, but on a wider scale, for instead of concentrating on one family the aim is to reconstitute all or at least a range of local families. To reconstitute a whole register for an average to small community, producing around one hundred register entries per year over some three hundred years has been estimated as the work of perhaps 1,500 hours. Some local historians love the sustained, steady and rewarding labours of such an approach, others will find the technique extremely helpful on a more limited scale. Many aspects of parish register analysis lend themselves to computer usage. Developments in micro-computers and affordable data-base packages make this approach increasingly accessible to the 'ordinary' local historian.

Reconstitution helps us to understand many things. Life expectancy at birth was in the range 40–45 years between 1550 and

1800. The consequences of this emerge in individual and local experiences from registers. For example, the experience of 'broken' families, through the loss of one or both parents, was a common one. So was re-marriage, bringing with it step-relationships. Some of the hazards of childbearing, for mother and child, show up in FRs, as does evidence for the contraceptive effect of breast-feeding. Look to see whether the first baby is born quickly after marriage while subsequent babies are spaced out, perhaps by three years or so. If there is such a pattern is it broken when an infant dies, so that breast-feeding ceases and the next conception follows more quickly?

Even when the register yields nothing about individuals or families this negative evidence can be useful. Are the 'missing' people, recorded only at baptism, younger sons and daughters of established local families? Does their absence show that marriage horizons for daughters tended to be outside the parish, perhaps because it was too small to offer enough likely partners, or because of the families' employment, trading or religious contacts? In the case of sons was it that a local community based on primogeniture could not provide opportunities for its non-inheriting male members? There will also be families who disappear totally from the register. This is one of the sources of evidence that has firmly knocked on the head the idea that pre-industrial English communities were overwhelmingly static. We see natural wastage in terms of genetic misfortune and the failure of family lines, but also a constant coming and going of people. To understand the degree and composition of this turnover is important. Until the coming of the national census in the nineteenth century the parish registers represent the most comprehensive and commonly available way of answering this and a whole range of fundamental local history questions. Parish registers have been used and known for so long that they can seem hackneyed; used fully, systematically and imaginatively they can offer some of the freshest and fullest insights to be had.

References

1 David Vaisey (ed.), *The diary of Thomas Turner, 1754–1765* (1984), pp. 267–8.
2 Margaret Spufford, *Contrasting communities. English villagers in the sixteenth and seventeenth centuries* (1974).
3 L.G. Mitchell (ed.), *The Purefoy letters, 1735–1753* (1973), p. 16.
4 Peter Clark and Paul Slack, *English towns in transition* (1976), p. 4.
5 R. Machin, *The houses of Yetminster* (1979).

CHAPTER FIVE

Traditional into Modern? Local Life, *c.* 1750 – 1914

The period *c.* 1750 to 1914 is associated with nothing less than the transition from a rural, primarily agrarian and traditional society, to a modern, primarily industrial and urban existence. Debate continues to rage as to how quickly and with what consequences, for good or ill, this move took place. When, and how deeply, did new patterns take root? What sort of changes were there in work, housing, political participation, local and central government, transport and mobility, education and literacy, economic and cultural influences, religious behaviour and the physical surroundings in which people lived? No local historian can be immune from this debate, because no place, urban or rural, industrial or agrarian, has been immune from the consequences of these changes. The imprint of the 'long nineteenth century' has to be appreciated in order to understand both earlier periods and a locality today. Above all this period is highly rewarding in its own right, both because of what was happening to places then and for the range of new and detailed sources of information it produced.

Patterns of economic change

For the local historian the challenge is to understand the interaction between local circumstances and wider factors, which together produced the particular local experience. Some primary general factors to consider will be technological change, available raw materials, sources of capital, markets, and means of transport. These largely economic determinants lie at the root of many local experiences; where all are present sustained expansion, and radically different physical environments, institutions, and social structures and relationships, are likely to emerge. However, where an experience of proto-industrialization or industrialization is based upon a single product or resource, then local transformations may be less permanent. For example, lace-making in Buckinghamshire,

100. Young straw plaiters, Titmore Green, Hertfordshire, c. 1900. Surviving cottage industries employing women and children provided a key supplement to male earnings, especially in agricultural areas.

a successful cottage industry in the earlier part of the period, subsequently fell victim to mechanization of lace production based in Nottingham and to Buckinghamshire's own lack of suitable power sources. Or, as we shall see from the pit villages of the Deerness Valley in County Durham, entirely new settlements could spring up around an exploitable but finite mineral resource, only to dwindle or change completely within a few generations. Finally we should not forget the places which never experienced industrialization directly, but whose fortunes were nevertheless determined by it, undergoing stagnation or an absolute decline in size and prosperity. An inability to sustain and keep local population was an experience common in the later nineteenth century to both such economically bypassed places, and those, like the Buckinghamshire lace-making communities, whose early prosperity had not been sustained.

Population: growth or decline?

One of the best indicators of the pattern of experience of a particular place is its population levels. The introduction in 1801 of a decennial national census, which grew in accuracy and detail with each decade, is an invaluable tool in plotting these patterns. Decadal totals and the rate of change between them can reveal a great deal, in comparison with what happened nationally, within a local area, or with similar places, whether market towns, pit villages, suburbs or seaside resorts. For example, a comparison of the market towns of Oxfordshire, using their population totals every ten years from 1801 to 1901, shows changes in relative importance and distinctly differing experiences within the group, some shared, some very specific. All the towns had populations in the range 1,000 to 3,000–4,000 at the start of the century, but by 1901 that range had widened greatly. This reflected rapid and continuing growth for Banbury (apart from a hesitation in 1881 in the early years of agricultural depression). For a middle group of towns there was survival and modest growth, although fortunes tended to falter somewhat in the later nineteenth century, except for Chipping Norton and its tweed industry. Dwindling decline was the fate of the smaller towns, whose population peaked in the second quarter of the century and were static or absolutely declining thereafter.

Banbury was not a predominantly industrial town. Its success was built on a number of factors: established markets for retail produce, for livestock and for grain; the continuing growth of major processing industries – brewing, tanning and milling; an expanding foundry making agricultural implements; a concentration of professional services – lawyers, vets, banks – and of specialist shops and crafts; increasing administrative functions, through continued borough status, but also as a seat of the magistracy, a poor law union, a registration district, an inspector of taxes, and eventually of a rural district council; the town was also a centre of political activity; it had secondary schools; it was the centre of a domestic industry, plush, (although as this was superseded by production in Coventry after the 1830s it constitutes one of the few declining elements in Banbury's fortunes); and the town was on main transport routes between the West Midlands and London, the canal and later two railways. Such a multiplicity of roles created a momentum of expansion new to the nineteenth century. However, the predisposing factors in this local history were longer-term, the continuing work of a primary market centre serving a rural hinterland with 140 places in a ten-mile radius, most linked to the nodal point of Banbury by carriers' carts and trading contacts. These had always been the roots of Banbury's experience and the town's new or increased roles sprang from them.

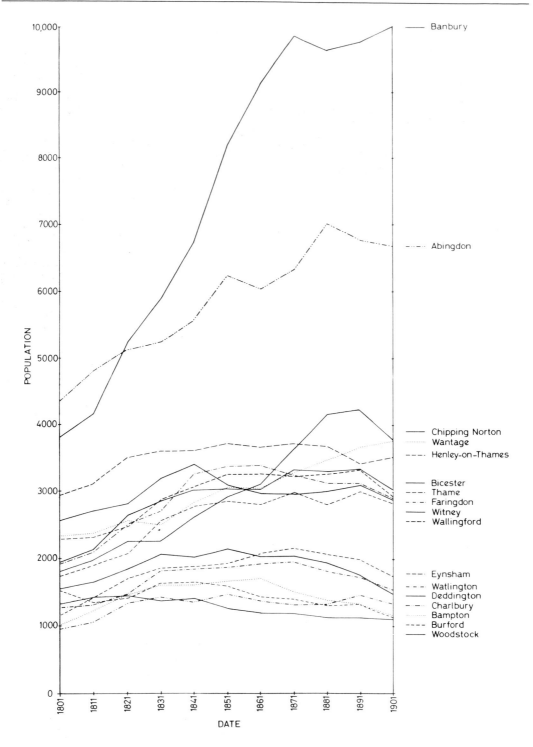

Population of Oxfordshire market towns in the 19th century

102. Carriers' carts in Banbury Market Place, *c.* 1878. The young Joseph Ashby from nearby Tysoe on first seeing Banbury, market centre for 140 surrounding villages, likened it to 'Nijni Novgorod', the great Russian fair of which he had read.

Other traditional towns experienced a shrinking in their areas of influence and in the extent of their outside contacts as the success of other centres like Banbury pushed them lower down the urban hierarchy. Wallingford (before 1974 in Berkshire) was overtaken by Abingdon and Reading. It ceased to return an M.P. after 1885, but retained real importance for its immediate area, still in 1915 receiving carriers' carts from twenty-two surrounding villages. Its population in 1901 was 38 per cent larger than in 1801.

Still other towns emerged into the twentieth century with similar or smaller populations than a century before. In common with the larger villages, from which they were increasingly difficult to distinguish, this masked initial population growth followed, in the last three decades of the century, by a decline from which the vestiges of urban diversity were not strong enough to save them. Agricultural depression, the weakening of rural industries and the absence of new ones, isolation from transport routes, and lack of administrative importance conspired to remove them from the urban league.

The reliability of census figures tempts the local historian to begin assessing population change and its impact from 1801. However, as we have seen, England was already well advanced into an unprecedented growth by *c.* 1750, generated principally by increasing levels of fertility. Men and women were marrying

101. (OPPOSITE) The varying fortunes of Oxfordshire market towns in the nineteenth century, as mirrored in population levels recorded in the decennial censuses.

younger, a higher proportion of the population was marrying, and more babies were being born. Also in the eighteenth century illegitimate births rose 'on a sufficient scale to have substantial impact on overall fertility'.[1] Death rates declined after 1750, although infant mortality rates improved little until as late as 1900. Overall, recent demographic research attributes some three-quarters of population rise in the eighteenth century to increased fertility and the rest to mortality changes.

Discerning trends, and still more understanding what determined them, is often difficult. Local historians, with their wealth of detail, know better than most historians that actual experiences are not easily reducible to simple categories. Equally a mass of unconsidered detail can hide more than it reveals, the perennial wood, unseen for the trees. It is here that models against which to test local evidence come into their own. For instance, some possible consequences of rising population are brought together diagrammatically here.

103. Responses to population growth (from D.B. Grigg, in W. White and R. Wood (eds.), *The geographical impact of migration* (1980)).

At the top of the diagram is the response of increasing and refining agricultural output, a process detected in landscape change, and in changing crops, rotations, tenures, and enclosures described in maps and documents. A second reaction is to turn to other employments, when surplus of labour makes it impossible for many to make a livelihood in traditional farm work. Here rural industry, temporary migrations, and short-term hirings feature. Another reaction is to limit fertility, as happened in England in the late seventeenth century, but then ceased, producing even greater pressure of numbers after 1750. Finally there is the response of moving away, pushed by deteriorating fortunes and no doubt pulled by hopes of relative prosperity. This was a major part of English experience in the nineteenth century, particularly internal migration to towns, and movement overseas. The push factor from over-populated rural areas is confirmed by peaks of migration at times of particular distress there – in the 1830s and from the 1870s.

In many ways local communities, agrarian or industrial, underwent a change of gear in the second half of the nineteenth century. There was an end to the earlier explosive rates of growth, particularly between 1760 and 1815. Rates of reproduction slowed and after 1870 England crossed a major watershed, into fertility decline. Those marrying in 1861–9 had an average of 6.16 children, couples married in 1890–9 produced 4.13, and those in 1920–4 bore 2.31. The immediate causes of this great change were improved means of contraception and a declining proportion of people getting married. The reasons for this behaviour are less measurable. They have been related to a decline in the family work unit, lessening the importance of earnings by women and children. The male breadwinner working outside the home was, on average, responsible for two-thirds of total household income in the late nineteenth century, compared with only a quarter earlier. The home became a separate sphere of domesticity and consumption, a powerful source of aspiration at a popular cultural level, a symbol of respectable independence, status and prestige. David Levine has interpreted this[2] as underlying a 'resurgent prudence' reflected in later marriage (in Edwardian times twenty-seven for men and twenty-five for women), fewer children brought up at greater cost (notably through longer education and entering work later), a lower proportion marrying, and a reduction in illegitimacy. This pattern of behaviour took longer to extend to unskilled, working-class groups, but over fifty years wrought a profound change of which population size is one sign.

Town and country

Not only did population grow after *c.* 1750 but the way in which it was distributed shifted radically. In 1800 the great majority of people in England still lived in places with less than 5,000 population. By 1850 as many lived in sizeable towns as in rural places, and by the end of the century almost three-quarters did so, a complete reversal of the situation a century before.

Table 1. Population of England living in towns of 5,000 inhabitants or more

Size of Town	1801		1851		1891	
	No. of towns	Population	No. of towns	Population	No. of towns	Population
20,000+	15	1.5 m	63	6.2 m	185	15.5 m
10,000–20,000	31	0.38 m	60	0.8 m	175	2.3 m
5,000–10,000	60	0.41 m	140	0.96 m	262	1.8 m
Under 5,000		6.5 m		9.8 m		9.2 m
per cent of total Population						
Urban		26.85		50.08		72.05
Rural		73.95		49.92		27.95

To put it another way, during the nineteenth century the total population of England and Wales increased just over four times and the proportion classified as urban by nearly nine and a half times. London again figured largely. It grew prodigiously from 1,117,000 inhabitants of greater London in 1801 to 6,586,000 in 1901. One-fifth to one-sixth of the total population lived in the capital in the nineteenth century. Elsewhere the urban hierarchy changed, with Bristol and Newcastle remaining prominent but places like York, Exeter, Chester and Norwich fading from the forefront. In their stead came the towns, often groups of towns and burgeoning villages, of the industrializing and commercial regions of the West Riding of Yorkshire, Lancashire, the Potteries and the West Midlands. Manchester with Salford, Liverpool, Birmingham,

Leeds and Sheffield were to the fore. By 1850 Liverpool and Manchester, the two most remarkable growth stories, were respectively the seventh and the ninth largest cities anywhere in Europe, exceeded only by capital cities.

Urban growth continued throughout the nineteenth century, but with changes in emphasis after 1850. Industrial developments still injected exceptional growth (defined by Philip Waller as growth of over 25 per cent in an intercensal period of ten years).[3] Railway workshops changed Swindon and Derby, iron and steel developed Barrow-in-Furness and Middlesbrough, shipbuilding Birkenhead, fishing Grimsby and so on. Other booming towns were the pleasure resorts, Blackpool and Southend amongst them. Perhaps the most striking growths were in suburbs and satellite towns. By the 1890s eleven of thirty central London districts were showing regular decreases in population and some of the most rapidly expanding areas in the country were East and West Ham, Leyton, Tottenham, Hornsey, Willesden, Walthamstow and Croydon. This physical separation of commercial and business areas from residential, and of rich from poor, and the various intermediate nuances of the English class system, was mirrored in many towns, whose developing social geography is seen in their extending boundaries, and in the architecture and occupancy of the new houses, often emerging in concentric bands around old centres.

The forces for segregation and suburbanization were formidable given the experience of urbanization during the earlier phases of the industrial revolution. One of the most graphic and influential exposures of this was the Utilitarian reformer Edwin Chadwick's *Report on the Sanitary Condition of the Working Classes*, published in 1842. In his carefully empirical and scientific way Chadwick gathered detailed information from all over the country, and this, despite his measured tone, remains a shocking testimony to what it was like to live in English towns in the late 1830s.

Particularly telling were the levels of life expectancies in years in different towns:

104. Nineteenth-century slum conditions, both urban (ABOVE) and rural (BELOW).

	Professional men	Tradesmen	Labourers & artisans
Rutland	52	41	38
Kendal	45	39	34
Truro	40	33	28
Derby	49	38	21
Manchester	38	20	17

Everywhere the expectations of social classes are starkly different, while the situation for all in the most industrial and rapidly growing, Manchester, is frightening. As Chadwick commented, 'It is an appalling fact that, of all who are born of the labouring classes of Manchester, more than 57 per cent die before they attain five

THE RAILWAY JUGGERNAUT OF 1845

105. Railways brought people, raw materials, goods, information and ideas into and out of many of the places they touched, while those bypassed by the expanding network could be reduced to economic and social backwaters.

years of age, that is before they can be engaged in factory labour, or in any other labour whatsoever.' Much local history from the early nineteenth century on reflects reactions to, and attempts to cope with, these early disruptive phases of modernization.

It would be easy to assume that increasing numbers of people were sucked into towns where the real changes were happening and that rural areas like Rutland were left in relative if out-dated peace. In fact population growth was largely generated within an agrarian setting. The countryside rather than being a late and passive recipient of the upheavals caused by modernization elsewhere, itself produced essential elements that enabled change, and was in the process greatly changed itself. Between the early sixteenth century and the early nineteenth century the population of England grew by over three-and-a-half times, without other than marginal dependence on food imports, and with little change in the size of the agricultural workforce. Rises in agricultural productivity enabled more rapid population growth, which was in turn essential in providing the workforce needed for industry. By 1800 little more than one-third of the English labour force was engaged in agriculture, but the story was not one of a backward agriculture being overtaken by industry. The rural world responded to increasing urban demand. The agrarian sector was linked to transport improvements, growth in credit, the development of capital markets and commercial exchange. Rural-based industries were capitalized and geared to market demands, and agriculture was improved, through new and better crops, advances in animal breeding, increased specialization, more flexible rotations, more effective cultivation, the consolidation and engrossment of holdings, and the enclosure of land.

Rural change and parliamentary enclosure

It is enclosure, particularly parliamentary enclosure, which has been most associated with the extinction of old, organic farming communities, and with a flight from the land to the city. After 1760 four million acres of arable common field and two million acres of waste were enclosed in England by this process. The unit of enclosure was the parish or township. A private act was promoted, usually by the principal property owner(s), the lord of the manor and the tithe owners. The reasons stated are time and again that the lands of the petitioners are 'intermixed and dispersed in small parcels and in their present situation are incapable of any considerable improvement'. Subject to the consent of the owners of a majority, usually two-thirds, of the land the bill became an act and commissioners were appointed to implement the enclosure on the ground. They carried out a detailed survey and valuation, heard claims for allocations of land in lieu of former holdings and of rights of use such as common grazing, and to collect tithes, and then drew up a definitive allotment of land, which also designated the routes of roads and tracks, rights of way and public spaces. This document was the enclosure award.

What exactly parliamentary enclosure meant for communities is one of the longest running debates in local history. In one view it swept away the roots of the old community, which lay in communally organized agriculture and in the common livelihood of a shared field system. Smallholders with a few acres and those with common rights lost out, having insufficient power to influence the formal procedures of enclosure, and then being ill-equipped to meet their share of the costs of enclosure or to make a viable living in a new landscape of large, separate farm units, geared to commercial production for outside markets. The result was increased poverty and a loss of independence and self-determination which reduced the villager, now dependent on wage labour, to hardship and caused an exodus from the countryside. The old community had dissolved.

This picture can be tested and measured for individual parishes.

Who held land pre- and post-enclosure can be explored in land tax assessments and estate records; parish registers and, after 1801, censuses show whether the population rose or fell; records of poverty, from parish government, parliamentary or private enquiries, mirror levels of distress and employment or under-employment; the printed enclosure bill and act and the parliamentary proceedings reveal the instigators and any formally expressed opposition, while the commissioners' award, and with luck surviving map, surveys, minutes and correspondence, chronicle the claims, negotiation and final allotment.

The experience of enclosure was undoubtedly widespread. After 1760 some 5,400 acts were passed, including those framed under the General Acts of 1801, 1836 and 1845, which aimed at standardizing, simplifying and making the process cheaper. Before 1760 only 259 parliamentary enclosure acts were passed. However, some areas of the country were much more affected than others, notably areas with full-blown, open field arable farming rather than the upland landscape zones. As the maps opposite show, areas like Cornwall and parts of Devon, the south-east, the Welsh marches, and Lancashire and Cheshire either saw very low levels of parliamentary enclosure, or they experienced it chiefly through measures to enclose not arable but commons and wastes, as in Cumberland and Northumberland.

With this major qualification it is clear that in many places the structure of local life did change to one of major landholdings in

106. Kettleshulme, Derbyshire. An upland landscape, overlain by the rectilinear fields of nineteenth-century parliamentary enclosure.

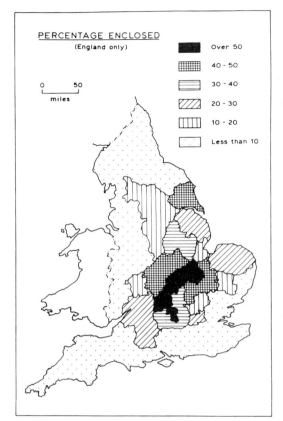
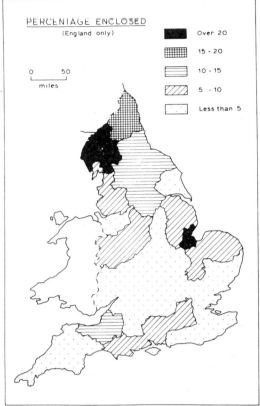

107. Density of parliamentary enclosure in England: open field arable (left) and common and waste (right). (From M. Turner, *English parliamentary enclosure* (1980).)

one or few hands, organized in large, enclosed units, often run by tenant farmers, and with an increasing mass of wage labourers at the bottom of the social scale. Whether this resulted from parliamentary enclosure, rather than being part of a longer and wider process, is much less clear. Local research has shown that enclosures already existed in many parishes, separated from the field system either by the lord of the manor or by mutual agreement of influential proprietors. Since at least the late seventeenth century major landowners pursued policies of consolidating holdings, buying-in land, and accumulating estates, producing structures in which landholding was already heavily polarized. In such a context improved farming methods could be implemented and a local enclosure act may be only a late stage in a longer process of modernization. There is little to support the image of the deserted village, inhabitants driven away by enclosure. The decades following enclosure frequently saw local population growing. In arable areas 'improved' agriculture was a labour intensive business. Villages grew, and at such a rate that an ample surplus of people power remained to move to the towns.

If the single, drastic dislocation of local life is not found a sense of change is apparent. In a rare surviving autobiography Joseph Mayett, farm labourer of Quainton in Buckinghamshire, records a life spent at this time of rural transition. Born in 1783, he lived in a village untouched by parliamentary enclosure, a place of mixed farming with a cottage-based lace industry to supplement agricultural earnings. In the typical pre-industrial way Joseph moved away from home in his early teens and took a number of annual hirings, living-in farm jobs, all within nine miles of his home village. He had twelve such contracts, but found his position

108. A labourer's life from a Berkshire settlement examination of 1773. Thomas Bradley was born in Abingdon, began his working life with annual Michaelmas hirings to employers at Yattendon and Theale, but was now a day labourer with no right to poor relief in his present parish of residence, St Laurence, Reading.

increasingly eroded. When there was a growing surplus of labour, and when an annual hiring earned a poor law settlement, employers were no longer keen to follow the traditional commitment to year-long contracts. Unhappiness with his position pushed Mayett into joining the militia in 1803, and he spent twelve years on postings in England and Ireland. Since marriage still implied setting up a separate household he returned to Buckinghamshire and married only in 1815, aged thirty-two, an unusually late age at this period. To make ends meet he did farm work on a labouring basis, peddling and itinerant harvesting. Like many in similar circumstances Joseph's lot proved precarious, as he found when his health failed in 1830. Mayett was forced to apply for parish relief and when he received what he felt were unreasonable terms, found himself in conflict with the parish overseers of the poor, the squire and magistrates. His other support came from the self-help of the labourers' friendly society at Quainton, to which he subscribed over the years, and which was a source of sick pay.

Joseph Mayett's perspective is a strongly individual and fiercely independent response to a process of modernization which caused upheaval, uncertainty and resentment. Enclosure in many parishes will be a central event in that process, an obvious focus of change and a sense of destabilization, but will seldom be a sole cause of change.

109. Self-help: banners of the village Friendly Society of Stogursey, Somerset, now kept in the local church.

Roughs and respectables

Economic triggers, technological change, population trends and landscape developments play a central part in any local history of this period, but it will also have to include the social and cultural life of the place. This means looking at the 'fixed capital' of institutions like schools, churches and chapels, pubs and institutes, libraries and newspapers, holidays and fairs, and pastimes, and through them at attitudes and groupings amongst local people, at 'outside' influences, and at sources of conflict, separateness and consensus. Here may lie clues to how soon the new kinds of settlement which were springing up, whether towns, villages, or new additions to either, became communities, and in what mould those communities developed. Were they dominated by a respectable, self-improving, disciplined and organized approach to life? If so, was this reinforced, or even imposed, by the philanthropic provision and paternalist influence of a principal employer or landowner? Or was the settlement an unregulated, physical sprawl, experiencing influxes of highly mobile outside workers to jobs where little skill was required and job security was low? In such conditions did a distinctive kind of place emerge, with speculative housing put up on an ad hoc basis for a mobile population, where the pub rather than the church or chapel was the main focus of

110. Figures of authority: the teaching staff and rector of Hook Norton, Oxfordshire. The local elementary school, built in 1855, was sponsored by the Anglican National Society.

111. Two boys in Portsmouth prison, 1899, sentenced to five days hard labour for throwing mortar at a door.

out-of-work hours, and where most of the population was impervious, if not actually resistant to the agencies of religion, education and respectability?

Some historians have coined the terms 'roughs' and 'respectables' to characterize these groups within local communities in the nineteenth century. They represent two ends of a spectrum and many places were not fixed exclusively in either mould but included elements of both. The struggle between the two cultures provides one of the keys to understanding how the old met the new. For example, in the first half of the nineteenth century traditional fairs and feasts came under attack for their rumbustious and vigorous enjoyment, and for their association in some places with indiscriminate charitable doles. Charity was very much part of the local scene in nineteenth-century England, but it was increasingly carefully targeted and often conditional giving by those recognizing themselves as middle or upper class to those recognizing themselves as working class. As for high days and holidays, the aim was to foster 'rational recreation'.

A perennial problem for local historians is that, whilst community itself is defined by the relationships of all people, the sources persistently tell us most about those at the top, economically and socially. In the nineteenth century sources begin to be 'democratized', so that, for example, in the census enumerators' books we have unprecedented detail about the whole population. This was just one government record revealing a new quality and quantity of information about 'ordinary' people. Other less official observers were also investigating and reporting on conditions in the homes and workplaces of individual families and places. Some of this was in the carefully ordered form of reports from the early statistical societies, and from professionals such as doctors and engineers. Others, such as the observations of a *Morning Chronicle* journalist on visiting Saddleworth in the Pennines in 1849 (quoted on p. 203), were more obviously impressionistic. All of this evidence brings with it certain moral baggage on the part of the compilers. The value judgements, on matters such as poverty and its causes or the nature of family life, may seem blatant. However, seen in context, the pamphlets, tracts, articles and reports, pouring out from the late eighteenth century onwards are welcome indeed to the local historian. This will be clear from just one example taken from the verbatim evidence of a witness to the Royal Commission on the Employment of Children in 1842. He describes some of the newest settlements of the period, growing up around newly opened collieries.

. . . within the last ten years collieries have been opened in very many places between the Weare and the Tees; and wherever a colliery has been opened a large village or town has been instantly built close to it, with a population almost exclusively of the colliery people, beer-shop people and small shopkeepers. The houses have either been built by the colliery proprietors, or have been so by others and let on lease to them that they might locate their people.

The village of Coxhoe, close to Clarence Heton Colliery, extends about a mile along both sides of a public road, but the houses are not continuous, there being a break every 10 or 12 houses to make a thoroughfare to the streets which run off right and left . . . The cottages are built with stone plastered with lime, with blue slate roofs, and all appear exceedingly neat, and as like to one another as so many soldiers . . . There is no yard in front of any of them, or any yard behind, or dust hole, or convenience of any kind, or any small building, such as is usually considered indispensable and necessary. Yet there was no unpleasant nuisance, no filth, nor ashes, nor decaying vegetables. All was swept and clean. It was explained that carts came round early every morning with small coals which were left at every house, and the same carts after depositing the coals at every door, moved round and came along the backs of the houses and received the ashes and all other matters, and carried them off and deposited them in a heap in an adjoining field.

The dimensions of the houses . . . were as follows: Front room, length 14ft x breadth 14ft 10in. Back room, length 14ft x breadth 10ft, communicating with which is a pantry 6ft x 3ft. Upstairs is a bedroom partly made up by a wall and a sloping roof. The ground floor is made of clay, sand and lime. The height of the front wall is generally 13ft 10ins: the height of the back wall is less. The whole expense of erecting such a cottage is £52. It could be rented for £5 a year.

112. Pit cottages, reconstructed at the open-air museum, Beamish, Co. Durham.

113. Pithill Methodist chapel 1854, reconstructed at the open-air museum, Beamish, Co. Durham. Methodism was frequently an early and formative presence in new mining settlements which had little initial community identity.

The population was estimated about 5,000. The work people of several collieries live in the village. . . . There were altogether 30 beer shops in the village. There was no Church of England church or chapel, but here as everywhere else in the collier district, the Wesleyans and Primitive Methodists had established their meetings, and had many adherents.

I was conducted into one of the cottages. . . . This house, like most of the colliers' houses in the several villages, was very clean and well furnished. In fine weather the doors are frequently left open, and . . . in every house maybe seen an eight-day clock, a chest of drawers, with brass handles and ornaments, reaching from the floor to the ceiling, a four-poster bed with a large coverlet, composed of squares of printed calico tastefully arranged, and bright saucepans, and other tin-ware utensils displayed on the walls. Most of the women take pains to make themselves, as well as their houses, look very agreeable. It must be admitted that there are exceptions and there are some women who are neither so attentive to themselves, their children or their houses, as their husbands have a right to expect.

In the collier villages are many little brick buildings used as public ovens. Small coals are put into them, and burnt until the ovens are thoroughly heated, and then the coals and ashes are swept out, and the bread put in, and by the heat of the bricks it is well baked.

Although there is not one inch of land attached to the houses in villages, there is frequently a large field divided by stakes of wood, into small plots of ground, which the colliers cultivate as potatoe gardens. The usual size maybe about a twentieth part of an acre.

Nineteenth-century Parliamentary Papers are full of such invaluably detailed testimonies. That of Coxhoe shows how new settlements were emerging totally outside existing networks of authority. If the coal owner did not control local housing, and take a direct interest in the lives and conduct of his employees and their families outside worktime, then these were self-structuring communities, at least initially. Coxhoe was probably so, as is indicated by the limited social mix, 'colliery people, beer-shop people and small shopkeepers'. The leisure institutions in Coxhoe are equally limited in kind, if not in number. Perhaps the thirty beer-shops provided supplementary income in some mining households? The Established Church is totally absent from the scene. The Methodist presence, and the descriptions of cleanliness, pride, display and taste in the colliers' homes remind us that the characteristics of a community were not just a matter of superior values instilled from above, but that people generated their own loyalties and codes. In a mining community such as Coxhoe these may be essential to understanding how it developed.

The government enquiry to which evidence was given was part of the reaction to change of the increasingly influential middle classes and, more partially and gradually, of the traditional ruling class. This response constantly colours local experiences between 1750 and 1914. The consequences of change – for working conditions, for housing, health, death rates and medical care, for street cleaning and lighting, for sewage disposal and water supply, for safe public transport, for policing and prison conditions, for education, for relationships between social classes, and for family life – were inescapable in every kind of place, urban or rural. All over the country, through national, legislative and local private actions, schools were built, places of worship restored, extended or created from new, drainage, water supply and housing conditions were grappled with, children's and adults' hours and conditions of work were gradually improved and controlled, and the old institutional fabric of parish, municipal, county and parliamentary government, which had proved so inadequate to the task of coping with change, was replaced or significantly reformed.

Coping with change: the growth of government

To some extent the local historian will find 'outside' and national factors setting the pace. At no time was this more apparent than in the 1830s, when the growth of government and the pace of reform gained unprecedented momentum. The old parish system of local government had everywhere been faltering. It continued to depend largely on unpaid, annually elected local officers, now faced with rapidly increasing populations of people who were more mobile, and included larger proportions of poor. In the 1830s a series of acts effectively ended the parish's central role in secular local affairs. The Poor Law Amendment Act of 1834 removed from the parish its principal responsibility, the relief of local poor; in 1837 the Civil Registration Act substituted central government recording of births, marriages and deaths for the parish's registers of baptisms, weddings and burials as the definitive record of vital events; the General Highways Act (1835) superseded parish responsibilities for roads; the Metropolitan Police Act (1829), the Lighting and Watching Act (1833), the Municipal Corporations Act (1835), and the County Police Act (1839) each required or enabled new forces of law and order to be set up, effectively replacing the old parish constable. This was also the decade of the 1832 Reform Act, extending the parliamentary franchise and redrawing constituencies to take account of population shifts and corruption, of the 1835 Municipal Corporations Act, reforming the government of old boroughs, and of the first central government grants to, and inspection of, local schools. All of this changed local experiences and generated new kinds of records for the local historian.

Reform and central government intervention in the localities generated strong reactions, from defenders of old-established vested interests, from champions of local autonomy and the 'old' community, and from opponents of new taxes, expenditures and officialdom. Theories of systematic structures and efficient provision of services had to contend with feelings of localism and existing patterns of provision. As the constitutional historian F. W. Maitland, who investigated many examples of local governance, observed, much had changed since 1832. 'We are becoming a much governed nation, governed by all manner of councils and boards and officers, central and local, high and low, exercising the powers which have been committed to them by modern statutes.'[4] Yet the significance of 'immemorial liberties' remained undeniable so that each borough retained its own character. This mixture of change and continuity gradually produced a range of jurisdictions which encompassed localities, often in overlapping layers.

The government of towns was reformed by the Municipal Corporations Acts of 1835 and 1882 and by the Local Government Act of 1888. Of 246 boroughs investigated in 1835 only 178 were incorporated under the new act, those rejected being considered too small and insignificant for separate status. The 'new' boroughs had to adopt a representative council structure, based on resident ratepayer franchise, with mayor, aldermen and councillors, and responsibilities for markets, police, lighting and by-laws. By 1888 there were 280 municipal boroughs, the additional ones being principally in the industrial areas of the Midlands and the north. The boroughs had grown not just in numbers but in responsibilities. Much of this growth was incremental and not uniform. For

114. Accrington, Lancashire, became a municipal borough in 1878. Changes in town government reflected the growing importance of provincial and industrial towns. Accrington's market hall of 1868–9 asserts local civic pride.

example many statutes were aimed at particular problems and provided for specific powers to tackle them. Often these powers were vested locally in existing authorities, but on a permissive or voluntary basis. A major instance was the Public Health Act of 1848, which was passed only after prolonged propaganda by reformers (including local branches of the Health of Towns Association, founded 1839) and finally spurred by a cholera outbreak in 1847. Even then the act merely permitted, not required, town councils to become public health authorities. Where councils did not exist and sufficient local people wished it, new authorities, Local Boards of Health, could be created. The larger towns tended to act first, but development was highly uneven; Liverpool had its first Medical Officer of Health in 1847, but Manchester did not appoint an MOH until 1868, and Birmingham not until 1875. A three-member General Board of Health, set up in London under the 1848 act to oversee local actions, was dissolved in 1854. The pressure to avoid compulsion from the centre, and to recognize local autonomy and voluntary effort, persisted. Nowhere was this clearer than in the important area of educational provision. Thus legislation to ensure universal access for all children to basic elementary education, when it eventually came in 1870, aimed in the words of its author, W.E. Foster, 'to complete the present voluntary system, to fill up gaps'. The existing system, of largely religious denominational schools was retained, alongside new, ratepayer elected school boards in those areas not able to make provision from existing resources. Thus boards for health or schools could appear, sometimes within, sometimes parallel with borough authorities.

One new jurisdiction affected all areas. Under the 1834 Poor Law Amendment Act poor law unions were created. These areas generally took in a town and its hinterland. They covered numbers of parishes, sometimes over-rode county boundaries, and were intended to be big enough to achieve economies of scale in expenditure and consistency of administration. Such consistency was overseen by a central body in London, the Poor Law Commission with its secretary, and nine itinerant assistant commissioners. Through this mechanism standard elements, like layouts for workhouses, or diets for their inmates, were stipulated. Local control was by a Board of Guardians, elected by a ratepayer franchise. The Guardians employed a master and other staff for the workhouse, relieving officers to visit those applying for relief in their own homes, and a medical officer. It is in the records of poor relief, on the one hand the local minute and letter books of the Boards of Guardians, the registers of admissions and discharges at the workhouse, the master's punishment books, the relieving officers' lists of relief given, and on the other hand the annual returns of the central commissioners published in Parliamentary Papers, and the voluminous correspondence of their office with the unions (now preserved in the PRO, MH12) that the relations of locality and centre, and through them much about the locality, can be discerned.

The *ad hoc* accumulation of jurisdictions became ripe for overhaul. The Local Government Act of 1871 placed poor law, sanitary matters and registration under a single Local Government Board. The next year a Public Health Act set up urban and rural sanitary districts, each to have its elected board. Through all this the ancient counties and their Quarter Sessions had continued, little changed. The Local Government Acts of 1881 and 1894 comprehensively changed and tidied structures, both urban and rural. In 1888 the county councils were created. Powers formerly vested in JPs passed to elected councils. The legislation also created the new status of county borough, which it was intended to limit to towns with populations of over 150,000 and thus avoid depriving counties of the population and revenue of smaller towns. Again local civic pride came into play and towns of 50,000 were granted distinct status as county boroughs, a total of sixty-one in 1888. The effect was to separate town and country, taking little account of the logical link between a town and its hinterland. The 1894 Act turned the rural and urban sanitary districts into Urban District and Rural District Councils. It forged a link between these councils and the Boards of Guardians (which were to continue in being until 1929) by making each District Councillor a Poor Law Guardian. The

115. Coping with change: a new jurisdiction at Stanhope, Co. Durham, 1868.

vestigial powers of the parish in civil matters were dealt with through the creation of elected Parish Councils, and in smaller places Parish Meetings. These two bodies must be distinguished from the Parochial Church Council, which now dealt purely with the concerns of the Anglican church. Both the districts and the parishes remained within county units, with the result that, as Philip Waller has remarked, 'the Government sped the country into the twentieth century with virtually unaltered medieval units'.[5] It was two of these units, the borough and the county, which were adapted as local education authorities under the 1902 Education Act, which finally co-ordinated educational provision nationally, and harnessed voluntary, denominational schools more firmly to a state system.

Coping with change: Christians and Utilitarians

To represent the 1830s and later years as a time when the provincial localities were mere recipients of reforms visited on them by Parliament and a burgeoning civil service in London would be very misleading. Much of the change to which all this was a response was most radically and acutely felt in local, provincial England. Newly assertive provincial opinion and power played a large part in framing reforms, and the battle to put them into action in the face of long-established interest groups and general conservatism was energetically fought out in places great and small throughout the nineteenth century. A rich sense of this is conveyed by George Eliot's *Middlemarch*. There the tensions between Bulstrode and Lydgate on the one hand, and Brooke and Casaubon on the other, are also those between new political, religious, medical and social ideas and traditional alignments. The old, unreformed equilibrium of county society, with its previously unchallenged right to rule the roost, is still clear to see. The alliance of landed classes in the surrounding countryside with clergy, magistrates and employers within the town is firm, but by the period in which the novel is set, 1829–32, under increasing attack. Middlemarch (based on Coventry) is expanding in size and changing in character. Men decidedly not gentlemen in the traditional mould are undeniably influential, controlling increasing amounts of money and jobs, holding opinions which they find inadequately represented within existing political structures (both national and local), and in many cases feeling strongly that the moral and practical government of the community in which they are living is wholly inadequate to the times, and that the existing establishment of 'old provincial society' is neither willing nor able to change things. This battle permeates the local history of nineteenth-century England. Many contemporary sources bear the mark of having been written by those of

116. Christians v. Utilitarians. The plaque on the village cricket pavilion at Warborough, Oxfordshire records how the Revd Herbert White saved the green 'from Goths and Utilitarians' in 1853.

one persuasion or the other. Today the green of the small Oxfordshire village of Warborough appears the epitome of an idyllic, rural cricket pitch, yet it too was part of the battleground. In 1848 the village fields were still open, but their common grazing, of which the green was a part, was ripe for more worthwhile use in the eyes of improvers. A plaque on the cricket pavilion records how the then vicar rescued the surviving green for the recreation of the inhabitants and 'from Goths and Utilitarians'.

Utilitarian ideas lay behind many legislative reforms of the 1830s and later. They informed the actions of the influential in many localities. Utilitarian solutions to problems were based on science rather than sentiment, as defined by Jeremy Bentham (1748–1832) who argued that everything could be measured in terms of utility. People made individual choices on the basis of how much pain or pleasure would result for themselves. Each individual would act on the basis of enlightened self-interest. This philosophical view of human nature had very direct effects locally, for example as the basis of the Poor Law Amendment Act of 1834, which created union workhouses. The aim was to provide relief to the able-bodied poor, but only in the workhouse in conditions of such a deterrent nature that enlightened self-interest on the pain and pleasure principle would keep people away, determined to help themselves. Public expenditure would fall, but essential needs be met. The local study of the 'new', post-1834 poor law is interesting not least in terms of whether this stringent regime was actually imposed and outdoor relief denied to the able-bodied. Solutions like the new poor law were based on general Benthamite principles allied to carefully collected, quantitative data. This was done by local groups, such as statistical societies, but primarily by numerous parliamentary investigations, Royal Commissions and Select Committees, into topics like housing, mortality, poverty, working hours, conditions and wages of men, women and children, schools and schooling and emigration. Their reports give verbatim local detail, as well as tabulations and analysis. The increasingly rigorous decennial census returns stem from the same belief in measuring the problem in order to find solutions. The accompanying tone of stern resolve and ultimate confidence in success will become familiar to every local historian of the period. The impact of the Utilitarians is undoubted, yet paradoxical. Their approach, as the new poor law shows, was rooted in individualism, an appropriate philosophy in an age of *laissez-faire*, yet Utilitarians appear as interventionists. Their argument was that conditions had to be created, out of old-fashioned inconsistency and changing circumstances, in which enlightened self-interest could operate. Hence legislation to remove distortions, the old poor law, unsafe factory conditions, inadequate education would ultimately produce a healthier, better-informed, and more efficient workforce.

The other great impetus to reform and action in the community came not from a new, secular philosophy but from Christianity. This was not the Christianity of the early eighteenth century, but one in which old certainties and structures were changing. Both Anglicanism and Nonconformity experienced major transformations under the impact of the Evangelical revival.

For the Church of England there was revival and internal reform. A state church enmeshed in the Establishment, in patronage and power, was slow to respond to the needs of those growing numbers living outside traditional communities. The Church also had to meet the challenges of other dissenting denominations, both for hearts and minds and for an accepted place institutionally and legally. The Church of England was only really stung into action in the 1820s and 1830s, action which will be very apparent locally. Schools sponsored by the National Society (full title the National Society for Promoting the Education of the Poor in the Principles of the Established Church) sprang up. New churches were built and old ones restored. Bishops clamped down on pluralism and non-residence amongst the clergy. The local norm became a resident, trained clergyman, ideally married and setting an example in family life, conducting more services, involved in educational initiatives, in local concerns and (with his family) in pastoral work, and living in a suitably appointed parsonage. For many Anglicans reform was an attempt to protect their Church's unique position as a comprehensive, national church against the encroachments of others who threatened to reduce the Church of England to the

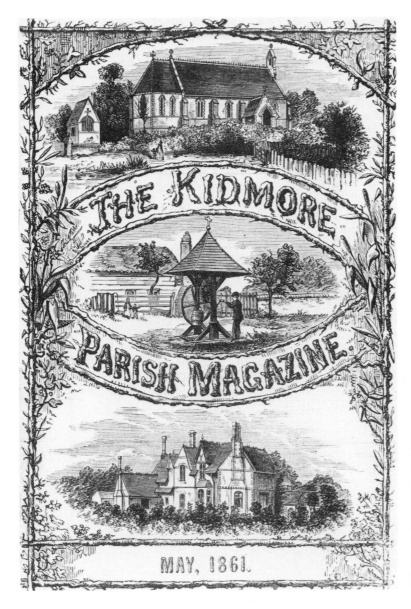

117. Church magazines are a useful record of local events, albeit denominationally biased. Kidmore End, Oxon. (1854) was one of many new Anglican parishes created to reach a neglected populace. Its magazine, depicting new church, parsonage for a resident clergyman, and improved water supply, shows the wide-ranging activities of an Established Church throwing off the comfortable complacency of the previous century.

position of one denomination in a pluralist world of different kinds of Christianity, of non-Christians and of indifference.

A major challenge here came from revived 'old' Dissent (the denominations of seventeenth-century origins, like the Baptists and Congregationalists), but most particularly from 'new' Dissent – the Methodists. Methodism was a product of evangelical revival. In its early years, it appealed strongly to a mass following through its itinerant preachers, its lay preaching, its intensely involving worship, its emphasis on sin and salvation, and on a life of grace

118. Church and chapel rivalry extended well beyond the spiritual in many places. This could mean that dissenters found only marginal sites for their buildings, unlike this Methodist chapel, boldly placed at the gates of the parish church in Thornham, Norfolk.

maintained by direct participation in local classes and meetings and by Christian living. As we shall see in case studies the early charismatic edge of Methodism was blunted by the mid-nineteenth century. It became a more bureaucratic denomination and provoked breakaways, notably the Primitive Methodists. The irreversible tide of dissenting strength was clear in the only national census of religious observance, taken in 1851. Protestant dissenters provided nearly half the church accommodation in England and Wales, and as many attended worship as the Anglicans. The church/chapel divide is an alignment constantly found by historians of urban and rural communities between 1750 and 1914. It related to class identity, social status, political allegiances, and many fiercely contested issues such as educational provision, payment of church rates, and membership of vestry government. Religious diversity was now a permanent fact of life. Alongside it may be found increasing doubt and, probably more widespread, indifference to religion and religious observance. The 1851 religious census report stated that of an estimated 12,549,326 potential worshippers 5,288,294 stayed away altogether.

Although the Christian basis of action was quite different from the calculated self-interest of the Utilitarians, the local historian will often find elements of both, even amalgamated in the same individuals. Both idioms permeate the period, as J.G. Farrell captures tellingly in the words of one of his characters in *The Siege of Krishnapur*:

> I believe that we are all part of a society which by its communal efforts of faith and reason is gradually raising itself to a higher state . . . There are laws of morality to be followed if we are to advance, just as there are rules of scientific investigation . . . the foundations on which the new men will build their lives are Faith, Science, Respectability, Geology, Mechanical Invention, Ventilation and the Rotation of Crops.

Not surprisingly some see in the Victorian period the emergence of a new religion, that of progress.

Responses to change: working-class life

Farrell's character, an official of the Indian Raj, operates in relation to a non-Christian and native populace, and it sometimes seems that the predominantly middle-class Utilitarians and Evangelicals in the mother country felt they were working on a similar basis. Because they so much dominate the sources, and were so active and effective in their crusades, it can be easy to forget other dimensions to local experience. The majority of local people were working class, the subject of moves to redeem and incorporate them in the image of an ideal modern society. There were also distinct, separate strands to their lives; in politics Chartism, the first working-class movement, with its national strength but strong community base; in trade unionism, in Co-operation, in dissenting chapels, in self-help groups like mutual improvement societies, and friendly societies, in clubs and pubs, and simply in where they lived as the separation of living areas by class became unprecedentedly clear. Out of this could come a strong sense of community, owing little to the 'social cement' of what were seen as middle-class institutions.

These strong local identities come across clearly in the increasing number of direct testimonies. In Flora Thompson's Lark Rise, a north Oxfordshire hamlet of the 1880s, there was a low level of adult church-going but a firmly imbued code of behaviour:

> Many in the hamlet . . . said they had no use for religion (but) guided their lives by the light of a few homely precepts, such as 'Pay your way and fear nobody'; 'Right's right and wrong's no man's right', 'Tell the truth and shame the devil', and 'Honesty is the best policy' . . . It was a stark code in which black was black and white was white; there were no intermediate shades.[6]

Robert Robert's *The Classic Slum* deals with similar themes in another working-class community, Salford, in the first quarter of the present century. The urban, industrial slum in which Roberts was brought up seems remote from Lark Rise yet Salford too had its stern internal discipline, enforced largely by a formidable indigenous matriarchy. It was intolerant of breaches of conformity and it was soon known if anyone erred. As Roberts recalls,

> Parents of the most respectable and conformist families were the staunchest upholders of 'discipline', though adults whose social standing was suspect or who had in any way transgressed against accepted conduct would often brag about the severity of the chastisement meted out to the erring young, in an effort to restore tarnished prestige.[7]

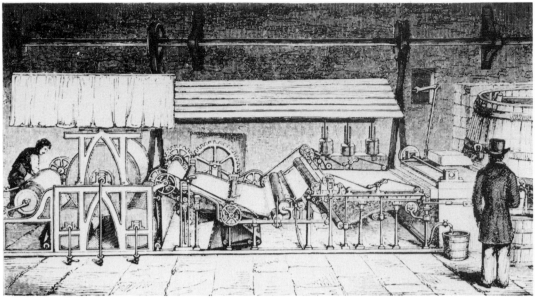

119. Changes in production processes not only altered work but profoundly affected the lives of families and whole communities. This paper-making machine of 1848 turned pulp (in the reservoir on the right) to finished paper (on the reel on the left) in minutes instead of seven or eight days by hand.

The working-class part in any local history of the nineteenth or twentieth centuries will be important, but is unlikely to be a homogeneous one. Some working-class people were influenced by the same beliefs and ideals as the concerned middle classes. As the nineteenth century progressed they were liable to be drawn more and more into networks of new provision, not least, after 1870, that of universal elementary education. Strategic concessions on issues like trade union rights and the extension of the franchise brought 'respectable' labour gradually into the mainstreams of public life. Other working-class people may make most sense to the local historian in the setting of a separate neighbourhood, as in Salford or Coxhoe, with a distinctive experience of religion, self-education, recreation, local trade union bargaining or political consciousness. Such places had their own pecking order, frequently related to work and workforce structure. Self esteem and pride in a status based on skill at work gave the male artisan bread-winner a key role in the character of the place, and created a divide between their families and those who could not, or would not, aspire to the status and stability which such work was felt to merit. Again we encounter roughs and respectables.

120. Hand processes, like this earlier nineteenth-century paper-making, involved groups of skilled artisans, secure in their status and rewards and often leading figures in their localities. Such certainties disappeared in many industries and trades by *c.* 1850.

Different phases? Pre- and post-1850

Whatever their degree of roughness, independence, or indigenous respectability, few settlements remained in one mould throughout the Victorian period. Early in industrialization the degree of flux tended to be greatest. In most sectors this phase applied in the years to *c.* 1850. However, because of the uneven pace of technological advance and, very importantly, of the implementation of mechanization, local historians need to understand the processes and chronology of any industries on their patch. For instance, mechanization and the growth of large factory units came earlier in cotton than in wool; it happened sooner in spinning than in weaving, and sooner in weaving than in carding. Likewise some coal seams became workable only when techniques of shaft-sinking, pumping water from workings, and ventilation developed, while some types of coal or lead or stone were worked only in response to a particular demand from other sectors of the economy. All of this may produce varying and lengthy periods of industrialization, and thus of local changes triggered by it. That said, by 1850 the economy was moving into a mature phase. The changes it had engendered in the physical and in the social environment were clear, as were the increasing political, institutional, religious and philosophical responses to them. In the second half of the century many local historians will discern a more stable and controlled pattern of local life emerging. Work-force structures in the main employments may be more settled, and social structures more diverse as artisan and professional groups establish themselves. A wider range of shops and services may appear. Invariably more churches were built or restored, and new chapels erected. Formal schooling increased. More work people were unionized, including from the 1880s the unskilled, and there was a relative increase in the standard of living for urban and industrial workers, who had access to cheaper foodstuffs and a growing range of mass-produced goods, as the fittings of many a cumbersomely comfortable late Victorian home show.

121. The pace of mechanization varied considerably between processes, and thus in different trades and places. Shoemaking (here in Northampton in 1869) was still in a transitional stage from workshop to factory organization following the introduction of the sewing machine in the 1850s.

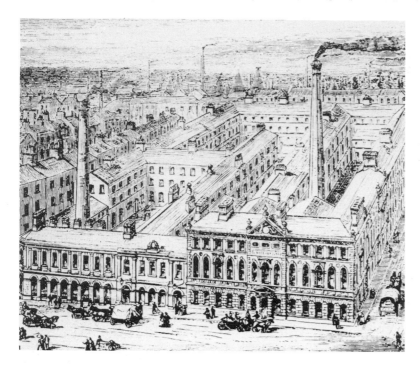

122. Cutlery making in the Sheffield area, like many other industries, developed first in small rural workshops. By 1874 it was based in steam-powered factory units like this of Messrs Rodgers and Sons in Sheffield itself.

In a more public sphere the 1850s were a boom time for the appearance of local newspapers, often the first for a locality. From their pages comes evidence of the formidable array of organized activities in a society emerging from a time of upheaval with changed institutions and channelled energies. This trend continued. It can be seen in party politics, in more broadly based Conservative and Liberal organization, in the parliamentary reformism of Lib-Lab politics, and in Labour and Socialist groupings, reformist or, less often, revolutionary. The active and organized are there too in friendly and mutual improvement societies, in the Co-operative movement, in church and chapel gilds and choirs, libraries and clothing clubs, in brass bands and cycling clubs, in public parks and organized sports, in pressure groups for causes from better drains to non-denominational schools and Anglican disestablishment. The very number and diversity of activities suggest a time of high local community identity. The local paper, in which the local historian can most readily find out about them, is itself another mark of that localism. This new-found identity, if that is what it is, certainly suggests that the raw new places and the disrupted old ones, together with the national institutions, had found a fresh *modus vivendi*, based on a recognition, if not always an acceptance, of changes in work, life-style, allegiances and representation. In this new regime the forces of nonconformity and conformity, of

123. A boom in the printed word.

124. This advertisement of *c.* 1893 speaks loudly of the development of a mass market and national suppliers. Grocery chains were appearing. Note the reference to mail order.

custom and education, still counted, but in many places its respectability seems increasingly dominant.

Cases and places

The pace of change

In 1849 Angus Bethune Reach, writing for the *Morning Chronicle* of London, ventured into the 'wild and hilly country' on the borders of Lancashire, Cheshire, Derbyshire and Yorkshire. There he found 'a hardy, industrious, and primitive race, engaged in the manufacture of flannel and cloth – sometimes in mills, sometimes by their own hearths'. Both domestic and factory production went on, some combined woollen cloth making with farming. Change was still coming, with the concentration of work in bigger units, centred on water and steam power, and with the opening up of the territory and of people's horizons by the arrival of the Leeds and Huddersfield Railway. Reach focused his attention on the Saddle-worth area and writes like a pioneer, penetrating strange wilds of the country only recently 'thrown open. . . . to the world'. From

this parochially metropolitan perspective he summed up neighbouring but very different local communities.

Life revolved around the nature of work. 'Birling' involved
picking imperfections from the surface of woven cloth, and was
done by women. In the country birling went on at home and in the
towns in the mills. There Reach found women, some married,
working happily together in some numbers. There was giggling,
'symptoms . . . of a relaxed state of discipline', and the tell-tale
aroma of pipe smoke. By contrast, in a home where birling was
carried out by the daughter, she earned enough to pay the rent, the
father worked in the mill as the main provider, and the mother
cared for a home which was 'neat, warm, comfortable and clean'.
Here were the ingredients of separation of home and work, and of
the roles of men and women. Reach clearly approved of what he
saw.

Quite another way of life emerged away from the town. In
Saddleworth Fold, up the hillside, were clusters of old-fashioned
houses still occupied by families 'who are at once spinners, weavers
and farmers'. A household here was presided over by a formidable,
elderly patriarch, 'a splendid specimen of humanity – tall, stalwart
with a grip like a vice, and a back as upright as a pump bolt'. The
household included grown-up sons and daughters, grandchildren
and journeymen, who ate and worked together. There were looms
and spinning jennies, as well as dairy cows. The adult sons received
no money wages but took board, lodging and clothing and time off
to hunt. In this transitional world, from pre-industrial into industrial, disciplines of time and work had not taken root. This was also
true in local mills, as the workers took off with their dogs in pursuit
of hares or lures, and in defiance of mill discipline. As a millowner
confided to Reach, 'several mills were left standing, and . . . more
than 500 carders, slubbers, spinners, and weavers formed the field'.

At the village of Delph Reach found the domestic system more in
retreat, with patched windows, beds and looms crammed together,
and handlooms and spinning jennies no match for power mules and
looms. Amid this air of decay he encountered a weaver, 'a very
intelligent man – much more so, indeed, than most of his class', who
appreciated that 'Machinery . . . had been a great advantage to the
weaver as long as it was pretty simple and cheap, for then he could
use it for his own behoof.' Yarn that had taken a dozen people with a
dozen wheels over a week to spin, his wife could produce with a
'hand-jenny' in two-and-a-half days. This represented a medium
state of machinery. Now a power mule did the job in a morning. Life
had been prosperous in the medium state of machinery. Now it was
hard, even with the earnings of several people, for hand labour rates
were depressed and falling, and capital costs and specialized market
demands beyond the small man. The focus was now in the towns, in
the valley. The weaver's neighbours produced milk, taken on

125. The Piece Hall, Halifax, 1775 is a monument to the hey-day of domestic cloth production. It has 300 rooms in which clothiers traded in cloths produced in rural homes for miles around the town.

donkey-back down into Staleybridge or Oldham for the factory hands to consume. The balance in Delph was shifting back to agriculture, but pursued in a very different context. Some chose to remain, eking out an increasingly difficult living; others swelled the populations of the growing industrial towns.

Coketown

The environment and spirit of the industrial town have never been more graphically characterized than by Charles Dickens in *Hard Times* (1854). To him Coketown was 'a triumph of fact'.

> It was a town of red brick, or of brick that would have been red if the smoke and ashes had allowed it; but as matters stood it was a town of unnatural red and black like the painted face of a savage. It was a town of machinery and tall chimneys, out of which interminable serpents of smoke trailed themselves for ever and ever, and never got uncoiled. It had a black canal in it, and a river that ran purple with ill-smelling dye, and vast piles of buildings full of windows, where there was a rattling and a trembling all day long, and where the piston of the steam-engine worked monotonously up and down like the head of an elephant in a state of melancholy madness. It contained several large streets all very

like one another, and many small streets still more like one another, inhabited by people equally like one another, who all went in and out at the same hours, with the same sound upon the same pavements, to do the same work, and to whom every day was the same as yesterday and to-morrow, and every year the counterpart of the last and the next.

These attributes of Coketown were in the main inseparable from the work by which it was sustained; against them were to be set off, comforts of life which found their way all over the world, and elegancies of life which made, we will not ask how much of the fine lady, who could scarcely bear to hear the place mentioned. The rest of its features were voluntary, and they were these.

You saw nothing in Coketown but what was severely work-ful. If the members of a religious persuasion built a chapel there – as the members of eighteen religious persuasions had done – they made it a pious warehouse of red brick . . . All the public inscriptions in the town were painted alike, in severe characters of black and white. The jail might have been the infirmary, the infirmary might have been the jail, the town-hall might have been either, or both, or anything else, for anything that appeared to the contrary in the graces of their construction. Fact, fact, fact, everywhere in the material aspect of the town; fact, fact, fact, everywhere in the immaterial. The M'Choakumchild school was all fact, and the school of design was all fact, and the relations between master and man were all fact, and everything was fact between the lying-in hospital and the cemetery, and what you couldn't state in figures, or show to be purchaseable in the cheapest market and saleable in the dearest, was not, and never should be, world without end, Amen . . .

Dickens's view is one of angry condemnation. Its images, of rattling and trembling, of monotonous, mechanical melancholy madness, and of a populace for whom 'every day was the same as yesterday and to-morrow' are memorable. This is a literary work and not an historical account, yet literature can help the local historian to see beyond the seemingly interminable wrangles over rates and drains, mortality statistics or government inspection, to appreciate the experiences and points of view they reflected. Since we know that Dickens's Coketown was largely 'inspired' by Preston this archetype of an industrial town can be tested further from the local historian's point of view.

Physically Preston presents row upon row of terraced houses built to house the work-force needed to keep the cotton mills in operation. As the story of its housing shows Preston was above all a 'workful place'. A guide described Preston as late as 1795 as 'a handsome well-built town. . . . rendezvous of fashion and so-ciety'. Cotton spinning had already been introduced in 1777, and

126. 'A workful place', Preston, Lancashire in 1927.

by 1801 the population of some 6,000 had already doubled. By 1851 68,000 people lived in Preston. The extra people were crammed into existing areas; houses were sub-divided; cellars were occupied; courts and gardens behind existing frontages, including those of major streets, were infilled, creating cramped and over-crowded slums with no or little water supply, unventilated, with open drains and accumulated refuse. In 1849 an inspector for the newly-created local Board of Health reported that Bolton's Court, off Church Street, had

> a range of piggeries and open dung-heaps, with a large trough for the storing and mixing of manure. Near is the National School with 700 or 800 children, and on the opposite side are the gas-works, once in the suburb, but beyond which the town has rapidly spread. In Bolton's Court are also eight public slaughter houses.

The growth of such towns was unregulated. John Robertson, a Manchester surgeon, told the Committee on the Health of Towns in 1840 that

> New cottages, with or without cellars, huddled together row behind row, may be seen springing up in many parts. . . . With

such proceedings as these the authorities cannot interfere. A cottage row may be badly drained, the street may be full of pits, brimful of stagnant water, a receptacle for dead cats and dogs, yet no one may find fault.

Much of Preston's additional housing was this new terraced, usually two-up and two-down cottaging. The front door opened straight off the street into the main living room, with an open fire or range for cooking. Through and beyond this room was the second downstairs space, the wash-house or back kitchen, with a boiler for heating water, a tin tub for baths, a wash-tub for laundry, and a slop-stone or stone sink. If there was piped water the single, cold tap would be here. From here stairs went up to two bedrooms, the front one usually with a fireplace, which was only occasionally used. Outside was a backyard, surrounded by other buildings, and with a privy, opening into a cesspool. Preston also had some back-to-backs, usually one-down and two-up, with no backyard, and subsequent problems over siting of the privy.

With this pattern of housing development Preston suffered badly from the health problems of the time. In the 1840s, Preston mortality rates were 28 per thousand; in the 1850s they worsened to over 30, when the average for England (in 1851) was 21.8; as the national experience improved, falling to a rate of 19.7 by 1881, Preston's mortality still stood in the 1870s at 30.26.

Some communities tackled their housing problems through improved or model schemes. These were commonly associated with philanthropists and benevolent employers, whose motives may present an amalgam of moral and religious conscience at the plight of their fellows, with the economic interest of having a fit, conveniently located, and grateful work-force, with an element of fear about the reactions of a majority with unaddressed and profound grievances. Most housing initiatives of this kind have a strong sponsor's message. For example, the by-words of Henry Ashworth of Turton near Bolton were Thrift, Order, Promptitude and Perseverance. The rewards of these virtues would be Prosperity and Respectability, and nowhere were these to become more clearly displayed than in Victorian homes.

Preston was little helped by such schemes. Improvements came only with fiercely and persistently resisted intervention by public authorities. The 1848 Public Health Act permitted the establishment of local Boards of Health with powers to make by-laws. Many things could be regulated: new houses might be required to have drains and a privy, building plans could be subjected to scrutiny, cellar dwellings might be banned, action could be taken to improve public water supply and regulate burial grounds. Preston was clearly ripe for such treatment. Where they existed privies and middens were in tiny yards where ventilation and cleansing were

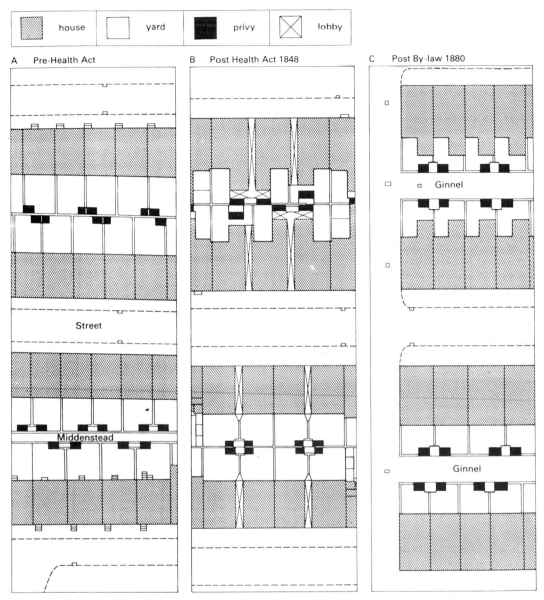

| house | yard | privy | lobby |

A   Pre-Health Act

B   Post Health Act 1848

C   Post By-law 1880

Street

Middenstead

Ginnel

Ginnel

127. Three layouts of houses in Preston. A: With privies in back yards reached either through the houses (top), or by way of a middenstead (bottom). B: Post 1848 Health Act, with privies reached by lobbies between every two houses leading to yards. C: Post 1880 by-laws, with privies in back yards reached by back lanes or ginnels. (From A. Quiney, *House and home* (1986).)

difficult, if not impossible. The town had only twelve scavengers, so to have a privy cleared every three months would be lucky. With some reluctance the town council set up a local Board of Health in 1850. One result can be seen in the town's surviving terraces. Between the front doors of adjoining houses appeared an additional opening giving direct access for the scavengers to a rear yard. Such 'tunnel-back' houses often had more rooms, three-up and three-down, with the front room taking on the role of parlour, receptacle of prized furnishings, its tidiness preserved by only occasional use. An internal hall or passage now led to the stairs.

Between 1851 and 1881 the population of Preston rose by over 40 per cent, but its number of houses by over 80 per cent. A system of sewers was completed in 1865, after fifteen years of debate. Yet mortality rates did not improve. Many houses were not connected to the new drainage system, many were still the old, pre-1850 stock, and even the 'new' housing was cramped, with typical plots of 15-foot frontage by 36-foot depth for a house and yard. Between 1880 and 1900 one in five babies died in Preston during their first year of life. A prime cause was infantile diarrhoea. Germs from privies were polluting water and penetrating houses. Yet the correspondence columns of local newspapers retail continuing objections to regulation, as a preventative of economic growth, a deterrent to investment, an annoyance to the building trade, and a worry to the ignorant working classes. Despite such opinion legislation was extended. The Public Health Act of 1872 made the appointment of a Medical Officer of Health mandatory for Preston, and this was eventually done in 1874 on a half-time basis. Further by-laws were drafted, aimed at ventilating drains and preventing pollution of houses, and also at opening up the offending back yards, so that all subsequent houses had yards of a minimum of 240 square feet, served by a ginnel 12 feet wide. The streets of Preston still bear the marks of these changes today. The by-laws were confirmed in 1876, but the requirement for ginnels omitted until 1880, during which time plans for various developments on the old pattern were pushed through, and further 'unimproved' houses subsequently built. The effects of reform worked their way through in wider streets, back lanes, and houses with more rooms and higher ceilings. This happened only after the loss of many

128. Corner shop and terraced, two-up, two-down houses, Albert Road, Preston. Note the entrances to lobbies leading to yards between the paired front doors of the post-1848 Health Act houses on the left.

lives, the spirited resistance of vested interests, and the slow adaptation to urban life of the inhabitants, urban incomers themselves. As late as 1883 the Preston MOH reported:

> There is a strong disposition on the part of many of the working classes to crowd up their already confined yards with pig-styes, hen-roosts and similar structures.

Only at the turn of the century was there significant improvement and even then local facts of life remained hard. In 1901–10 infant mortality (measured as deaths in the first year of life per 1,000 live births) in Preston was measured at 158, when the England and Wales average was 127; in 1921–5 the comparative figures were 107 and 76, and in 1926–30, 94 and 68.

If the buildings of a town like Preston tell much of its sometimes painful transition from pre-industrial market and social centre to large, working-class, industrial town, then circumstances of the families and households living in those same houses and homes reveal even more. Michael Anderson has used the census enumerators' books for 1841, 1851 and 1861 to analyse family and household in Preston. He applies sociological approaches to historical evidence. We already know of the rapid, local population growth, to some 68,000 in 1851. Local historians interested in large places such as Preston need to look, as Anderson does, to techniques such as sampling. His study is based on a 10 per cent sample. This indicates that in 1851 70 per cent of those living in Preston had been born elsewhere. 40 per cent came from within ten miles, and in all 70 per cent from under thirty miles. Within this area of movement many had moved a good deal, from village to town, and from town to town. Economic survival was the driving force. Perhaps the most marked instance of this was the increase from 3.3 to 7.4 per cent of Preston's Irish-born population between 1841 and 1851, the time of the potato famines.

It was long held that the typical family of the pre-industrial England was large, extended by generation and kin, and mutually supportive. By contrast the family produced by modernization was small, nuclear (consisting only of parents and their children), more private, individualistic and less community-oriented. Peter Laslett and others have radically corrected the view of the pre-industrial household, showing it typically to have been relatively small (around 4.5 to 5 people) and kept so by infant mortality and the absence of older children in education or work. Anderson's Preston families suggest that the typing of industrial families has also been misleading. In 1851 10 per cent of them were sharing houses; a higher proportion than those known from earlier sources had co-resident adult children; more households had other kin as lodgers; and more had grandparents living in. Far from retreating into a new, introverted, smaller household in Preston the response to a strange environment was the development of new solidarities. Larger households meant practical savings, on rent and food; kin coming to live with family contacts in the town got employment through relatives already working in the mills; since earning opportunities were overwhelmingly in cotton nearly a quarter of married women with children (1:5 of those with children under ten) worked in cotton mills. The child care offered by grandparents was highly valued, and helped the grandparents avoid the union workhouse in that trough of the poverty cycle, old age. Within the new streets of terraces, corner shops, pubs, factories and work-shops, new communities rooted in coping and adapting to new necessities were generated.

Anderson, writing in the 1970s about how ordinary families have varied, concluded that 'the working class have come, at least at present, something of a full circle, from pre-industrial kinship weakened because the problems were so great and the resources so small, through a functional 'traditional' kinship system, to a situation where kinship is again weakened but now, by contrast, because the problems are reduced, resources are so much increased, and ready alternatives are open to all'.

Many local historians working on the last hundred and fifty years will recognize this pattern. Certainly when Elizabeth Roberts studied Preston between 1890 and 1940 she found the neighbour-hood life emerging in Anderson's period of study alive and well. Preston was still primarily a cotton town. It had grown by 1911 to 117,088, of whom 45 per cent of those working were in cotton. Preston, and other towns with large proportions of women in the work-force, always attracted much contemporary comment on the consequences, frequently presented as dire, of working womanhood. It is on women's work that Roberts concentrates in a study based substantially on oral history, a source becoming available for the first time by this period. In Preston in 1911 54.3 per cent of females over ten were at work, and of these 67 per cent were in textiles. The picture which emerges is of a world in which the women were decidedly unequal in the public sphere, in law, politics and employment and pay, but were at the centre of individual households and whole neighbourhoods. They held sway in managing family budgets, in raising children, and in operating a strict code of community behaviour. Roberts found that this distinct life-style centred on a 'universal social norm of respect-ability' with roots in a pragmatic, broadly Christian approach to life. There was New Testament neighbourliness alongside Old Testament justice and punishment, there was rejection of stealing, swearing and adultery, there was suppression of sexuality, there was belief in the saving properties of work and damning con-sequences of idleness, there was the discipline of punctuality, obedience, the Methodist emphasis on 'cleanliness is next to

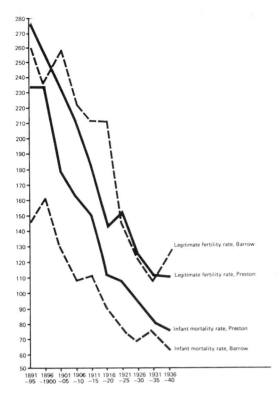

Legitimate fertility rate, Barrow

Legitimate fertility rate, Preston

Infant mortality rate, Preston

Infant mortality rate, Barrow

129. (LEFT) Falling fertility and infant mortality rates, Barrow and Preston 1891–1940. Legitimate fertility rate = number of live births per 1,000 married women aged 15–44, infant mortality rate = number of babies dying before first birthday per 1,000 born. Source: Medical Officers of Health annual reports.

130. (RIGHT) Women's talk, Kiln Lane, Skerton, Lancaster, 13 June 1927, photographed by a local amateur photographer, Sam Thompson.

godliness'. In some households a strong element of class conscious-ness and political activism came into play. No community is monolithic. There were the dictatorial husbands and fathers, whose womenfolk were allowed little role, there were the homes where drink diluted conformity, there were the graduations within and on the bounds of the working class, of the skilled, semi-skilled and unskilled, and of the shopkeepers. Yet despite these variations, life in the industrial, urban working-class neighbourhoods which were now the majority experience in England, had the kind of distinct character seen in Preston. It was strongly local in feeling, influenced by 'outside' factors like Board of Health by-laws, or the fortunes of the textile industry, but by the late nineteenth century stable and stubborn in its self-generating life-style. These old working-class social patterns have been slow to change. Elizabeth Roberts believes they only did so after the Second World War, although the lives of her interviewees began to alter between the wars.

They were part of the decline in fertility; in Barrow-in-Furness, another of her areas of study, the three women whose mothers had the largest number of children (21, 16 and 15 respectively) them-selves had two, one and two children. Life-chances, health, oppor-tunities through education, work methods at work and at home, were changing radically. To repeat Michael Anderson's comparison of then and now, 'the problems are reduced, resources are so much increased, and ready alternatives are open to all'. This has completely altered the nature of local life. Present-day local historians have to grapple with the wholesale, physical redevelopment of many neighbourhoods, with the disappearance of the economic activities around which communities were centred, and with a great gulf in outlook, if not a positive reaction against 'Victorian' attitudes. Because we may be dealing with the relatively recent past it is important not to forget the degrees of difference from the present day when it comes to interpreting the evidence. Fortunately there is no lack of such evidence.

This section has drawn on the work of Anthony Quiney in 'Two-up, two-down', chapter five of his *House and home. A history of the small English house* (1986); Michael Anderson in *Family structure in nineteenth-century Lancashire* (1971); and Elizabeth Roberts in *A Woman's place. An oral history of working-class women, 1890–1940* (1984). The sources used in their local studies, or quoted elsewhere in this section, are:

* *census returns*.
* *Parliamentary Papers*. Both the annual returns of 'new' departments like the Registrar-General's, or the Poor Law Board and the evidence of specific enquiries.
* *newspapers*, like the *Morning Chronicle* series on 'The life and labour of the poor', from which our account of Saddleworth is drawn, but particularly the burgeoning local papers.
* *records* of the multiplicity of local jurisdictions created in the nineteenth century, for example the local Medical Officer of Health's annual reports for Preston. Public health and housing by-laws led to the requirement for:
* deposited *house plans*, which should be used alongside the evidence of:
* *standing buildings* and
* *large scale Ordnance Survey maps* (at 6 in and 25 in to the mile) and plans of some 400 towns at a scale of 1:500.
* *contemporary photographs*. It is not just photos from the earliest period of photography in the mid-nineteenth century that bear close examination. Those of the 1930s, like that of Bolton on the back of this book, showing by-law, terraced housing, cheek by jowl with the mill, showing daily dress, and the pervasive smokiness of the atmosphere, record a lost way of life. The Gateshead street scene is even more recent. Such evidence may link particularly well with that of:
* *oral history* and
* *literature*. For those periods where direct testimony is lacking, and even where it is available, a reading of Dickens, or J.G. Farrell, or Hardy or many others may well help the local historian to inject into her or his questions some of the imagin-

ation and understanding which bring greater insights in interpreting the local evidence from other sources.

Rural experiences

Not all industrial lives were lived in towns. Industrial villages continued to exist and as communities to have things in common both with town and countryside. Such places were the villages of Deerness Valley in County Durham. Settlements like Waterhouses, Quebec-Hamsteels, Esh Winning and Cornsay Colliery owe their existence, as the names of the last two clearly signal, wholly to the opening up of coal workings in the valley after 1850. Round the workings, drift mines in the west of the valley and deeper shafts further east as the geology changes, grew first utilitarian terraces of housing for the immigrant labour working the mines, and then distinctive communities. Their rise and decline has been recorded by two very different local studies. They are Ken Clark's *Deerness. A short industrial and social history* (1987), an affectionate compilation of information, photos and recollections by a local resident, and Robert Moore's *Pit-men, preachers and politics* (1974), a sociologist's account of the valley villages, centring on the interaction between two formative influences for the communities, work and religion, in the dominant form of Methodism.

The villages grew from virtually nothing, in a very short time. They were products of wider economic circumstances, created to exploit the high quality gas and coking coal much in demand for gas production in London and the south-east, and coking coal for steel making in Middlesbrough, in turn supplying the shipbuilding yards on the banks of the Tyne, Tees and Wear. Mine ownership shows this connection, with some employers also having interests in steel, a sign of the trend to integrated industrial enterprises and larger units of ownership and employment after 1850.

In the final analysis the fortunes of the villages were wholly prey to such outside factors, yet they give the impression of isolation, in their rural setting and from established institutions. The essential ingredients of life soon became more than the pit and adjacent housing. Each place had its chapel or chapels, with Methodism, Wesleyan and Primitive, earliest and strongest. There were pubs, schools, Co-op shops, reading rooms and miners' institutes, cricket, football, horticultural societies, leek growing, pigeon and rabbit raising. In some places the benevolence of the mine owners was a factor. That is how *The Colliery Guardian* saw Waterhouses in a rosy account of 24 October 1863:

A new school, erected by Messrs. Pease, was opened at their colliery known as Pease's West Brandon or Waterhouses, on Monday.

131. Industry in the countryside.

132. A pit head at the open-air museum, Beamish, Co. Durham.

133. The pits of the Deerness Valley, Co. Durham were opened from the 1850s, but within a century closures had begun. Already large-scale tree planting masks the industrial landscape.

The village of Waterhouses (County Durham) is in many respects a model one. It is entirely new, and the houses of the men, well built of fine brick . . . A good sized plot of ground suitable for a vegetable garden, is attached to each, and for the benefit of such miners as are disposed for the fattening of livestock, a pig-sty is placed at the end of the garden. Great attention has been paid to sanitary arrangements and complete drainage renders these model cottages and premises dry, healthy and comfortable. There are about a hundred such houses the property of the coal company; but in the immediate neighbour-hood enterprising grocers, butchers and one publican have built or rented other houses.

The physical well-being of their labourers being thus cared for, the owners of the colliery have lost no time in providing for the education of the children of the miners.

The sinking of the pit, a most difficult and really troublesome work, was completed only some three or four years ago, and now there exists in this almost Utopian village a good and commodious schoolhouse, and, what is of more importance, a competent school master.

In other parts of the valley paternalism had even less of a role. At Waterhouses a new Anglican parish was created in 1879, but at East Hedley Hope and Hedley Hill the landscape was one of pit, terraces, coking ovens, Primitive Methodist church, pub and school. The heyday of these villages was between 1880 and 1920. They generated their own way of life remarkably rapidly. Robert Moore has identified the communal values imbued by Methodism as a formative force. Rather than Methodism being a religious affiliation limited to those formally associated with this particular denomination, he finds it a much more pervasive source of activities, leadership and generally accepted values. Methodism has been viewed by historians in a variety of ways. Some point to the way in which it fostered dissent, provided opportunities for participation and leadership in local classes and societies, and generated concepts of equality which translated into leadership in the emergent labour movement. Others have seen Methodism, with its emphasis on sin, individual salvation and achieving a state of grace through self-discipline and hard work, as a cause of personal repression and sexual guilt, and a channel of social control by employers over employees at work and in general life. A third view is that Methodism had a particularly strong psychological appeal to those whose lives were being disrupted by change, and helped by providing participation and involvement in this world, but hope of ultimate salvation in the next. This focus effectively defused dissatisfaction and active, class-based, resistance to their present lot. Moore found in the Deerness Valley that Methodism

134. Religious revivalist service in a coalmine, *c.* 1860.

did provide a community consensus, despite the presence of other Christian denominations and despite the inequalities of employer and employed. This ethical and individual view of the world dominated any political or economic view. It was a world of saved and unsaved rather than of employer and employed. A belief in the equality of men before God served to defuse resentment, at least while relative prosperity lasted. The Methodists provided leadership in the villages, in politics, industrial bargaining and in social mores until the economic fortunes of the coalfield began to falter. Then conflicts of economic interest became undeniable and could no longer be negotiated away as the righting of a misunderstanding or of a temporary imbalance in market forces, which was equally regretted by mutually respecting Liberal Methodist working-class leaders and locally known employers. The 1920s saw prolonged and bitter strikes over wage cuts.

At East Hedley Hope the pit closed in 1936, and finally, after reworking, in 1945. In 1962 the school was demolished, as Chapel Row terrace had been in 1952. In 1963 the Miners' Institute shut, in 1966 the Wesleyan Methodist chapel closed, as had the railway, to be followed by the local post office in the 1970s. In 1911 808 people lived there in 109 houses; by 1984 there were 91 in 45 houses. The same fate overtook other villages, and the scars of the workings are now planted over in an apparent reversion to ruralism. As Ken Clark has written of Esh Winning, '(the colliery) closed in 1968, dying like an aged parent, leaving its mature offspring, the village, to survive on whatever scraps of industry might fall its way'.

Many local historians will be looking at village histories but at places which remained overwhelmingly agricultural and which had centuries of previous development. There too religion will be a

135. The former Esh Winning Miners' Institute, built 1923.

revealing aspect, as James Obelkevich argues in his study of South Lindsey in Lincolnshire between 1825 and 1875. He finds that class differences became increasingly clear and that styles of religious behaviour directly reflected this. The gentry had an 'ex officio' commitment to the Church of England, with occasional excursions into Roman Catholicism, but never into Protestant dissent. Farmers had mixed allegiances, with some of the better-off prominent in Wesleyanism and setting an example in domestic respectability. Craftsmen and shopkeepers were important in Methodism, as preachers, stewards and class leaders. Nearly one-third of Primitive Methodist local preachers were drawn from this group. Labourers had the most mixed reactions to organized religion. There was some nominal conformity. The pressures of landlord or employer could be great, especially in small rural places. Charitable help was sometimes tied to church attendance. There was also genuine religious fervour, an emotional mainstay in a difficult world, as Joseph Mayett found. Then there was a strong survival of unofficial beliefs and practices, of pagan superstitions, customs, explanations of misfortune, and observance of the natural world, which Obelkevich feels amounted to a popular religion.

During the mid-nineteenth century Obelkevich finds the Church of England active and reforming, assertive of its 'natural' leadership. The chapels fulfilled a different role. 'The church was the forum of respectability and deference, and the chapel the arena for saving of souls.' During this period the fervour of the Methodist experience lessened as first Wesleyanism, and then to a lesser extent the always more radical Primitives, evolved from 'a religion of the heart' to 'tranquil denominationalism' and increasing introversion. The balance between these religious positions, and between them and those indifferent or resistant to religious observance tells a great deal about the character of a community. For example, in Flora Thompson's Lark Rise the nearest parish church is in the next village, 'Candleford', which would appear an obvious candidate for stability and conformity, and indeed Sunday morning service there sounds much like Obelkevich's 'pre-eminent ritual of social stability':

> The Squire's and clergyman's families had pews in the chancel, with backs to the wall on either side, and between them stood two long benches for the schoolchildren, well under the eyes of authority. Below the steps down into the nave stood the harmonium, played by the clergyman's daughter, and round it was ranged the choir of small schoolgirls. Then came the rank and file of the congregation, nicely graded, with the farmer's family in the front row, then the Squire's gardener and co-achman, the schoolmistress, the maidservants, and the cottagers, with the Parish Clerk at the back to keep order.

However, Flora Thompson is clear about the nature of many people's attachment to the Church:

> If the Lark Rise people had been asked their religion, the answer of nine out of ten would have been 'Church of England' for practically all of them were christened, married, and buried as such, although, in adult life, few went to church between the baptisms of their offspring. The children were shepherded there after Sunday school and about a dozen of their elders attended regularly; the rest stayed at home, the women cooking and nursing, and the men, after an elaborate Sunday toilet, which included shaving and cutting each other's hair and much puffing and splashing with buckets of water, but stopped short before lacing up boots or putting on a collar and tie, spent the rest of the day eating, sleeping, reading the newspaper, and strolling round to see how their neighbours' pigs and gardens were looking.

There was Dissent in Cottisford parish. According to the 1851 religious census thirty Wesleyan Methodists met in an ordinary cottage for worship every Sunday. This was still the case during Flora's childhood some forty years later, and she and her brother, having duly attended the Anglican morning service, escaped there in the evening to a very different and intriguing religious world. The meeting was held in the main living room of a local cottage, with whitewashed walls, lamp-lit, an open fire, cleared of everyday furniture except for the clock and a pair of red china dogs on the mantelpiece. The congregation were greeted by the householder with a handshake and a 'God bless you', sat down on scrubbed wooden benches, sang Sankey and Moody hymns unaccompanied, heard extempore and direct conversations with God – calling for rain or deliverance of a pig from disease. This direct, individual communication with the deity was at the heart of the religious experience. Flora, who thought God would know all these things already, found it unsophisticated, entertaining, but as a spectacle less impressive than the Anglican rituals of the morning. Yet Flora's final conclusion on Methodism in Cottisford is clear and revealing of the very different functions Dissent of this kind fulfilled as opposed to Anglicanism. 'Methodism, as known and practised there, was a poor people's religion, simple and crude; but its adherents brought to it more fervour than was shown by the church congregation and appeared to obtain more comfort and support from it than the church could give. Their lives were exemplary.'

The 1851 religious census returns for Cottisford also reveal that, even when every attendance at church or chapel is counted (and as Flora's Sunday shows some may represent the same people going to more than one service), some 48 per cent of this rural population did not attend worship of any kind. This is not exceptional; local historians may find higher levels of non-attendance in other places, evidence which counters any popular picture of a devout and unquestioning period.

Whether people went to church or chapel or neither is an indicator of whether a village fell into the category of open or closed. This model is one of the most useful to historians of rural communities. It draws on a distinction recognized and employed by nineteenth-century observers. It has been developed by twentieth-century local and social historians, one of whom, Dennis Mills, has summed up the descriptive characteristics of open and closed as follows:

OPEN	CLOSED
Large populations	Small populations
High population density	Low population density
Rapid population increases *c.* 1851	Slow population increases
Many small proprietors	Large estates
Peasant families	Gentlemen's residences
Small farms	Large farms
High poor rates	Low poor rates
Rural industries and craftsmen	Little industry and few craftsmen
Shops and public houses plentiful	Few shops and public houses
Housing poor, but plentiful	Housing good, but in short supply
Nonconformity common	Strong Anglican control
Radicalism and independence strong in politics and social organizations	Deference strong in politics and social organizations
Poachers	Gamekeepers

These types of community are readily recognizable on the ground, most obviously in the case of the closed, estate village, but no one can reasonably suggest that every place is one or the other. Rather the two types stand at either end of a spectrum. The possible intermediate gradations have been drawn out by Mills, using the most common means of quantifying differences, distribution of landownership.

A CLOSED (i) *Squire's village*; resident landlord owning at least half the acreage.

             (ii) *Absentee landlord's village*; at least half acreage owned by absentee proprietor.

B OPEN   (i) *Freehold village*; more than 40 proprietors or 20–40 proprietors with an average of less than 40 acres each.

             (ii) *Divided villages*; fulfilling none of the above criteria.

OPEN VILLAGES   CLOSED VILLAGES

Peasant   Divided   Absentee Landlord's   Estate

The Peasant System   The Estate System

This approach is useful, but has the effect of focusing on landowning as the prime mover in making open or closed communities. Local studies may show otherwise. For example, Castle Acre in Norfolk became well known in nineteenth-century accounts as an archetypal open community, large, uncontrolled, the nearest magistrate seven miles away, and poor but plentiful housing. Castle Acre was certainly open but, as Sarah Banks has shown, was 97 per cent owned by the Cokes of Holkham. The Cokes chose not to exercise a paternalist role in housing, education or charity. The active ingredient was the 3 per cent of small proprietors who owned a stock of cheap housing. The availability of housing exercised a strong pull on those in the surrounding area. Castle Acre grew in size and landowners in surrounding villages drew on its labour surplus for their work-forces without having to house them in the small, estate-dominated villages elsewhere in the neighbourhood. Thus open and closed villages are often in symbiotic relationship with each other. They cannot be measured solely in terms of landowning, as traced in land tax assessments, or rating and valuation records. Rather a range of indicators, including religious nonconformity should be sought, with the descriptions and listings in commercial directories often a good starting point. The way in which people responded to these different types of community is summed up by Flora Thompson's father's choice to live in Lark Rise, although rents were higher:

> The first charge on the labourer's ten shillings was house rent. Most of the cottages belonged to small tradesmen in the market town, and the weekly rents ranged from one shilling to half a crown. Some labourers in other villages worked on farms or estates where they had their cottages rent free; but the hamlet people did not envy them, for 'Stands to reason', they said, 'they've allus got to do just what they be told, or out they goes, neck and crop, bag and baggage'. A shilling, or even two shillings a week, they felt was not too much to pay for the freedom to live and vote as they liked and go to church or chapel or neither as they preferred.

Each town, village or hamlet will be part of a pattern of such differences and interrelationships.

The fortunes of rural communities are well summarized by the experience of Ashwell in north Hertfordshire. B.J. Davey has studied this open village between 1830 and 1914. In the early nineteenth century it was a place of some 750 people which Davey considers a 'genuine, vital community, a parish society which most people found a

136. (OPPOSITE, ABOVE) Chenies, Buckinghamshire: the picturesque tidiness of an estate or 'closed' village on the estates of the Dukes of Bedford.

137. (OPPOSITE, BELOW) Hook Norton Club Day, 1908. Festivities in an open village, where the club or friendly society met in the Sun Inn (top left), provided some insurance from members' contributions against ill-health and for a decent burial, and once a year, in Whitsun week, a church service, a pub feast, and afternoon jollifications for families.

satisfactory framework for a difficult existence'. All those who lived in the village worked in the village. There was absentee landownership and no squire. The community lived by agriculture and associated crafts and trades. The open fields were not enclosed until 1863. There were ten large farms, largely tenanted. Ashwell's openness was emphasized by the high proportion (about a quarter of the adult male population in 1841) who were craftsmen or tradesmen, or their apprentices or employees. They ranged from carpenters, bricklayers, wheelwrights, blacksmiths, millers, bakers, publicans and grocers to a rope-maker and a rat-catching family. Just under half the adult male population were agricultural labourers. Generally work was regular and poor rates low, largely because of supplementary income earned at weaving, lace-making, and increasingly straw-plaiting. This was done by the women and girls for sale in Hitchin. Housing standards were poor, but the community was largely self-sustaining. The parish was governed by its own members and according to mutually recognized interests and concerns.

Between 1801 and 1851 the population of Ashwell rose from 715 to 1425. This doubling was caused by natural increase and by 1830–50 the village simply could not support its growing numbers. This was the time of 'surplus labourers'. The old equilibrium was upset, and in this lay the seeds of the dissolution of village society.

All of this came to a head between 1850 and 1870, for Davey years of crisis. There were, as always in history, random events. On 2 February 1850 a catastrophic fire left two hundred homeless and seventy men out of work. In 1855 there was a smallpox outbreak with over two hundred cases. Apart from these sudden dislocations 'change replaced stability as the normal condition of life'. The Great North Eastern Railway constructed a branch line near Ashwell. One thing it brought was outside supplies of bricks for the post-fire rebuilding, at first stimulating craft industries but then bringing an influx of finished goods 'which destroyed village trades'. This was also the time of parliamentary enclosure, and of encounters with the forces of 'improvement' and respectability in the form of a new major landowner and potential squire figure, and a new reforming and interventionist parson. Ashwell's population continued to grow, but at a slower rate, to 1,576 in 1871. However in the 1850s 205 Ashwell-born males left the village. People were coming in, but the population was more mobile with, by the 1871 census, 'a good quarter of the population born outside the parish . . . The situation was critical because the increased numbers could not be supported by the 1870 level of economic activity; it therefore became essential for the village economy to expand vigorously in the 1870s and 1880s, if the old community was to avoid total collapse'.

The final phase of Ashwell's story is summed up by Davey as, 'They could bear it no longer'. The trend to move away accelerated. By 1901 the population had declined to 1,281, with a rapid drop of 300 in the

138. (OPPOSITE, ABOVE) Ashwell, Hertfordshire, a traditional, rural community transformed during the nineteenth century. Random events played their part. A fire of 2 February 1850 left 200 homeless. New brick façades can be seen in the High Street beyond old timber-framed buildings.

139. (BELOW) Longer term trends were undermining Ashwell's former stability. Despite re-building after the fire this agricultural village declined in size and vigour in the later century.

1890s. They left behind a village hit by the agricultural depression of the mid-1870s onwards, with a similar number of agricultural jobs but falling standards of living. The introduction of compulsory elementary schooling in the 1870s and the mechanization of straw-plait reduced supplementary earnings. Education and economic circumstances took people away from the village, to London, into the army and into domestic service. Individual family histories show craftsmen and tradesmen, a key group in the old Ashwell, disappearing, giving up business, or moving away, often overseas.

In 1910 a local man, H.W. Bowman was elected to the Royston Rural District Council, in whose area Ashwell now lay, on the slogan 'Ashwell Water for Ashwell People'. He was campaigning for a local, parish solution to water supply problems instead of that of the outsiders, the Biggleswade Water Company. Davey sees this as a final attempt 'to cling to a way of life that had already disappeared'.

> By 1914 the 'old community' had collapsed. The village had lost the right to govern itself; the growth of communications had broken its insularity; the decline of farming and the extinction of the local trades had destroyed the true economy and community of interest which had been the basis of life 70 years before. Village life was no longer the mainstream of existence; indeed, it was despised, and for many people fulfilment could only be found – or rather, sought – in the 'golden city' to the south, or in a wider world. National attention was only focussed on this situation by the agricultural depression and the rural depopulation of the last decades of the nineteenth century, but in fact these were only the most spectacular manifestations of a process of decay that had been going on for 60 years. The attack had begun with the stresses imposed by the rapidly increasing population of the 1820s, and had intensified during the tempestuous times of the so-called 'Golden Age', the depression of the 1880s was but another, albeit more powerful, example of the steadily increasing, and now paramount, influence of the outside world.

Ashwell gained a safer water supply, but, Davey argues, these and other improvements were gained only at a price to the community and those who remained in the village.

This section has drawn on the work of Ken Clark (op. cit.), Robert Moore (op. cit.), James Obelkevich in *Religion and rural society. South Lindsey 1825–1875* (1976), Flora Thompson in *Lark Rise to Candleford* (1945), Kate Tiller (ed.) in *Church and chapel in Oxfordshire 1851* (1987), Dennis Mills in *Lord and peasant in nineteenth-century Britain* (1930), Sarah J. Banks in 'Open and closed parishes in nineteenth-century England' (unpublished Ph.D. thesis, Reading University 1982), and B.J. Davey in *Ashwell 1830–1914. The decline of a village community* (1980). The sources they used are:

* Census, both enumerators' returns and printed tables
* religious census of 1851. The only such census ever taken, it records accommodation provided and actual attendance at places of worship in England and Wales on Sunday 30 March. In the PRO (HO 129)
* commercial directories
* tithe commutation award and map
* newspapers, in Davey's case the splendidly named *Royston Crow*
* parliamentary enclosure papers
* diaries, memories and descriptions, e.g. for Ashwell. Arthur Young's *General view of the agriculture of the county of Hertfordshire* (1804), one of a county series; and Edwin Grey, *Cottage life in a Hertfordshire village* (1926) for straw-plait
* diocesan papers
* Wesleyan and Primitive Methodist Circuit records
* photographs
* Ordnance Survey maps
* oral history
* farm accounts and estate papers
* parish registers, vestry minutes, parish overseers of the poor papers
* poor law union records
* land tax assessments
* buildings
* landscape.

Sources

Some record types already familiar before 1750 continued to be produced and are useful, for example diocesan visitation returns and parish registers. Others were affected by reforms which reduced their importance, like the land tax assessments no longer used as proof of voting rights after the 1832 Reform Act, or which ended their production, like ecclesiastical probate records after the introduction of secular procedures in 1858. Other new sources were introduced or developed as the earlier part of the chapter has repeatedly shown. What follows is a checklist of the principal sources of use to local historians. The first part is annotated and emphasizes particularly useful and accessible types.

* *The census*
Begun nationally in 1801, the census has been taken every ten years since, except 1941. The results of each census were summarized in printed volumes in the Parliamentary Papers series. These provide both reliable population totals and analysis of age structures of local populations, and employment patterns in counties and larger towns. Unusual features and fluctuations may be explained in accompanying

Parish or Township of *Holy Trinity King's Court*	Ecclesiastical District of	City or Borough of *York*	Town of	Village of

No. of Householder's Schedule	Name of Street, Place, or Road, and Name or No. of House	Name and Surname of each Person who abode in the house, on the Night of the 30th March, 1851	Relation to Head of Family	Condition	Age of Males	Age of Females	Rank, Profession, or Occupation	Where Born	Whether Blind, or Deaf-and-Dumb
		Mary A. Speckh	Daur	U		12	Scholar at home	York, City	
		William do	Son		11		do "	do do	
		Robert do	Son		10		do "	do do	
		Elizabeth do	Daur			6	do	do do	
		John do	Son		4			do do	
		Mary Ann Newham	Assistant	U		12	Dressmaker (Assistant)	Lincolnshire, Linwood	✓
		Elizabeth Sudbury	do	U		19	Milliner do	Yorkshire, Pontefract	✓
		Sarah A. Overend	do	U		15	do do	do Pocklington	✓
		Hannah Huth	Servt	U		19	General Servt	do Nunnikton	✓
37	King's Square	Joseph Kimber	Head	Mar	52		Grocer	York City	
		Ann do	Wife	Mar		40		do do	
		Mary J. do	Daur			12	Scholar	do do	
		Joseph do	Son		9		do	do do	
		Henry Guy	Appr	U	17		Grocer (Appr)	do do	
		Job Ayres	do	U	14		do do	Yorkshire, Riccall	✓
		Jane Smith	Servt			20	General Servt	do Bulmer	✓
38	King's Square	John Marsh	Head		40		Furniture Broker	Middlesex, London	✓
		Charlotte Marsh	Wife			35		Yorkshire, Pontefract	✓
		Sarah Anne Marsh	Daur			6		York City	
		Elizabeth Wolstenholme	Servant	U		12	General Servt	do do	
Total of Houses 12	U — B				Total of Persons	8	12		

140. Census enumeration schedule, 1851. A sample of the CEBs completed by local enumerators. It is unlikely that so many of these York residents were blind, deaf or dumb. Information from schedules was subsequently counted for inclusion in printed summary tables and clerks frequently 'ticked' various columns.

reports. These volumes, frequently found in local studies libraries, make comparisons between censuses and places relatively easy and cover the years when detailed local returns are unavailable.

This detail is found in the census enumerators' books (CEBs), written up by local recorders who went from door to door, collecting information. Between 1801 and 1831 detailed returns do not survive centrally. Only a limited range of questions was asked, by parish overseers, and apart from summary totals there are only rare, local survivals of their records. All this changed with the census of 1841, the first organised by the Registrar-General's department. An increased number of questions was introduced, covering individual names, ages (to the nearest five years), sex, profession or trade, and birthplace (in the same county, Scotland or Ireland). Information was collected by paid local enumerators.

In 1851 the census attained the form most familiar to local historians, with the name of every individual, marital status, sex and exact age, relationship within the household (e.g. wife, lodger, apprentice, visitor), rank, status or occupation, and parish of birth. Although exact addresses are infrequent, especially in rural areas, entries are clearly grouped by household. The personal details in the CEBs, returned to the central Census Office and now in the PRO, are protected by a hundred-year rule, under which the 1891 returns will shortly emerge. CEBs for 1841–81 are commonly available on microfilm in local studies libraries.

Such uniform and extensive detail for the whole population lends itself to hand indexing, and increasingly to computer storage and data analysis, using packages. Larger places may require use of sampling techniques. Common approaches to the CEBs involve working out age and sex structures in five-year groups. This may reveal the profile of a growing population with a broad base of 30 per cent or more children, in the age range 0–14. Imbalances in age groups may show out-migration, indicating growing or dwindling work opportunities. The life of children, whether at home, school or work emerges, e.g. with the impact of changes in legislation and attitude between 1851 and 1881 apparent in proportions 'at school'.

Occupational structure is a key to social structure. To interpret the varying designations needs careful categorization, for example of craftsmen and tradesmen, of industrial or agricultural workers, skilled and unskilled, or of professionals. A number of well-tried classifications may be drawn on. Different parts of the census need to be used together. For example, household sizes may reveal most when related to the social status of the head of the household – were poorer households smaller than middle-class ones? The incidence of servants may relate to high social status, or is it to do with households which are still workplaces? Are certain social groups concentrated in certain areas of the town or village? Do birthplaces indicate a stable or mobile population? Does the degree of stability vary between men and women, or between social groups? Do incomers to the community come from particular places or directions? Do the birthplaces of children in a family plot its movements? Does tracing the turnover between censuses reveal core families as a stable factor in community, with 'lost' people mainly mobile, single people of less lasting relevance to the character of that community? Used with another source such as the large scale tithe maps of the late 1830s and early 1840s it may be

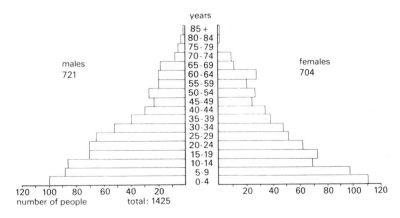

141. The age and sex structure of Ashwell analysed from the 1851 CEBs. The profile is still that of a growing population, its broad base showing the large proportion of children (aged 0–14).

possible to link properties with named individuals from the 1841 or 1851 CEBs, thus re-populating your place.

Not surprisingly the CEBs have produced more local studies than almost any other source. A recent review and bibliography of such publications (D. Mills and C. Pearce, *People and places in the Victorian census*, (Historical Geography Research Series No. 23, November 1989) runs to 144 pages.

★ *Commercial directories*

The succinctness of this source can complement the detail of the census. A typical mid-nineteenth-century directory entry offers a brief history of the town or village, locates it in relation to railways and jurisdictions, from poor law union to parliamentary constituency, lists the principal or private residents, and then the tradesmen and commercial people of the place, including farmers. From such entries one can quickly compare places, their size, economic and institutional structures, for example open and closed villages may suggest themselves. Because the directories existed to inform the world about suppliers and potential customers they are incomplete. No labourers appear and not all farmers or traders. The history, much copied from edition to edition, can be inaccurate, and many smaller places only begin to appear after *c.* 1840. Nevertheless the directories make an exceedingly useful source of accumulated outline information, of names, and potential comparisons over a place and time. Most were published by counties, although some were for individual towns.

★ *Tithe commutation award and map*

The vexed question of tithes was tackled by the Tithe Commutation Act of 1836, which led to the replacement of tithes by fixed rent charges apportioned to specified pieces of land. In order for this to happen large scale maps were prepared along with written surveys, listing the owners and occupiers of all property. Land was listed by field-name and other properties by use, for example malthouse or weaving shed; land was described by its use (arable, pasture, woodland) and its size. Three copies of map and apportionment were produced, for the Tithe Apportionment Commission (now in the PRO), and for the Diocesan Registrar and the parish (now usually in the County Record Office). The surveys covered some 79 per cent of the area of England and Wales. Some parishes, where tithes had been settled by an earlier parliamentary enclosure, lack full coverage, but for the majority of places there will be great opportunities to analyse landownership and occupation, buildings (possibly repopulating them using CEBs), land use, industrial development and local place-names.

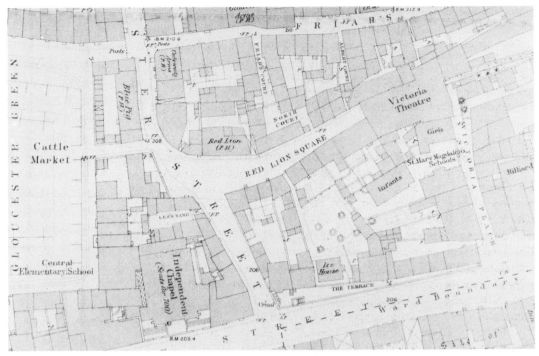

142. An extract from the 1:500 Ordnance Survey map of 1880 for central Oxford.

★ *The Ordnance Survey*

This department was founded in 1791 for the purpose of mapping Great Britain at the scale of 1 in to the mile. The first sheet, for Kent, was published in 1801 and the first edition worked its way north to the Scottish border by the 1860s. The OS really comes into its own for the local historian with the arrival of its larger scale maps and plans. Between 1853 and 1893 the whole of England was surveyed and maps published at 6 in and 25 in to the mile. The quality and detail of these is surpassed only by that of the 1:500 plans of almost 400 towns, published between 1855 and 1895. These give detail down to pieces of street furniture and lay-out of rooms within large public buildings like hospitals and workhouses. For dates of publication and survey at various scales see J.B. Harley, *The Historian's guide to Ordnance Survey maps* (1964).

★ *Newspapers*

Although not a wholly new phenomenon, with examples going back to the late seventeenth century, it is from the mid–nineteenth century that this invaluable source comes into its own. Encouraged by the improved technology of steam presses, the repeal of taxes on knowledge in the 1850s, and a widening readership of those involved and concerned in local affairs, local newspapers burgeoned. From the tight-packed pages of these broadsheets will come exhaustive details of national and local politics, of speeches and campaigns, of the activities of a bewildering range of agencies – the official such as the Board of Guardians, the borough council, the local sanitary authority, and the voluntary, such as the British and National schools societies, or the local branch of the Anti-Corn Law League. The correspondence columns will mirror contentious issues, from strikes and trade unions, to allotment gardens, to liturgical practices in the local church. The advertisement columns will show land and house prices in different neighbourhoods; the range of goods and services, whether exclusive and expensive, mass-oriented and cheap, locally provided or delivered via chain stores and outside enterprises; and the availability of medical, contraceptive and other preparations. Practical information will explain transport connections, prices in local markets and fluctuations in weather, vital in agricultural areas and for many industrial processes. Obituaries will give biographical details of those hard to trace fully elsewhere.

★ *Oral history*

This is a unique source for the local historian. It also requires exceptional care. Oral history is more than the chance reminiscence jotted down. Properly used it provides direct and immediate testimony, often of aspects of local life otherwise unknown, as for example sexual attitudes and mores, or school from the child's point of view, or of details of shopping, clothing, cooking and washing thought too ordinary to note but part of a way of life increasingly distant from present-day understanding. Much of this has changed in the last forty years.

No local historian should presume that everyone they approach will wish to be interviewed. A relationship of trust and sensitivity must be built up, perhaps involving some time in preliminary contact before tape-recording begins. Taping is undoubtedly the best approach. A checklist of areas of interest is a help, especially if a team of people is carrying out interviews, but it should never be a straight-jacket questionnaire which prevents the interviewer listening to, and looking at, the interviewee, and letting him or her talk spontaneously. The replies should not be distorted by questions consciously or unconsciously loaded – 'You must have enjoyed the harvest, mustn't you?', as opposed to, 'What was the harvest like?'. The less the questioner says the better. You must know exactly how your recording equipment works and try to avoid inhibiting or interrupting factors, from clocks chiming on the quarter hour to a disagreeing spouse; one interviewee at a time is always best.

Once the interview is taped it needs to be made into a usable source, and here the long business of transcription and indexing is unavoidable. This makes the information accessible and permanent, without editing or interference. It should only be referred to in this form, or incorporated into a published study, with the knowledge and consent of the interviewee, and with identities disguised if necessary. Unlike returning a document to the shelves a local historian's involvement with an interviewee does not end when the tape recorder is switched off. This makes oral history a demanding but rewarding option. It may be especially effective when tied in with photographs or other contemporary items. It is sobering to reflect that it is not just the very old who are sources of history, but ourselves. Oral testimony is one way of purposely recording the recent past, and even the present for the benefit of succeeding local historians.

Other sources for the post–1750 checklist are:

* photographs
* parliamentary enclosure bills, acts, awards, surveys, maps and papers
* land tax assessments, 1652–1832
* estate records
* Parliamentary Papers
* civil registration of births, deaths, marriages
* poll books, prior to introduction of the secret ballot in 1870
* business archives
* educational records – National and British Societies, school log books, school board records. See also Parliamentary Papers
* records of religious denominations
* records of local authorities, e.g. Boards of Guardians, Paving and Lighting Commissioners, Boards of Health, MOHs, Borough, District and County Councils.

References

1 E.A. Wrigley and R.S. Schofield, *The Population history of England, 1541–1871: a reconstruction* (1981), p. 266.
2 D. Levine, *Reproducing families* (1987).
3 P.J. Waller, *Town, city and nation – England 1850–1914* (1983), p. 3.
4 F.W. Maitland, quoted in P.J. Waller, op. cit., p. 240.
5 P.J. Waller, op. cit., p. 249.
6 F. Thompson, *Lark Rise to Candleford* (1945), pp. 207–8.
7 R. Roberts, *The Classic slum – Salford life in the first quarter of the century* (1971), p. 29.

Conclusion

Local history continues to be made in the twentieth century, yet it has been much less recorded or written about than for earlier periods. Given a pace of change which means that signs of local life are constantly being masked or removed by later developments, this relative neglect is unfortunate. Yet there are understandable reasons for the widespread emphasis on earlier times. Many people find it hard to think of a photograph of a 1950s domestic interior or an itemized supermarket till receipt of the 1980s as important historical evidence. It may seem that the vastly increased amount of record – in print, on tape or on film – renders local, personal recording redundant. Some major areas of local historical enquiry – for example, family life, religion, politics or property development – may seem too contentious to be tackled in the recent past. Yet when we reflect on the immense value we find in every kind of evidence for previous centuries and on the sort of insights it provides, the claims of recent and present local history to be written and recorded must seem very strong. Present and future historians need this dimension which forms a natural continuation of the common agenda with which this book began. The basic, shared questions remain the same. Who lived here? How many of them? How, when and why were settlements made? Did they grow, decline or shift? How has man moulded the landscape? How has the physical setting in turn affected people's lives? What work did men, women and children do? How were they governed and educated? Did they take part in religious worship? What were their social relationships and attitudes? All these questions remain relevant whether in the 1930s or the 1980s or, indeed, in the present tense.

There are many useful ways of collecting material to help provide answers. The Suffolk Local History Council in 1988 suggested the following headings for a county-wide series of locally-produced parish surveys:

* *Place*

* *District Council* and location of Planning Office.

* *Acreage*

* *Population* at last census.

* *Housing*: number of dwellings; if possible note local authority and sheltered housing.

* *Firms and Industrial Concerns*, including farms and farming.

* *Services, Amenities and Recreation Facilities*: shops; post office; public telephone; library; museum; theatre; doctor's surgery or clinic; bus shelter; park; car park; cemetery; allotments; electricity; gas; water; sewerage; street lighting; rubbish collection; public transport; football pitch; tennis courts, etc.; village hall; playing field; police station (or nearest).

* *Places of Worship*

* *Educational Establishments*

* *Clubs and Organizations*

* *Environment*: village green (registered?); village pond; reserve; conservation area; sites of Special Scientific Interest; picnic site; tree preservation orders; hedges and woods; footpaths and bridleways; present field names; other things of interest, such as ponds, lakes and gravel pits including, perhaps, those already filled in.

* *Sites of Historic Interest*: scheduled histroic monuments; listed buildings and others of particular interest; moated sites; old industrial sites. (Many of these sites could be recorded on a map.)

* If possible keep an up-to-date list of such 'office holders' as county, district and parish councillors, the Parish Clerk and secretaries of clubs and organizations.

* *Compiler's Name and Date*
In addition to these factual compilations, backed up wherever possible by photographs and maps, the keeping of diaries of day-to-day happenings, the gathering of printed or handwritten ephemera (handbills, receipts, newsletters, and the like), and recording of changes in the physical environment and in social and economic life, were all recommended. An annual update was to be added to the survey.

All this can now be undertaken with the help of tape recording, video filming and microcomputer storage, to complement the more traditional forms of manuscript, map or plan, and photograph.

In collecting evidence local historians should perhaps reflect on their predecessors and how the content and style of the histories they have left us strongly reflect their own attitudes and thinking. Will twentieth-century local history bear a similar imprint? Certainly people now undertake local history for a variety of reasons. These include the desire of incomers in a highly mobile society to find attachment and involvement in the place they come to live.

Reasons may also involve strong conservation motives in the face of development, or a concern with new forms of presentation notably the boom in museums and in commercialized heritage. There is also a strong vein of nostalgia. This last can generate a desire to escape into an idealized past, safely over the drawbridge between then and now, an unpalatable present. Nostalgia can obviously colour both accounts of the past and attitudes to whether and how to record the present. Many, or most, of these reasons may co-exist alongside that perennial motive for doing local history: interest and curiosity about a familiar place. They need to be recognized in ourselves and in the work of others as we set about reading, observing, recording or writing local history.

Anniversaries or important dates are often the focus for intensi-fied activity. The year 2000 brings not only a century but also a millennium on which to reflect. Could this be an ideal spur to local historians to look not only back but forward to the record they will be leaving for their successors?

Further Reading

This list is deliberately limited in length and is designed as a way into the dauntingly large literature of the subject. Each local historian will inevitably develop a longer list of useful books and articles, but the stress here is on basic works which should be of use all over the country. These books and journals are intended as a complement to those cited in the main text and in references to each chapter. It is there that examples of studies of particular places will be found. Most of the works listed here are in print. The dates of publication given refer to the most recent edition.

Local history in general

An excellent account of the subject is provided by W.G. Hoskins, *Local history in England* (1984). Useful general books include D. Hey, *Family history and local history in England* (1987) and A. Rogers, *Approaches to local history* (1977). D.P. Dymond, *Writing local history: a practical guide* (1981) deals with much more than the mechanics of composition.

Of general guides focusing on sources W.B. Stephens, *Sources for English local history* (1981) is essential to every local historian. Other source-based books are A. Macfarlane, *A guide to English historical records* (1983) and J. West, *Village Records* (1983) and *Town Records* (1983). J. Richardson, *The local historian's encyclopaedia* (1986) will prove a much thumbed reference book.

For local history approached through landscape history W.G. Hoskin's *The making of the English landscape* remains a classic, preferably read in the 1988 edition, which incorporates updated information and comment from Christopher Taylor. In addition many county surveys have been published in *The making of the English landscape* series (Hodder and Stoughton).

National journals of particular relevance are *The Local Historian* and *Local Population Studies*.

Anglo-Saxon England

For a general view of the period see H.R. Loyn, *Anglo-Saxon England and the Norman conquest* (1962), and *The governance of Anglo-Saxon England* (1985). James Campbell (ed.), *The Anglo-Saxons* (1982) provides an attractive account using many local examples.

On place-names see Margaret Gelling, *Signposts to the past. Place-names and the history of England* (1978) and the county volumes of the English Place-names Society.

Medieval England

The social and economic factors which so influenced local experiences are best covered in E. Miller and J. Hatcher, *Medieval England: rural society and economic change, 1086–1348* (1978); C. Dyer, *Standards of living in the later middle ages. Social change in England c. 1200–1520* (1989); and J. Hatcher, *Plague, population and the English economy* (1977).

W.L. Warren, *The governance of Norman and Angevin England 1086–1272* (1987) and A.L. Brown, *The governance of late medieval England 1272–1461* (1989) have much to say about local administration and society.

Introductions to the church at local level are offered by J.H. Bettey, *Church and parish* (1987) and C. Platt, *The parish churches of medieval England* (1981).

For towns see C. Platt, *The English medieval town* (1976), and R. Holt and G. Rosser, *The medieval town 1200–1540* (1990).

On agriculture (and buildings) much local evidence is incorporated into *The Agrarian history of England and Wales*, although the expensive volumes of this series are likely to be referred to in library copies. Vol. II (1989), edited by H.E. Hallam, covers 1042–1350, and vol. III (1991), edited by E. Miller, 1348–1500.

Local historians needing guidance in reading medieval documents may look to E.A. Gooder, *Latin for local history* (1978). K.C. Newton, *Medieval local records: a reading aid* (Historical Association 1971) is one of several pamphlets and books illustrating documents.

Early modern England

The best general accounts of the social and economic context will be found in K. Wrightson, *English society 1580–1680* (1984) and R. Porter, *English society in the eighteenth century* (1982).

Population history, particularly the use of parish registers, is clearly explained in E.A. Wrigley (ed.), *An introduction to English historical demography* (1966). The fruits of much local demographic research are encapsulated in E.A. Wrigley and R.S. Schofield, *The population history of England 1541–1871: a reconstruction* (1981), a weighty volume to which reviews, such as that in the journal *Local Population Studies*, may provide a helpful introduction.

For parish life and government, and its records see J.H. Bettey (as above) and W.E. Tate, *The parish chest* (1969). The treatment of the poor is succinctly discussed by Paul Slack in *The English Poor Law 1531–1782* (1990). Religious themes are dealt with in C. Cross, *Church and people 1450–1660* (1976).

Agrarian matters are usefully introduced in Joan Thirsk's pamphlet *England's agricultural regions and agrarian history 1500–1750* (1987). Dr Thirsk is aditor of two volumes of the *Agrarian history of England and Wales*, vol. IV, covering 1500–1640 (1967) and vol. V (pts. 1 and 2) for 1640–1750 (1984–5).

Basic works on towns are P. Clark and P. Slack, *English towns in transition 1500–1700* (1976), and P.J. Corfield, *The impact of English towns 1700–1800* (1982).

Buildings, particularly vernacular buildings and their study, are well covered in R.W. Brunskill, *Illustrated handbook of vernacular architecture* (1978) and Anthony Quiney's survey, *The traditional buildings of England* (1990).

The Civil War is of great fascination to many local historians, but caused disruption or changes to many sources as explained in G.E. Aylmer and J.S Morrill, *The Civil War and the Interregnum: sources for local historians* (1979).

In addition to the books on sources already mentioned historians of the early modern period will encounter documents written in secretary hand. Guides include F.G. Emmison, *How to read local archives 1550–1700* (Historical Association 1967), and H.E.P. Grieve, *Examples of English handwriting 1150–1750* (1978). J.S.W. Gibson with the Federation of Family History Societies has produced a valuable pamphlet series on the location of sources, e.g. *A simplified guide to probate jurisdictions* (1985).

Modern England

Two recent general background texts are G.E. Mingay, *The transformation of Britain 1830–1939* (1986) and F.M.L. Thompson, *The rise of respectable society 1830–1900* (1988). P.J. Waller, *Town, city and nation. England 1850–1914* (1983) emphasises towns but not exclusively so.

Enclosure, parliamentary and otherwise, is the subject of W.E. Tate, *The English village community and the enclosure movements*

(1967). A summary of more recent work is M. Turner, *Enclosures in Britain 1750–1830* (1984). A particularly monumental volume of *The Agrarian History of England and Wales*, vol. VI (1988), edited by G.E. Mingay, deals with 1750–1850.

A.D. Gilbert, *Religion and society in industrial England. Church, chapel and social change 1740–1914* (1976) brings together much relevant information including local data.

Alan Rogers (see above) has interesting examples of the use of nineteenth-century sources. For that prime local historical tool, the census enumerators' books, see E. Higgs, *Making sense of the census* (1989).

Some of the best reading on the period 1750–1914 is to be found in 'personal' accounts of wider relevance, e.g. M.K. Ashby, *Joseph Ashby of Tysoe 1859–1919* (1974), Flora Thompson and Robert Roberts (both cited in chapter 5).

Many good thematic essays likely to be interesting to local historians, including accounts of work, politics, crime, education, housing, sport and pubs, are brought together in G.E. Mingay (ed.), *The Victorian Countryside* (2 vols., 1981) and H.J. Dyos and M. Wolff (eds.), *The Victorian city: images and realities* (2 vols., 1973).

Index

Page references in bold indicate illustrations. Where counties are given, the pre-1974 boundaries have been adhered to.